IN QUIET WAYS

In
Quiet
Ways

GEORGE H. MEAD

*The Man
and the Company*

Privately Printed

THE MEAD CORPORATION *Dayton, Ohio*

1970

Editor's Preface

T HIS IS THE BIOGRAPHY of a man and the story of the growth and development of one of America's leading industrial corporations. These two stories are so intertwined that to separate one from the other would necessarily make each incomplete. Our major objective has been to record the life and contributions of George H. Mead. But to tell this story fully, it has been necessary to document the growth and development of The Mead Corporation—the most tangible evidence of his unique contributions during the 85 years of his life.

Yet, while The Mead Corporation stands as a monument to his genius, he was at all times much more than an industrialist. He was, first of all, a family man—devoted both to his personal heritage and his wife and their offspring. And he was a warm and affectionate human being—so much so that many of those who contributed to this biography constantly remarked that the story of George Mead couldn't really be told unless it was possible to capture the twinkle in his eyes. Perhaps two brief comments, penned in his wife's hand at the end of one of the drafts of the biography manuscript, make the point most succinctly. They read simply, "Sense of humor" and "Optimist."

Unfortunately, trying to capture these qualities in words amidst the host of documentary material so vital in recording George Mead's important contributions to his Company, his industry and his country, has proved extremely difficult. He was basically a quiet man, not given to showmanship. The force of his personality was revealed not in specific incidents, rather in its effect on those around him and the results of their mutual activities. Perhaps his most distinguishing characteristic was his ability to blend the efforts of others to produce exceptional results. This was true not only of his business affairs, but also in his many governmental activities and with his family, which today remains closely knit and dedicated to the perpetuation of the spirit he fostered.

It has also been difficult to portray adequately the vastness of George

v

Mead's contributions to his country. While he served in a variety of very important positions in Washington over a period of 20 years, he functioned in his typical quiet way—no press conferences, no speeches, no publicity photos. More often than not he chose to be an active, hard-working committee member rather than stepping into the limelight as a committee chairman. Thus, the record of his valuable contributions is hidden in the anonymous results of his many assignments and in the memories of those with whom he worked. While George Mead was a close confidant of many notable national figures who obviously valued his advice, counsel and abilities, he remained the man behind the scenes, and there are few lasting records to document his contributions.

It is hard to imagine a man often joining in conversations with Bernard M. Baruch on his famed park bench, meeting almost daily during World War II's hectic years with James M. Byrnes, being a frequent White House guest of Franklin Delano Roosevelt, continuously serving in one important government position after another, including intense activity on the Hoover Commission—a man obviously contributing importantly to the entire direction of a changing nation—yet a man who maintained a personal anonymity in historical records. Yet, this was the very nature of George Mead. His important work went on in silent ways, with no personal credit sought and little publicity received.

An additional complication faced by this biography's editors was George Mead's communications techniques. Above all else he valued face-to-face conversation and most of his activities were conducted in that manner. His speeches were invariably impromptu. He disliked memoranda and his letters were brief and usually dictated and dispatched with such speed he had no time to examine them. The telephone, even in the early and more trying days of its long-distance history, proved an important asset to him. The net effect, however, is a paucity of recorded details surrounding most of the important events in his life.

These observations are not offered as an excuse for a less than complete biography. Rather they are, in themselves, important in understanding George Mead, the man. The very fact that so few records exist probably tell much more about his personality than what can be found in the recorded material from which many of the details of this biography were drawn.

On the other hand, the compilation of biographical material was aided by the dynamic force of Mr. Mead's personality, which left lasting and graphic impressions upon his business and government colleagues, friends and family. Interviews with those who knew and worked with him invariably brought forth more than just facts and figures. Each response was made more meaningful because memories of George Mead, the man, were a constant ingredient.

From the very beginning, both Howard E. Whitaker, then chairman of the board of The Mead Corporation, and the Mead family made it clear that the editors were to have full and free access to all available files and the people who could contribute background information, together with free rein in reporting the facts and interpreting them. The aim of the Mead Corporation in commissioning the book was to provide an accurate record of the principles, procedures and policies of the Company through a picture of the man primarily responsible for them. The Mead family agreed that such a book serving as both a memoir and a public document, would prove useful for future executives and employees in understanding Mead's basic way of doing business as well as providing a valuable historical record. In matters of analysis and presentation, full discretion was placed in the hands of the editors.

The production of this biography involved a cooperative effort. The extensive initial research and most of the original writing was the work of Herrymon Maurer, a gifted business writer and experienced biographer. Additional research and writing was carried out by Miss Kathleen Ineman. The final editing was greatly aided by the careful review and comments of members of the Mead family and former colleagues of George Mead. We are particularly indebted to Mrs. George H. Mead and Sydney Ferguson for their invaluable assistance.

Fortunately, Mr. Maurer's work on the biography was begun before the death of George Mead. He had the benefit of a series of long and intimate conversations with Mr. Mead. However, Mr. Mead in no way dictated what should be included or excluded from this biography other than through his life style which, in itself, directed much of the writing and editing.

Richard S. Hodgson

Chicago, Illinois

Foreword

IN THE FIFTH YEAR of this century, George H. Mead undertook to rescue a small family company that had not been successful in meeting the social and economic demands of the 19th century. During the ensuing 57 years of his life, he labored to create an organization safe from 20th century alarms and dislocations. In attempting this task, his Company grew a thousand-fold, and Mr. Mead himself became not only a recognized leader of the paper industry, but also, during a period between the beginning of the Depression and the end of the Korean War, one of the most influential industrialists serving in Washington. Inherent in all that he achieved, responsible in fact for some part of it, was a modesty that forbade his talking about it. He never gave a press conference, declined public appearances, granted no interviews, signed no articles, hired no publicity agents and collected no materials for memoirs. Esteemed in Washington, revered in his industry and his Company, he talked only with colleagues, employees, and friends; and even among them he was hesitant in discussing the chief aims of his life.

These aims were essentially heterodox. Like his friend C. F. Kettering, Mr. Mead held that "chances are the rule book is wrong": a dictum he held not only concerning corporations in particular but also concerning life in general. His unsung success in Washington lay not only in a wish to aid the affairs of the nation but in his success in inducing other industrialists to cooperate with government and with one another in meeting those affairs. His preeminence in his industry reflected not only his talents for technology, merchandising and finance, but were so marked that he dominated the sale of newsprint in North America when he was barely out of his thirties, but also reflected a will to avoid dominating others and a capacity to instruct his peers in the lessons of integrity and mutual responsibility. In his own business he did not preach maximization of profits, seldom alluded to monetary incentives, warned against size for its own sake, and sought to create an organization that would be voluntaristic rather than systematic; humane rather than self-seeking: an organization that would demonstrate his own goals of cooperation rather than competitiveness, and expansiveness rather than acquisitive self-seeking.

"We see many successes in industry," Mr. Mead once said, "and we see many failures. The majority of these failures come from jealousies and conceits and from characteristics of simple inhumanity." At another time he said, "We are engaged in constructive enterprise, not a battle. No man is expendable."

It is the conviction of this author that this man's contribution to the United States social and economic scene, as disclosed by his life and by the work of the Corporation, which is in a remarkable way his monument, can be of incalculable pertinence.

I first met George H. Mead after my 25 years of experience as a writer and as a student of cultural anthropology. Mr. Mead's impact upon me through personal conversation and subsequent research into his life and into the history of his Company, have had such force as to alter many of my former conclusions about large enterprise, particularly about their systems of organization and communication.

Mr. Mead was not only modest; he was profoundly non-directive. He talked with warmth, cordiality and great openness about the daily matters of his life. He did not lead people around by the nose. He led by virtue of the effectiveness of his personality, by simply carrying on and not commenting about his way of doing business. Persons close to him sensed that the way of his personality was indeed great and, by unconsciously trying to emulate it, were led by him in a manner quite different from that typical of organizational life.

Herrymon Maurer

Princeton, New Jersey

Contents

IN QUIET WAYS

Revolution and Evolution

THE SLEEPING GIANT of American industrialism stirred and stretched its muscular, mechanized limbs across the land. It was 1877, and the times were ripe for change. Throughout the country, most businesses were small; manufacturing, mercantile and banking operations were overshadowed by farm enterprise; cities were still relatively self-contained and housed only 20 per cent of the population; and the hardships of the frontier were almost forgotten.

But the Industrial Revolution had been launched in America and pointed to an era of progress and plenty. The country had recovered from the depressed years following the panic of 1873. Discussions now centered on the wonders of new industrial machinery and ready-made clothes, shoes, furniture and even foodstuffs displayed at the Philadelphia Exposition of 1876.

In Dayton, Ohio, population increased from 30,473 in 1870 to 38,678 in 1880. Since the 1830's, Dayton had been served by canals, which gave power to small factories and linked the city to two great avenues of water transportation—the Ohio River and Lake Erie. By 1850, the city had entered the age of steam; railroads linked it to the East Coast, the South and the new West, even beyond Chicago. Newly devised belts, ropes, shafts, pulleys and gears transmitted the energy of coal to Dayton's expanding mills and factories. Telegraphy provided communication more rapid than the old horse and riverboat posts. Since 1869 and the completion of the first transcontinental railroad, the city had been physically linked with the West as well as the East Coast.

While by no means a sleepy community in 1877, Dayton was still quiet. On summer days, dust hung heavy along the tree-lined, dirt-packed streets fronted by two- and three-story residences, their solid, white surfaces fresh against green foliage and brown streets. The houses were connected only to their own plots of earth. Water came from the earth; sewage returned to it. Backyard gardens, common even near the center of the city, provided most

3

households with fresh produce for summer and for home canning and storage in the cold cellar. The telephone and electric lighting were as yet undiscovered; there were no gas mains, newly laid only in a few eastern cities. Wood and coal were used for heat. The kerosene lamp, a new marvel which dramatically eclipsed the candle and whale-oil lamp in efficiency, was used for light.

A Spirit of Change

By 1900 the country had virtually completed the initial phase of the Industrial Revolution and had reached a peak of prosperity after the severe panic of 1893. A marked spirit of change was in the air. New inventions, such as the telephone and electric light and power, were now appearing with quickened pace. Within the past 20 years, the Bessemer converter had ushered in a new age of cheap and plentiful steel. Edison's incandescent lamp had been invented in 1879, and in 1882 the first central power generating plant was built on Pearl Street in New York. Electricity not only lighted homes and factories but also began to serve as power for industry. Urban and interurban streetcar systems, which first appeared in 1886 in Birmingham, Alabama, had suddenly become common; the first elevated system had appeared in Chicago in 1895 and the first subway in Boston the same year. The telephone, patented by Alexander Graham Bell in 1876 and 1877, already had, by the turn of the century, 1,356,000 subscribers throughout the country. Long lines, which first linked Boston and New York in 1884 and joined with Philadelphia in 1887, now linked all major eastern and middle western cities, reaching as far west as Omaha and Denver.

Meanwhile, the steel industry had completely outgrown its craftlike operations of earlier years. After a visit to Britain in the early 1870's, Andrew Carnegie chose to build a major works in the U.S. and to concentrate all his diverse resources on steel in the very middle of the panic of 1873. While in 1877 there was still very little Bessemer steel in America, U.S. steel production passed England's by the turn of the century. In 1901, the Carnegie Steel Company became the United States Steel Corporation. Together with John D. Rockefeller's Standard Oil Company, it was one of the few large industrial corporations in the country.

Everywhere the industrial expansion of the country was being pushed with frenetic enthusiasm. In 1900, there were roughly twice as many persons employed in manufacturing as there were in 1877; horsepower had increased about two and one half times; and pig-iron production had trebled.

Success Spurs Innovation

Newly endowed with the basic ingredients of industrialization and now linked together by new means of communication, the country was firmly launched on a course of increasingly rapid change. But the economy was still dominated by agriculture, which employed far more than half of the working force. Most of the business of the country, moreover, was still carried on by small manufacturers, small traders, small jobbers, small retailers and small bankers. Oil and steel had not yet found use in any but hand-crafted, prototype automobiles, and it was only in 1900 that organized auto production got its initial start. Electronics did not exist; the first workable vacuum tube was not to be created until 1917. No airplane had flown. The very look of the land was relatively the same in 1900 as it was in 1877.

Population was greater, and factories were more numerous. But developments of the late 19th century were only a foretaste of the radical technological changes to come. Social changes were limited mostly to the multiplication of miserable slums in factory towns and cities. A marked division remained between the low-paid workers of the new industrial lower-class and the members of the settled middle-class, long established in business and the professions. In spite of all the enthusiasm for change, evolutionary, rather than revolutionary, changes were expected from technological development and application of knowledge already at hand. In the colleges and universities, there was an optimistic feeling that the roots, at least, of practically all knowledge had been uncovered, that practically all of the universe had been explained, that the basic laws of mathematics and of such sciences as astronomy, physics, chemistry and biology had been discovered and defined. The future had in prospect no explosion of knowledge, but rather the decimal point refinement of calculation and discoveries already made.

The word was progress, and the very expectation that it was not likely to get out of hand increased the general enthusiasm for it. In Dayton, no one suspected that two of its citizens would shortly be the first persons to build and fly a heavier-than-air craft, that enterprises soon to be founded by already prominent citizens would become parts of a giant automobile corporation, or that its own successful National Cash Register Company would someday engage in the application of electronic circuits to such things as computers. But it did seem that science, industry, enterprise and the American economic and political system had created a new soil in which all things would grow and flourish. By 1900, the population of Dayton had grown to 85,333, and established mills and factories were growing from year to year. The National Cash Register Company, which was altering the cash and bookkeeping practices of shops and stores throughout the country, was growing rapidly and profiting handsomely. It popularized and stimulated the search for new products and establishment of new enterprises within Dayton. The city now had electric lights, gas mains, two telephone systems, street car system and interurban lines. Besides new factories, most of them still located near the old canals, it had fine new office buildings. More than most cities of its size in 1900, Dayton had an atmosphere of continuing progress, growth and profitable change.

A Cut Above the Best

It was into this environment that George Houk Mead was born in Dayton, Ohio on November 5, 1877. From that year until 1900, when he was graduated from the Massachusetts Institute of Technology, George Mead saw and experienced radical changes in America's way of life. These were the innovations that shaped his personality, his business and personal values. As the country grew strong between 1877 and 1900, George Mead grew up, got an education and embarked on a career that was to take him from Dayton, Ohio, to Washington, D.C. via an involved, circuitous and successful route. At the beginning, George Mead took two run-down paper mills, combined them into one. Eventually, by 1962, he increased the Company's holdings to 39 mills and plants. Using imagination, forethought and business acumen, he expanded the product line, once limited to magazine paper, to include a greater variety of white paper products than any other manufacturer in the world. Every width, thickness and weight of kraft liner board and corrugating board, a variety of packages for customers' purchases and as great a variety of containers for shipping industrial and farm products, not to mention technical papers, special laminates and even a ceramic fiber paper used as lining in combustion chambers are produced in Mead plants. (In the space program, Mead ceramic paper was first used as the insulating gasket between the observing window in the space capsule and also as an insulator to protect the antenna used to locate the astronauts after splashdown. Beginning with the Mercury space program, there was ceramic paper on board every capsule launched by the United States. The lunar landing modules of the Apollo moon probes were protected by ceramic fiber paper during the critical descent and ascent stages on the moon. The instrument packs, specifically the power units left on the moon to operate scientific instru-

George Mead with employee at the Escanaba Mill—
"beyond an exchange of fact to genuinely personal communication . . ."

ments, were protected from the sun's heat by Mead ceramic paper also. Conversely, a less glamorous, but perhaps more common, application is the use of ceramic paper in the insulator of household toasters.)

During 20 years of activity in Canada, he created and ran one newsprint plant, combined it with two others and finally merged it with still others into the largest newsprint company in the world. Meanwhile, in an entirely separate operation, he sold more newsprint than anyone else in North America. By the time he was 40 years old, he was probably the most respected man in his industry, and the respect grew in the 40 years that followed.

During the latter half of his life, George Mead combined his concern for the paper industry and his work with his Company with intensive service in Washington. He held posts in the Business Advisory Council, the Industrial Advisory Council of the National Recovery Administration, the War Labor Board, the War Mobilization and Reconversion Board, the Price Decontrol Board, the original Hoover Commission, the Economic Cooperation Administration and the Office of Defense Mobilization. Bernard Baruch once remarked: "It is unbelievable the influence George Mead exercised during many years in Washington without people being aware of it." Herein lies the key to George Mead: he accomplished exacting objectives without people being aware of it. Through sheer force of character ("The head of the table," a colleague once said, "was wherever Mr. Mead sat.") he affected the course of events. Though quiet and dignified, he was always the boss of the situation. All people were not alike to him, but almost all conversations were alike. Whether talking in his office or on the plant floor, to industry leaders or Company colleagues, government leaders or roll tenders on paper machines, he was talking with equals, freely giving information, avidly seeking it and invariably going beyond an exchange of fact to genuinely personal communication and an open sharing of his own experience.

George Mead was a man of warmth, dignity and gentle humor. He had a quiet insistence on the primacy of person-to-person relationships during a period of social, economic, technological, governmental and cultural change. A relatively gradual change of pace characterized the United States before the Civil War. By 1900, when George Mead was 23, the pace was rapid; by the end of World War II, when he was 68, the change was of a new order beyond description in terms previously applicable. Through the years, George Mead became one of a small number of men capable of taking a whole view of the changes of the times, of synthesizing the innumerable aspects of change and of reaching theoretical or practical conclusions based on an accurate overview.

It was not George Mead's practice to talk about the state of the world in abstract terms, but to do something about it in his own sphere of action, particularly in his own Company. Of all his undertakings, his labors with the organization of that Company remain probably the most crucial in importance. But his life was more than just business—it was family-oriented and public-spirited, and the total impact of his life was keenly felt in the broad spectrum of his many interests.

CHAPTER 1

The Source of It All

BECAUSE THE DESTINIES of George Mead and the Mead Corporation are so completely interrelated, our story really starts with the arrival of Colonel Daniel E. Mead in Dayton in 1841.

Daniel E. Mead came from a family long settled in New England, but his father, Anzel, made the trek west. Born in 1781 in Manchester, Vermont, Anzel Mead moved to Cooperstown, New York, where his son was born in 1817 and subsequently spent his youth and young manhood. Eventually, the family moved to Meadville, Pennsylvania, where Anzel Mead died in 1866. Daniel Mead in turn traveled westward seeking a place to settle until, after crossing a third of the continent, he reached Dayton in 1841 and there found a home and a job. In 1842, four years before the founding of the first Mead company, Dayton (population then a little more than 7,000) boasted 188 shops. Although goods of one sort or another from hats to pig-iron were turned out by hand tools and craft techniques, these shops were dignified at that time by the term "manufacturing establishments." Among the larger of these were five cotton, two carpet and two cording, dressing and weaving factories; five flour, five saw and two oil mills; one last and peg factory; four foundries; four soap and candle works; one clock factory; four distilleries; one brewery and two paper mills. These two mills probably drew power from Dayton's Miami and Mad Rivers and used some machinery, but they used primarily old hand processes for the transformation of pulp into paper.

Daniel Mead earned his keep and his initial share in the paper company-to-be as a bookkeeper in a hardware store (in which he soon acquired a third interest) and deposited his savings regularly in one of Dayton's new commercial banks. At the age of 29, Daniel Mead joined a few other men in the 1846 founding of Ellis, Chafflin & Company, the predecessor of all Mead companies.

At this time, the first phase of the Industrial Revolution in England was nearly complete. The United States would not feel the currents of the revolution until around 1860. Before this time, however, the eastern and then the western paper mills were becoming increasingly mechanized. It is known that in 1829 in Massachusetts, then one of the largest paper-producing states in the country, only six of sixty mills used machinery. By 1847 only two mills in the United States continued to make paper by hand. Daniel Mead's mill, constructed in 1846, is known to have made machine paper. So did the mill of Entrekin & Green, located in Chillicothe, 75 miles distant. This company, which was shortly to become Ingham & Company, was eventually purchased by Daniel Mead in 1890 and after 1905 it became the largest plant in the Mead Company. In their respective communities, the two mills were pioneers of the industrial revolution.

The Crucial Need for Paper

Paper is the earliest, most widespread, and today one of the cheapest materials used in mass production. The printing press, invented in Europe in the 15th century and dependent on paper introduced into Europe during the 14th century first demonstrated the equation of production and price basic to modern development of enterprise in the U.S.; that is, as more goods are produced, lower prices and higher wages result. Daniel Mead grasped the logic of this equation at the very beginning of his papermaking career.

Even in pre-industrial countries the need and demand for paper is critical. It is indispensable as a tool for education; for writing personal, business and government letters; for keeping all kinds of accounts, documents and records; for currency, and for the communication of information of all sorts, from the setting down of daily events and scholarly discoveries to recording philosophical explorations and religious inspirations.

A humbler but still critical need existed for used or rejected paper for wrapping goods purchased in shops. Far more than half of today's paper production in the U.S. (49.4 million short tons in 1968) is used for wrapping sheets, bags, cartons, containers and other packaging devices. Of yesterday's production (only 425,000 reams as late as 1813), no part was produced for packaging purposes, but all paper not preserved was reused for wrapping. As early as 1690, when the Rittenhouse mill in Philadelphia was the first in the American colonies, a jobber contracted for the mill's rejects to sell as wrapping paper.

In America, paper was scarce from Colonial through Civil War times; it was critically scarce during the Colonial and Revolutionary periods. British policy was to prohibit manufacturing of any sort in the colonies, and while the number of American mills during the 17th and 18th centuries grew steadily (by 1813 there were 202 of them), their output was entirely insufficient to satisfy need. Most paper was imported at high cost from Britain and Holland. The combination of intense need, attendant scarcity and high price greatly stimulated the interest in papermaking machinery. Generally speaking, the lag between the Industrial Revolution in England and America was almost a hundred years; in paper production it was only a decade or two by the end of the first quarter of the 19th century. During the second half of that century, American inventiveness matched and then exceeded the British, and the lag disappeared.

Early Mead Papermaking

Apart from the fact that both the Dayton and the Chillicothe mills made paper by machine, little is known of their early operations, equipment and size. Located near the middle of town, some of the Dayton mill's original machinery came from a nearby Kneisley, Ohio paper mill established by William Clarke, who had a part interest in the original firm. In 1856, Daniel Mead bought out his partners and with a friend from Philadelphia, formed the new firm of Weston and Mead, which was followed in 1860 by Mead and Weston and in 1866 by Mead and Nixon. In 1866, two decades after the founding of the firm, annual sales totaled $57,379.55, indicative of a sizeable operation. Seven years later, in 1873, Daniel Mead was prime mover in reorganization of the firm as the Mead & Nixon Paper Company with a capitalization of $250,000.

At the beginning of its operations in 1848, the Chillicothe mill drew power via aqueduct from a dam five miles distant on Paint Creek. It employed about a dozen people and made coarse paper from straw and rags. A year later, when the firm was reorganized as Crouse, Entrekin & Company, the entire mill and stock were purchased for $9,000. At this time, the population of Chillicothe—the original capital of the Ohio territory and capital of the state through 1816—was about the same as Dayton; but, from 1850 on, Dayton's increase was rapid while Chillicothe's was slow. (Between 1850 and 1860, Dayton grew from 10,977 to 20,081, Chillicothe from 7,100 to 7,625.) Mead's Dayton mill also grew at a faster clip than the Chillicothe operation. But the Chillicothe operation did continue to flourish. Following an 1852 change in name to Ingham & Company (the company was purchased by descendants of the Ingham brothers who in 1812 initiated hand production of paper in the Chillicothe area), a new steam plant was installed in 1858 for $7,000. In 1877 or 1878, following a visit to the Philadelphia Exposition by the then senior Ingham and his son, the company bought a second-hand, 76-inch Fourdrinier paper machine, which ran at a speed of 75 feet per minute, and about the same time added a new pulp mill. Paper was sold for the most part to Cincinnati newspapers. The manufacture of book and magazine paper wasn't begun until some years later when the mill passed into the hands of Mead.

Operations at the Dayton mill were considerably larger than those at Chillicothe. Profits from 1866 through 1872 averaged $43,000 a year and by 1874 had increased to $53,690.92. During the next eight years, however, profits diminished, hitting an 1881 low showing a loss of $11,502.17. While the panic of 1873 resulted in a lasting depression throughout most of the country, old Mead records attribute the Company's profit decline to the conservatism in the face of changing papermaking methods of Mr. Nixon, then the paper-making expert of the firm. In 1881, Daniel Mead became sole owner of the mill and solid profit figures of $21,732.38 and $30,366.88 were earned the two subsequent years. Probably Mr. Nixon had objected to the use of wood pulp either to supplement or replace rag pulp, since it was during the later 1860's and the 1870's that mechanically ground wood pulp was introduced widely throughout the country. In any case, on July 14, 1881, Daniel Mead bought out Nixon and formed the Mead Paper Company with an initial capital of $150,000 and total assets of $393,882.09. The mill was immediately rebuilt, and profits for the next decade averaged $22,000, reaching $49,683.08 in 1891.

Daniel Mead was well acquainted with the Ingham & Company mill in Chillicothe, but he was not aware that it was for sale. While traveling through Chillicothe in December, 1890, Mr. Mead noticed a crowd gathered across the street from the railroad station. While his train stopped for a lunch-time break, he joined the crowd and discovered it was gathered for an auction of the Ingham & Company property. Mr. Mead put in the successful bid of $30,000 and on December 6, 1890, The Mead Paper Company became a two mill operation. The Chillicothe plant included a pulp mill and a Fourdrinier paper machine that Daniel Mead knew was the right size for magazine paper. During the next 11 months—until Daniel Mead's death on November 10, 1891—he spent $100,000 modernizing the property and redoing the pulp mill to turn high-grade, soda-process pulp and paper.

From Pulp to Paper

To gain a better idea of the operations of the Dayton and Chillicothe mills between 1846 and 1891, it is necessary to review the state of the art of papermaking during the years between the abandonment of the old hand-made process and the adoption of modern machine operations. Although there have been many changes and improvements in papermaking, the basic process of papermaking has remained essentially the same since the death of Daniel E. Mead in 1891.

Roughly speaking, papermaking by machine involves two chief steps: transforming vegetable cellulose raw material (mostly wood and, for fine writing paper, rags) into pulp, and transforming the pulp into sheets or rolls of paper. Groundwood pulp, principal uses of which are in newsprint and wallpaper, is the type most easily made. Cleaned and debarked logs are pressed against the face of a rapidly revolving grindstone; the cellulose fibers are torn loose, mixed with water, bleached if necessary, and sent along to machines known as beaters for final preparation for the paper machine. Other wood pulps—sulphite, soda, and sulphate or kraft—result from the reaction of various species of wood with chemicals in huge pressure cookers called digesters. In these processes, hardwood logs are debarked and chipped into small pieces, then conveyed to the digesters where they are cooked with the requisite chemicals for several hours at high temperatures. Thereafter, the pulp is put through a series of large washers and bleachers, from which it is conveyed to the beaters for refining and for mixture with additives like rosin, clay, starch, glue and color as required for the particular type of paper to be made. (When rags are used as raw materials, similar processes are used, except that the rags must be cleaned, sorted and cut up before going to the digesters, where they are subjected only to weak chemical action.)

From the beaters or from contemporary-type refiners, such as Jordans, the pulp moves to the head box, a container which holds the pulp in a 99 per cent water mixture and lets it float out on the paper machine itself. In the Fourdrinier operation, the pulp is carried along a horizontally moving wire cloth, much finer than a window screen. Water drains away and is drawn away by suction through the wire, and the fibers mat together, producing a very wet sheet of paper (75 per cent water) that is thereafter picked up on endless feltings, squeezed at high pressure between smooth cylindrical presses and passed around the dryers, a long series of huge steam-heated drums. After it emerges from the dryers, the paper passes directly through the calenders, iron rollers mounted vertically on top of each other, which smooth it to the desired surface, and finally to a reel on which the finished paper is wound up. It can then be rewound for super-calendering, coating (unless it has been coated during its passage through the dryers), cutting and other special types of finishing.

Certain types of paper now used for fiber boxes require the use of a multi-cylinder operation. The cylinders, covered with thin-meshed wire cloth, revolve partially immersed in vats containing the liquid pulp. The pulp fibers are formed into a sheet on the wire as the water drains through. Thereafter, the paper is combined with other sheets and is then pressed and dried exactly as in the Fourdrinier process.

Many of these processes are intricate; all of them are precise. In sum, they are highly complex, involving continuous-flow systems such as used in catalytic oil cracking, rolling systems such as used in sheet-steel manufacture, batch systems such as used in the making of synthetic rubber and storing and circulating systems such as used in chemical plants. They require ancillary equipment of wide variety and complexity, together with the attention of scientists, engineers and technicians trained in the various disciplines of mathematics, physics, chemistry and biology.

On the Ohio frontier, during the early 19th century, however, paper was made in the same way it was along the East Coast during the Colonial period, the way it was made for centuries in Europe, indeed much the way it was made in China around 105 A.D.

The equipment of the frontier paper mills consisted of one or two stone vats filled with heated water. Chopped-up rags and straw were soaked in the vats for days and then beaten by large hand hammers until the cellulose fibers were released and pulp was formed. The pulp was ladled from the vats into moulds—wire-mesh strainers stretched between thin wooden frames. The frames were agitated by hand until the fibers matted and part of the water drained away. Then layers of felting cloth were inserted between each rough sheet of paper. The alternating felts and sheets were put into a hand press, made of iron or stone and usually operated by a wooden wheel driving wooden cogs. Additional water was squeezed out and the paper was flattened to its finished dimensions. Sheet-by-sheet, the finished product was taken out to air-dry on long wooden poles in a loft or nearby shed. With such tools and an adequate supply of water, one day's production of five skilled men and ten to twelve women and children was some

20 reams of paper adequate for ordinary writing and printing purposes. Some mills had only one vat; some had as many as three or four; most of them had two.

The need for water in papermaking is so great that mills have almost always been located adjacent to rivers and streams. The first use of machinery usually involved the installation of a waterwheel to drive the heavy handpress by means of wooden cogs and gears. The next step was to use water power to drive heavy iron-tipped stamping rods to beat the rags into pulp. This apparatus led to the first form of the beating machine (still often called a Hollander, after the place of its origin and development during the 17th century). Using a revolving cylinder with metal blades that rotated against a stationary plate, thus macerating the pulp, this machine appeared in the United States around 1825, nearly 75 years after it was in general use abroad.

Mechanical rag cleaners and cutters made their appearance many decades after their European introduction, but soon the pace of U.S. mechanization quickened. The first Fourdrinier machine was built abroad in 1803, the first one in America in 1827, and in 1829 the first American-manufactured Fourdrinier was in operation. In England, the cylinder machine was put in use around 1809. A patent was issued for an American-designed machine in 1816, and this type of machine came so quickly into general use, that until well after the Civil War more paper was made in the U.S. by cylinder than by the inherently more efficient Fourdrinier process. Within two decades after these improvements to the wire-cloth or "wet end" of the process, came the presses and driers of the "dry end." In 1830, for the first time, pulp moved in at one end of a machine and finished paper came out at the other. Calenders were in use around 1850.

The Mead Mill Develops

Thus, when the Dayton and Chillicothe operations began in 1846 and 1847, almost all of the basic components of machine papermaking were at hand. Both mills undoubtedly used Hollanders; both probably used the generally prevalent cylinder machines. Chillicothe is known to have supplemented water power by steam power in 1858. Since both types of power were readily available a decade earlier in Dayton, the plant there probably used both from the beginning. The technical problems for the two mills thus centered on keeping up with the improvements that were constantly being made in the basic machinery and on keeping alert to discoveries yet to come.

The 1850 census reported that there were 426 mills in 20 states and districts of the country with total value of production of $10,187,177 ($23,000 per plant) and total capitalization of $7,260,814 ($16,000 per plant). Employees totaled 5,805 or 14 per plant. The Chillicothe mill, which began operations with a dozen employees was probably close to the average size. The 1860 census revealed that the average mill was capitalized at about $27,500; its production was valued at $40,000; and it employed 20 persons. In view of the 1866 Mead profits of $57,000 and 1873 capitalization of $250,000, it is obvious that the Dayton operation was much larger than average.

The likelihood is that both the Dayton and Chillicothe operations started with mechanical rag cleaners and rag cutters, Hollanders, and cylinder rather than Fourdrinier machines, since the cylinder machines, complete with the newly mechanized "dry end," were prevalent in the U.S. In view of the substantial profits earned in the Dayton mill from 1866 through 1876, it appears that Dayton kept up well with the mechanical improvements constantly coming out: most of these improvements led to the production of larger sizes of paper at greater rates of speed and, thus, to increased economies of operation.

Thereafter, difficulties appeared in the Dayton operation. In England and the eastern United States at this time there was some use of chemical pulp, the soda process having been discovered in the City of Reading in 1851 and having been patented in the U.S. in 1854. In the U.S., however, the soda process did not spread outside the Philadelphia area for a long time, and it may not have been used by the Mead Paper Company prior to 1891, after the extensive improvements to the Chillicothe mill. Daniel Mead effected the important change from rag pulp to wood pulp in the 1870's (by 1891 the Mead Company is recorded as one of the first mills in the West to have been producing pulp by chemical means). At that time rag pulp was added to ground wood pulp to give paper more strength. In the 1880's, about a decade after its invention in Sweden, sulphite pulp came to be used—as it still is—as a general substitute for rag pulp, and the once flourishing market for old rags began to disappear. (The third of the chemical pulp processes—the Kraft or sulphate process—did not appear until much later; it was invented in Sweden in 1884, but it was not until 1911 that a successful plant was constructed.)

The first building used as an office for
the Mead Pulp & Paper Co. in Chillicothe.
It was in this office that George Mead was said to have
started work at $15 a week when he became chief chemist of the company in 1905.
This building was used from 1859 till 1925.

No Chillicothe figures for sales or profits survive and only one for capitalization, but existing records do suggest that it kept up with improved techniques. The mill added steam power in 1858, installed a Fourdrinier machine in 1877 or 1878, and switched to ground wood or soda pulp at least before 1880. In 1880, Chillicothe assets were $50,000, production of paper three tons a day. At the time of its acquisition in 1890 by Daniel Mead, the Chillicothe mill was probably of a size close to the national average.

"Restrained Self-Interest"

Daniel Mead was alert to the great increase in the circulation of books, magazines and newspapers that took place in the U.S. during the late 19th century, and particularly to the new market created by the emergence of mass advertising and of mass-circulation magazines. (Even at that time press runs for magazines like Crowell's *American* ran over a million.) George Mead once stated, "My grandfather assisted Mr. Crowell in financing the first carload of paper he purchased." Indeed, Daniel Mead prospered so well personally that his estate was valued at $500,000, a substantial sum for the times. The bulk of the estate consisted of the Mead Paper Company, which then comprised a two-paper-machine mill in Dayton in excellent condition and a single-machine mill and a soda-pulp plant in process of thorough modernization in Chillicothe. In 1880, the principal building at the Dayton plant was a 200-foot by 100-foot four-story structure. Dayton records for that year show 125 employees with an annual payroll of $40,000, three steam engines developing 450 horsepower, water power developing 150 horsepower and a mill capacity of 3,650 tons per year of super-calendered and machine-finished book paper, magazine paper and colored paper.

Clearly Daniel Mead was an astute man of business; just as clearly his influence on his grandson's early life was intertwined with the history of the paper company that bore the Mead name. It was men of business like Daniel E. Mead who took the responsibility for the economic development of a rapidly expanding America through the first phase of the Industrial Revolution. During frontier days, in the early Ohio settlements as elsewhere, the dangers and uncertainties of life and the extreme paucity of goods called for a mutuality of effort. Each individual man was vital to the survival of each other man. It is a literal fact that no man was expendable, that cooperation was a necessity for existence. Hence the ideals of Jeffersonian democracy were actualized literally: for some decades after Ohio became a state in 1803, there was a working equality among its farmers, tradesmen and craftsmen.

Thereafter, in places like Dayton and Chillicothe, the deliberation of men of business and of public affairs began to take the place of the councils of small farmers and craftsmen, just as small enterprises began to take the place of early grist mills and trading places. The need for new shops, factories, banks and waterways now made the men who developed the techniques of commerce and who financed the machines of enterprise critical to the survival and growth of their communities.

The process of industrialization, however, was not something to be undertaken by a town meeting. It required men capable of directing and rationalizing the work of other men, of producing and raising capital, of accounting precisely for income and expenditures, of anticipating new needs and new opportunities. In Ohio of the 1840's, frontier ideas were considered a dream of little practical use in this world, although of unquestioned applicability in the next. Moreover, as more and more people pressed in from the settled areas of the East, more and more did human beings become the most plentiful of the raw materials required in many new undertakings. In papermaking, for instance, the supply of raw materials like water and straw could be cut down or cut off by unpropheciable acts of nature; the supply of people, who sold their labor for a few cents an hour, was more dependable than the supply of rags, whose market price ranged as high as many dollars a hundredweight. In enterprises of all sorts, men of business, men of finance, men of affairs were naturally looked to as more important than the men whose rags they bought or whose labor they hired.

Long before the Civil War made its calls for production, such men were already convinced that the increase of community well-being depended upon their efforts. They were already following a new concept of self-interest, which, when pursued competitively and without restraint or restriction, lead not only to the maximum of personal wealth but also to the greatest general good. Aside from a comparatively few extremists, the personal goal of most entrepreneurs of the period was not maximum wealth but personal probity, combined with solid material comfort. Convictions of stewardship and community responsibility were active in their minds. Highly responsible men, like Daniel E. Mead, guarded their reputation for integrity, guaranteed the quantity and quality of their goods, kept meticulous books and honored even verbal contracts. The social changes of the mid-1800's—the Civil War, the rapid increase of population, the initial impact of the Industrial Revolution—confirmed in them their attachment to rationality, responsibility and restrained self-interest. Few of them were participants in the very large enterprises in steel, oil and railroads that grew during the last half of the century, but they were prepared to respond as interest and responsibility required, whether to the increasing rapidity of technological change or to the incipient change latent in the organization of growing corporations.

CHAPTER 2

The Aristocracy of Absenteeism

FROM ITS BEGINNING in 1846, the Mead Company has experienced six distinct generations of management, of which George H. Mead was intimately familiar with five. The first generation, with which he was acquainted only indirectly, was comprised of Daniel Mead and the various men who were associated with him as partners: Messrs. Ellis, Chaflin, Weston and Nixon. These men assumed the role typical of the times, not of running the day-to-day activities of an enterprise, but of guiding and directing its affairs, giving on-the-spot authority to a manager, a superintendent, or a foreman. During this period, Daniel Mead himself acted primarily as the financial man of the various partnerships, just as he did in the other businesses in which he served as member of the firm and ultimately as president: The Merchants National Bank, the Cooper Insurance Company, the Dayton Hydraulic Company and a small railroad. It was then customary for experienced men of business to spread their talents among a variety of enterprises. Financial talent was crucial not only for creation of new capital and new companies, but for their efficient operation and continued growth.

Accounting is basic to rational enterprise. Full realization of the fact that paper is one of the earliest of infinitely reproducible commodities requires detailed and exact record keeping, a grasp of the financial aspects of technological change and a concept of responsible enterprise. These three factors were at hand by the 1880's when Daniel Mead became the sole owner-proprietor of his company. From the records of the company and from George Mead's recollection of its affairs, it is evident that Daniel Mead maintained an efficient operation, that he did not seek the highest possible profits (they were highest during the seven years before Daniel Mead bought out his partners). Rather, he put profits to work in continued improvements to plant, and made no move toward creating an enterprise as big as the corporations and trusts beginning to appear on the American scene. His constant emphasis was on integrity of operation and quality of product.

At the time of Daniel Mead's death, the fortunes of the Mead Paper Company appeared to have been near their peak. In 1892 the profits of the combined operations in Dayton and Chillicothe amounted to almost $38,000 and the next year to $51,000. The panic of 1893 struck the Dayton area in 1894, but it resulted only in an insignificant loss. Yet the transfer of management from the first to the second generation had in it the seeds of near-failure. In 1900, nine years after the death of Daniel Mead, George Mead was informed by his father that he could not look to the family company for employment, and five years later the company was in trusteeship, the only alternative to receivership.

Other companies suffered such reverses toward the end of the century. The main reason was often a hidden malaise that was marked by an outward appearance of prosperity. The frontier with its struggles and uncertainties was long gone, and few remembered its actuality. The hard work of launching the first enterprises, of joining in a multiplicity of partnerships, of planning for each of them day-by-day and watching over them hour-by-hour lest they collapse and fail had crowned the efforts of the first generation with success, but the second generation sometimes saw the success and overlooked the effort. In many enterprises throughout Ohio, indolence and high living appeared to be the habits of a new type of aristocracy of managers. Their homes were substantial, their incomes large, but they gave little attention to the companies that gave them their means. Charles A. Mead, oldest son of Daniel Mead, executor of his estate and successor to his father as president of the Mead Company and his father's other enterprises as well, was in effect an absentee owner. He played the role of a man about town, forsaking that of a man of business. He was recorded as secretary of the company in 1872 and as vice president in 1881, but after his father's death he appears to have limited his work with the company to drawing a salary and expense account and supplementing them with sizeable drafts on company funds, activities in which he was joined by other relatives, including, albeit to a lesser extent, Harry Eldridge Mead, George Mead's father.

Harry Mead indeed wished to be a man of business, but his early upbringing inclined him neither to the exercise of sound judgment nor to a comprehension of how to accept responsibility and execute it. His mother had died shortly after his birth on March 26, 1853, and, upon the recommendation of a trusted family nurse, the young son was sent in her company to live on a farm southwest of Dayton. Here he lived with three decrepit bachelors, an unmarried lady of uncertain years and the nurse, receiving such education as he did from the older persons, who spoiled him by over-much affection. He became an omnivorous but undisciplined reader and returned to Dayton at the age of eight, markedly amiable by inclination, warm and friendly by nature, but quite unacquainted with work or study. He attended Dayton public schools until he was 14, when he was sent east for schooling at Andover, but he was packed home in the middle of his first year. During the next four years, he attended no fewer than six colleges, the last of which was Hobart in Geneva, New York. He managed to stay there a full year, but failed to graduate, having been expelled for putting a cord of wood on top of a dormitory roof.

His father put the errant son to work in the Cooper Insurance Company as his personal assistant, and for a time his affairs seemed about to prosper. In 1876, he married Marianna Phillips Houk, daughter of a prominent Dayton lawyer, and with family life begun, his application to work increased. The family moved to a house of its own in the country, and Daniel Mead advanced money against Harry Mead's share in his estate so that he could begin business ventures of his own. In the first of these, a jobbing concern that sold wrapping paper, he proved an engaging and effective salesman and built up the volume of business so well that within two years he had established a branch in Chicago.

The First Failure

Unfortunately, he expected business to prosper without undue exercise of judgment. Impressed by the success of his friends Frank and Robert Patterson in making cash registers, he sought for a comparable product by which he, too, could win a fortune. (The sales of cash registers had increased so dramatically that the Patterson brothers had built a large new plant near the boundaries of Dayton, and the city had become widely known almost overnight as a thriving industrial center.) Learning of an untried device called a typewriter, Harry Mead rented the first floor of the Patterson brothers' old warehouse, put up capital on the strength of his paper business and formed a partnership with a salesman named Phillips and the English inventor of the machine, a man named Granville. As financier of the operation, Harry Mead became president, but only to preside over the collapse of a firm trying to produce a novel and untried product. To pay off

Miniature of George Mead and his mother during a trip
to Europe in 1893. Young George was 16 years old.

the debts, he had to sacrifice his own jobbing business, and thus, precisely
at the time of his father's death, lost his share of the estate and any hope of
raising additional capital.

The Mead family, forced to retrench, remained for a time in Dayton,
where Harry Mead had the nominal post of vice president of the family
paper company, but in 1896 he secured work as vice president and general
manager of a Philadelphia firm engaged in making industrial filters. He
moved his small family to that city, only to return roughly a year later, after
the untimely death of his wife. He rejoined the family company when it had
only a few prosperous years left. Profits in 1898 were consumed by the costs
of remodeling the North Mill at Dayton without sufficient regard to the
profitability of the expenditure. Profits reached $18,315.53 in 1898 and ac-
tually went up to $33,649.19 in 1900, but by 1900, demoralization had set in.

At this time, the capitalization of the Mead Paper Company was still $250,000, but total assets were about $500,000; yearly output of finished paper was more than 13,000 tons (computed on the basis of two months' output during a year of poor performance in the early 1900's); employment was about 200 persons. These figures compare with those of the average paper company, as shown by the 1900 census, of $220,000 capitalization, 2,800 annual tonnage and employment of 65 persons. The Mead Company was still a substantial concern, but it was not long to be a going concern. Major financial problems had resulted from personal overdrafts by members of the family amounting to well over $200,000, from the yearly salaries of $7,200 for Charles Mead and $3,600 for Harry Mead, not to mention Charles Mead's travel expense and cash accounts, which in 1900 amounted to $13,800. In 1901 and 1902, the company had losses of $22,586.74 and $13,853.10, and the banks began calling loans.

Harry Mead now began drafting recommendations whereby the company could survive and the estate of his father could be protected. His intentions were excellent even if some of the logic of his proposals was weak. In 1903, he called for the ending of overdrafts and family advances, the payment of interest on overdrafts by the persons responsible for them instead of by the company, the transfer of part of the Dayton operation to Chillicothe, and the savings of the salaries of the superintendent and treasurer by having the president and the vice-president take over their jobs. This last recommendation vitiated the soundness of the others: the president, Charles A. Mead, was largely responsible for the company's plight and largely lacking in either inclination or experience to run a paper mill, while the good intentions of the vice president, Harry Mead himself, could hardly have made him an adequate treasurer. The only result of these recommendations, which went no further than the president, was a $100 a month cut in salary for Harry Mead.

Mead Paper Company losses continued, and in July, 1904, the Teutonia National Bank instituted a suit which resulted in a compromise arrangement of a trusteeship for the company. On August 31 of that year, current liabilities exceeded current assets by $84,170.45; family overdrafts amounted to $104,121.63; and the company owed the Daniel Mead estate $81,856.04.

Thus a company created and nourished over a 45-year period by one generation of capable men of business collapsed and came close to bankruptcy after little more than a decade of second-generation mismanagement.

CHICAGO OFFICE: MEDINAH BUILDING ROOM 820

GENERAL OFFICES

THE MEAD PAPER COMPANY.

DAYTON, OHIO, Nov 5ᵗʰ 1898.

My own dearest Laddie

at twenty minutes after
four this morning you were
twenty one years old! a full-
fledged complete American citizen.
one of the uncrowned Kings of a nation - a Voter of these United States!
a Man - "free, white and twenty one" +
entitled from this day forth to all the
privileges. and also charged with all
the responsibilities thereto attached.
I wish I could be with you on
this one day of your life in which
you cross the threshold of independent
manhood. and bring then, could have
words given me to express the hundredth
part of the heartfelt joy I have had in
your existence from the moment I heard
your first lusty cry. that beautiful November morning to this present hour. and
also to take your hand and welcome
you into the Brotherhood of man and
promise you the friendship loyalty and

On his 21st birthday, George Mead received this letter
from his father, Harry Mead.

CHICAGO OFFICE: MEDINAH BUILDING ROOM 820

GENERAL OFFICES

THE MEAD PAPER COMPANY,

DAYTON, OHIO,

love due from one true man to another
whom he respects and honors.

There is something of sadness to most
parents who think of it at all, in
giving up the child idea and some
difficulty to many in accepting the
equality conferred by the crown of
american citizenship. but to me it is
a joy unspeakable that you are a
man! and such a man! clean-cut fine
noble in purpose, honest in intention,
untainted in morals. pure in mind
and healthy in body. manly decent &
straight — May God Keep you so thro'
a long useful & honorable manhood!
I had intended writing you a long
rambling chatty letter today but from
the minute of consciousness this morning
until now (noon) you have been so
constantly in my thoughts that there
has been a congestion of heart. head & hand.
a choking up of thoughts ideas & modes of expression as it were, so you'll take the "will for
the deed." In true fatherly brotherly friendly love
             Yours now & always. Dad —

A Heritage of Diversification

Although he wasn't inclined to talk about persons close to him, George Mead did reveal a few aspects of his father's life to intimate friends and associates. He did this factually and straightforwardly, not as if excuses were to be sought for his father's inadequacies in self-discipline but to keep the record of his father's life accurate. George Mead always looked for the best in any person, and there was a large measure of good in Harry Mead. In the community, Harry Mead was not only friendly, he was also amiable and markedly popular. He studied history enthusiastically, read poetry and liked to write verse of his own. He became a colonel in the Ohio National Guard, and he served for a time as a member of the Oakwood Board of Education in the Dayton School System. His work with his jobbing company and his connection with the family paper company gave him a reputation in the paper business, and from 1890 to 1892 he held the post, largely honorary, of vice-president of the American Pulp & Paper Association, the industry's trade group. George Mead's warm relationship with his father continued until Harry Mead's death from pneumonia on October 2, 1916.

Although she died during his first year in college, George Mead's mother was probably an even stronger influence on him. He never discussed this influence although he did indicate that it was in her memory he declined to drink or smoke. Marianna Houk Mead was attractive, intelligent, well-educated, calm and quiet in manner, and warmly devoted to family and friends.

In her character and in her concern for intellectual and spiritual realities, she much resembled her mother. It is through her mother's life, which stretched from 1833 to 1914, that her own life—cut short in 1897 in her 40th year—that her impact upon her son George can be understood most fully. Eliza Thruston Houk (his grandmother) was an affectionate and high spirited woman who raised a family of four children while keeping an open house for a large circle of relatives and friends. She joined her husband, a lawyer and legislator, in his studies of philosophy, history, mathematics, chemistry and geology. She read such authors as Gibbon and Hume and studied the classics in their original tongues. Eliza Houk set aside the hours from ten to noon each day for her intellectual and spiritual pursuits, wrote copiously, and published a long narrative poem and two novels, one of which she wrote after she was 80. She also wrote dissertations on *The Chemistry of Fire* and the *Diminution of Water on the Earth*. She presented the latter before the American Association for the Advancement of Science in August, 1873. These works sought to explore her conviction that the spiritual aspects of man's existence could be explained by a scientific approach.

George W. Houk, her husband, and George Mead's maternal grandfather, was a self-made man distinguished both in his public life and in his scholarly pursuits. In 1844, at the age of 19, he was bossing a gang of men on the Dayton canals to earn his law school fees. Admitted to the bar when he was 21, he supplemented his early legal work with school teaching, soon developed a wide and lucrative practice as a lawyer, served as representative in the Ohio State legislature, and was elected representative to the 53rd and 54th Congresses of the United States. A serious and impressive man, he wrote upon a variety of subjects, in particular French history and Greek civilization, but left publication to his wife.

Eliza Houk sought spiritual reality vigorously. Like many earnest and unconventional persons of the time who pursued truth through religion, she shifted from one denomination to another, being progressively Presbyterian, Baptist and Episcopalian until in 1888 or 1889 her own daughter, George Mead's mother, became convinced of the precepts of Christian Science. Eliza Houk, convinced in turn, launched upon an intensive study of the Bible and of Mary Baker Eddy's *Science and Health* for the rest of her life.

Christian Science's emphasis on the supremacy of love in all aspects of man's life had a profound impact on Eliza Houk, and through her, in varying ways, on the numerous members of her family. Its effect on George Mead was unquestionable. His scientific education ended his reliance on mental healing alone, but he continued to attend Christian Science services, until the last 30 years of his life when he became an Episcopalian. Throughout his life, he held Christian Science to be "a very pure religion," and was strongly touched by its precepts.

The direct, personal influence of his grandmother must have been large in his life. After the death of his mother, she stood to him *in loco maternis*, a role she was ready to assume with unflagging energy towards any of her relatives and friends. (When in her eighties, she was writing a book in memory of her brother and acting as mother to his son.) She was the only grandmother George Mead had known, and after the death of his grandfather Mead in 1891 and his grandfather Houk in 1894, just at the beginning of his second term in Congress, she was his only grandparent. She was also his closest link with the frontier past, and with its achievements, hardships and ideals. Her own grandparents had traveled by horseback from Philadelphia over the mountains to Pittsburgh, by flat-boat to Cincinnati and by wagon to Dayton, arriving in 1805 when the city contained about a thousand people. They settled in Dayton and kept store in a two-story log house, later to thrive and prosper as did the city. In fact, her grandfather became one of the earliest and most prominent men of business in the community.

CHAPTER 3

"A Chemist, Not a Papermaker"

IN 1876 HARRY MEAD, newly married, rented the house on South Jefferson Street in Dayton where he had been born, and on November 5th of the following year George Houk Mead was born. On his first birthday, his father wrote a poem for him, which was inscribed in a birthday book kept by his mother. The poem's message is summed up in the last two lines: "When the man with the scythe calls the last,/May He who sent thee say, 'Well done.'"

In 1879 the family, increased by the birth of Charles Anzel Mead, moved to a rented house in the country near Runnymede, the rambling country home of Grandmother and Grandfather Houk. The birthday book entry for George Mead's second birthday announced he had learned his first nursery rhyme. On the fourth birthday, his mother wrote, "George is a peculiar child. He is rather gentle and affectionate—very easy to manage on ordinary occasions. He gives up to the baby entirely, but yields because Charlie is the stronger in will. Harry tries against my wishes to make George fight for his rights, and he always answers he does not want to hurt his little brother. I regret to say that he is inclined to be saucy, answers back, and is quite obstinate at times, but when he discovers a look of sorrow in my face he is always ready to yield and beg my pardon. He rebels when I punish Charles and it ends sometimes in my having to punish him."

When he reached his fifth birthday in 1882, his mother was beginning to teach him reading and writing: "He takes to his figures more readily than his words." Of the two boys, she wrote, "He is the tease of the pair. He hates to be teased himself. He is easy to control generally because he loves to please." George Mead's younger brother was then ill with diphtheria but thought to be recovering. Tragically, his condition became worse and he died on January 6, 1883. Nothing was written in the birthday book for two years, until January 6, 1885, when Harry Mead announced the arrival on the preceding day of Eliza Thruston Mead. "The years that have passed since the last writing," he wrote, "have been rich in temporal blessings—Prosperity has attended all my efforts. Peace and plenty have been in our household." In this year George Mead, aged seven, began school, attending a combined first and second grade class in a country schoolhouse. On the occasion of his tenth birthday, when he was in the fourth grade, it was recorded that he was at the head of his class, that he was four feet, one inch in height and 58 pounds in weight, he was taking piano lessons and learning to play the piano by ear. He already had the enthusiasm for music that was to last throughout his life, and he was singing regularly in the Episcopal choir. His mother wrote, "I can truthfully say that I have never since before he was five years old known him willfully to disobey me." His grandmother added the exclamatory note, "An A No. 1 good boy."

In 1888, the family moved to a house on North Jefferson Street in Dayton, and for the next two years George Mead attended the Dayton View School. In 1890, the family moved to a house of its own in the country, again near Runnymede. George Mead attended the seventh and eighth grades at the Brown Street School, riding a bay Indian pony to and from classes. His mother's entry for his 13th birthday reads, "We moved the first of April to our own dear little house on the hill. Our *very own*. [George is] sweet and gentle, loving and considerate."

The next year's entry reports that he is "only recently back from an engineering party, after several weeks' work in the mountain wilds of Virginia with his uncle, Harry Talbott . . . He was popular with the men and wrote interesting letters . . . He chopped down a tree for me yesterday and chopped it up in pieces of equal length in a very short time. He got good pay for his work in the mountains—will pay for a course of dancing lessons and have some left over for Christmas. He shows so much judgment with his money." Only five days after this 14th birthday, however, his Grandfather Mead died, just at the time his father's financial difficulties had become critical. Sometime after the birthday, his mother added the line, "His music lessons have been given up for lack of funds." This was the last entry in the birthday book.

This was also the first record of George Mead's long and intimate association with his Uncle Harry Talbott and his Aunt Katharine Talbott, his mother's only and very close sister. He already knew his uncle and aunt well, since from his earliest years he had been in and out of his grandparents' home, Runnymede, where the Talbotts had been living since their marriage in 1887. Harry Talbott was a civil engineer, then 31 years old, who had been engaged in railroad building in such still-frontier places as central Kentucky, the Virginia mountains, the Dakotas and Montana. That summer, George Mead not only saw the frontier for himself and worked as part of a construction crew, but also enjoyed one of the first of many hunting trips with his uncle. Already very fond of the sports of riding and tennis, he now became an enthusiastic fisherman and hunter.

The next year, 1892, a Professor Warren came to Dayton to open a private preparatory school for about a dozen boys. Here George Mead, whose Brown Street School grades were good and who wanted to go to college, condensed his high school work into two years. In 1894, he passed the preliminary examinations for Yale, but held back from applying there because other Dayton boys who previously had passed the exams subsequently flunked out. Besides, his family felt that he was too young for a big college, and his father—because of his own experience or perhaps despite it—suggested Hobart. Here George Mead enrolled at the age of 15, and elected to take the course in three years instead of four. His father was having to scrimp to meet the college expenses.

A Turning Point

The following years were not entirely happy. In 1895, the family was stricken by the death of his sister Eliza (called Lilah) at the age of ten. In 1896, his mother and father moved to Philadelphia so that his father could take up his new job there; and the next year, his last at Hobart, his mother died.

In June of 1897, George Mead graduated from Hobart with a Bachelor of Laws with high honors. He had enjoyed his studies, his singing with the college choir, and his learning the new game of golf, but he was not certain what he wanted to do.

"I then came back to Dayton," George Mead later reported, "and started to work as a draftsman in the machine shop of W. P. Callahan & Company on the first day of July, thinking I was going into either engineering or architecture. During the summer the Mead Paper Company was rebuilding its mill on Front Street between Second and First Streets. I usually carried my lunch, and during the noon hour after eating lunch in the drafting room where I was working, I would walk up there and watch this construction. By the end of the summer, I had determined I was going to follow engineering rather than architecture, and I thought I would like to get a job and try working with my hands. So, without saying anything to my father, with whom I was living and who was vice-president of the paper company (there were only my father and myself; I was an only child and my mother had died in my senior year in college), I asked the superintendent for a job in starting this paper machine which had just been installed . . . The superintendent gave me a job on the paper machine as a roll boy on the night shift the first week in September. Some of the other male members of the family had taken similar jobs and lasted just one week, and the superintendent, who was a very definite Irishman in his birth and thinking, thought that was the quickest way to get rid of the new applicant, but to his great surprise I appeared on the morning of the second week for work and continued through the next 12 months, working 13 hours nights and 11 hours days. On Saturday nights, we worked from 4:30 in the afternoon until 10:30 Sunday morning, which made a pretty lengthy work week."

During the first part of this year of labor, George Mead had an experience which he did not report. Although his father was in stringently reduced circumstances, his family was known throughout Dayton as social and well-to-do, and the other working men at the mill did not accept him; in fact, for three months refused to talk to him because his name was Mead. Soon thereafter, however, he managed to become one of the men and came to know every employee in the mill well. This experience undoubtedly made a great contribution to his subsequent pioneering efforts in labor relations and to his later work in Washington during the Depression and World War II. George Mead later commented on the year's working experience as "gratifying and instructive."

During the spring of that year, despite his youthfulness—he was not yet 21—he introduced the game of golf to Dayton, where only two or three people had ever heard of it. The summer following his graduation from Hobart, he had visited his roommate in Rochester and had brought home a set of clubs. He won the interest of several Dayton sponsors, persuaded a local shoe company to hire a professional to show how clubs should be made, and with him directed the laying out of a nine-hole course on a farm owned by the Patterson family. (Several years later, an addition to the National Cash Register Company was built on the farm, and George Mead then took part as a founder of the Dayton Country Club, which was first located adjacent to Runnymede and later moved to its present location.)

Mr. & Mrs. Harry Mead with George and Lilah,
taken in the mid-1880's.

Encounter with M.I.T.

During his year's work with the family company, George Mead made up his mind to enter the paper business. He also made up his mind that "I had not only to get an education in engineering, but some chemical instruction, so at the end of the summer of 1898 I left Dayton and went to M.I.T., my father having provided me with enough money over and above the wages I had received during the summer to last for a limited time, which I figured would be two years. In discussion with the bursar of M.I.T. when I reached Boston, I found that it might be possible for me, if I put in sufficient hours of work, to obtain a college degree from M.I.T. as a Bachelor of Science in Chemical Engineering, and I started on the venture. It required my staying through summer school the summer of 1899 as I had great difficulties with chemistry, and my first year proved I would have to take extra time for it."

Actually, almost incredibly, George Mead failed nine of eleven exams at the end of his first semester and was about to be dropped from the Institute. Possibly his Hobart preparation was not sufficiently thorough, but that would by no means explain his problems since his intellectual capacity was high. Some sort of personal crisis may have been the principal cause, a crisis, perhaps, arising out of conflict between his scientific education and Christian Science healing claims—a conflict he resolved by abandoning the claims but holding onto the positive aspects of Christian Science. In any case, George Mead persuaded M.I.T. to let him continue, and at the end of his second college semester in June 1899, he took 21 exams in two weeks and passed 20. Summer school brought him up to his class's schedule and removed his difficulties with chemistry. In June of the next year, 1900, age 22, he received his Bachelor of Science degree in Chemical Engineering. He had taken 35 hours of instruction the first year and 36 the second.

He had also been strapped for funds. His father was determined that nothing should interfere with his son's education, but money for the purpose was extremely short. George Mead looked for the cheapest boarding house and for restaurants serving the least inadequate 25-cent meals. His grandmother came east to keep house for him, which eased the financial crimp somewhat during his second year; he was even able to get in a little golf at Boston's public links in Franklin Park.

The summer immediately after graduation, he took a vacation at Sault Sainte Marie, Canada, where his Uncle Harry Talbott was working on railroad, bridge and dam construction, and where his Aunt Katharine was visiting together with several of her six children (of whom there were eventually to be nine). Harry Talbott had stopped his travels around the country as civil engineer for distant railroads and had opened his own office and started his own company in Dayton. His income, considering both the size of his family and the size of Runnymede, had continued to be modest. It was after 1900 that his engineering business and his participation in various other thriving enterprises began to lead him to prosperity. (Much later on, his other enterprises included the Dayton Metal Products Company and the Dayton-Wright Airplane Company, both subsequently purchased by General Motors.)

Meanwhile, George Mead's aunt, Katharine Talbott, a warm, vital, and unconventional woman, had been finding time not only to raise a large family and manage a large household, but also to pursue a career of singing. Gifted with a remarkable contralto voice of extraordinary power and range—Metropolitan star David Bispham called it one of the great voices of the generation—she had even gone for further training to England the preceding summer. When she returned to America after that summer of intense study, she auditioned for an impresario. He was highly impressed and outlined his plans for her, which included additional coaching, adding new songs to her repertoire, the probable date of her debut and then a six-month engagement with the Boston Opera Company. Katharine Talbott was flushed with excitement at the prospect, and, while putting her music into her portfolio, she dropped a picture.

"Who are these people?" the impresario asked.

"My husband and our six children," she answered proudly.

Unfortunately, a husband and six children are not compatible with an operatic singing career, as far as time, training and performance are concerned. He would not undertake sponsoring her career unless she was prepared to give undivided attention to her work.

Making up her mind, Katharine Talbott later told her children, was not as easy as they might like to believe. But the next day she declined his offer and told him she was going home. However, she had already started a series of concert tours in the Middle West for her own pleasure and for an addition to the family budget. Much later, after 1923, when all her children were grown, she was to become famous not as a singer but as patroness and one of the directors of the Westminster Choir College, which she helped to locate first in Dayton and then in Princeton, New Jersey, and with which she traveled throughout America and Europe.

In the summer of 1900, however, her music served mostly as an additional common bond with her nephew, George Mead. (She had never been an "old" aunt: the aunt was only 13 years older than the nephew.) Canada that summer proved also another hunting and fishing bond with Harry Talbott and his older sons and opportunity for other sports, which George Mead had now fitted into his philosophy as an essential part of a balanced life. He had learned to his surprise at M.I.T. that he was congenitally blind in one eye; but that was no obstacle to his way of life, and he found it no handicap except when playing net at tennis.

The Synthetic Experiments

Earlier in 1900, he had been informed by his father that the family company was in serious financial difficulties and had been told that he was now on his own. But he had already been offered, together with nine other members of his M.I.T. class, a job in a Boston research laboratory being established by A. D. Little, then the foremost cellulose chemist in the country. A new enterprise, the Cellulose Products Company, had been formed to obtain the English patents for the manufacture of viscose, the only soluble cellulose that can be made in water, and to push forward with further experimentation. The new laboratory was established in a loft building in South Boston on the first of July, 1900, and George Mead spent the first months of his technical career washing the windows. It was hoped that viscose could be used in papermaking—one of the reasons for his being chosen as a member of the laboratory force was his previous paper mill experience—and after several months of laboratory work, he was sent out to make practical tests in pulp and paper mills throughout the country. The hopes came to naught, but in the course of the year George Mead visited most of the prominent papermakers in the country, in the process inspecting the most advanced techniques and making close friendships, many of which were to last for life.

He was then given the problem of manufacturing artificial silk—rayon—from viscose, which up to that time had never been made in the U.S. but had been produced in Europe by the nitrocellulose process, which was more expensive to make than viscose and much more dangerous. During the year, the Cellulose Products Company was able finally to turn out a skein of artificial silk, the first in America. But the company had spent all its capital without financial results, and it was, therefore, closed up and sold. However,

Although his own immediate family was struck with tragedy,
George Mead found companionship and a huge family at Runnymede.
This 1919 picture shows George Mead, his wife,
their family and the assembled Talbott clan.

the same promoter, who had provided money for the initial A. D. Little research venture, bought the patents and organized a second company in
Philadelphia called the General Artificial Silk Company. While the new company was being formed and a pilot plant was being built, George Mead was
given a leave of absence. The bankers' trustee committee for the Mead Paper
Company back home in Dayton had been corresponding with him about hiring a chemist for the Chillicothe pulp mill, and he took advantage of his
leave to volunteer to go west and look over the situation. He later recalled:

Upon arriving in Chillicothe I was asked by the Chillicothe members of the
bankers' committee if I would not consider coming to Ohio and taking over the
managership of the Mead Paper Company . . . I declined the offer of the banks

for two reasons: I wanted the experience of continuing in the development of the new product in Philadelphia; and I also did not want the responsibility of trying to solve the management problem of the Mead Paper Company, because, if solved and the banks eliminated, the control returned to the Mead family, and if I were not successful, I would have the responsibility of failure in bringing the company out of its difficulties and, therefore, embarrassment with the older generation of my own kin. It was my judgment at that time that the reason for the difficulties of the company was due to the neglect of the older generation . . . It was a natural conclusion that if the company were returned to this group, the management would not be improved and my own future would be somewhat doubtful.

After spending several months in Chillicothe setting up a laboratory and improving the pulp-mill operation, he learned that the General Artificial Silk developments were moving much more slowly than anticipated, and eventually he spent 12 months in Chillicothe. Hired as a chemist, he also acted at first as pulp-mill foreman, general trouble-shooter and suggestion-maker. In three months, he had the chemical laboratory working to his satisfaction. In six months, he transformed a $9,000 pulp-mill loss into a profit of over $4,000. His other roles proved more difficult. The general superintendent of the company repeatedly cold-shouldered his suggestions, saying, "You were hired as a chemist, not as a papermaker." Nevertheless, after long argument in which he was joined by his father, George Mead was able to persuade his Uncle Charles, the president, that one of the two Dayton paper machines, along with its ancillary equipment, should be moved to Chillicothe to benefit from readier raw materials and lower operating costs.

Learning the Basics

At the end of this period, he returned to Philadelphia, became general manager of the General Artificial Silk Company, and started operation of the pilot plant. Here he had his first introduction to the intricacies of finance, spending three hours each evening examining accounts with the bookkeeper and each weekend with the principal stockholders. During the next two years, the venture became technically more and more successful, but the original capital was insufficient and the president, Daniel Spruance, and the largest stockholder, Silas W. Pettit, could not agree on meeting additional money requirements. Mr. Pettit, moreover, felt that Mr. Spruance had used bad judgment and had possibly misled him as to capital needs. George Mead, having spent many weekends at the homes of both men discussing the business with them, had become friends with both of them, and now found himself between the two of them. A reorganization battle was in the offing, and both Mr. Spruance and Mr. Pettit wanted George to take sides and become general manager of a new company. However, he saw both sides of the dispute and, unwilling to choose between two friends—friends also much older than himself—he declined. In thus turning down two offers for a position that would probably have led him to leadership in the manufacture of synthetic fabrics, he demonstrated his strong distaste for combativeness and factionalism together with his equally strong attachment to cooperation—factors that were to contribute markedly to his business and civic life.

At this juncture, the bankers in Dayton, having heard of the situation in Philadelphia, again asked him to return west. Two years had passed without improvement in finances. The bankers now stated that they were ready to put the property to the hammer unless the company could be reorganized successfully. They again requested George Mead to consider taking over its management, the Mead family having waived interest in the future. During the late spring and summer of 1905, George Mead, now 27, began to evaluate the chances of reanimating the family paper company.

Runnymede, the beautiful family home of the Talbotts and
the second home of young George Mead.

CHAPTER 4

Getting Into "The Big Leagues"

A T THE AGE OF 27, George Mead faced the most crucial decision of his business life. Well liked by both principals in the Artificial Silk Company dispute, even though they were personally at loggerheads, he could have remained secure in his post of general manager in one of the earliest and most promising glamour industries in the country, beyond doubt would have been highly rewarded in money as the operation grew (it did, in fact, become the largest rayon operation in the country), and, beyond that, in view of his talents and his imagination, might well have reached pre-eminence in the entire field of man-made fabrics. Why, then, did he opt for a literally ancient industry (however great its 19th century progress) and in that industry for a small company with a dilapidated property, a recent dismaying history of excursions into the red, and an immediate prospect of break-up under the auctioneer's hammer?

But George Mead was not thinking primarily of glamour or money. He was already thinking in terms of these non-economic values which were to rule his life. It was not in his nature to temporize for his personal advantage, and he did not do so with the parties to the rayon dispute. Instead of temporizing, he himself hired as his replacement a capable chemist from General Electric so that his departure would not embarrass the rayon company's affairs. Moreover, the dilapidated paper company was the Mead Company. Given some measure of hope that it could be reanimated, he could not turn his back on it without, in effect, turning his back on his own heritage.

The banker-trustees of the family company, faced on one hand with the inevitability of loss on their loans if the plant were dismantled and on the other with hope at least of clearing their books if the Company could be rejuvenated, could only prefer the risks of reorganization. In addition, Alexander Renick, president of the largest bank in Chillicothe, foresaw dismal consequences to the community, dependent mostly on farming, if it lost its one industry of any size. Although his bank was not involved in the trusteeship, he

Little Woods, completed in 1922, became the headquarters for
George Mead and his own family.

said he would try to refinance the Company by selling preferred stock to prominent Chillicothe citizens, thus removing the onus of the old bank loans and providing the boost of at least some working capital. And he suggested sweetening the preferred stock offer by adding in a bonus of half the equity stock.

The Problems with the Company

It was in response to this proposition that George Mead began calculating the chances for rejuvenation of the old Mead Paper Company. Here he brought to bear the sharp, analytical aspects of his character. Critical mismanagement there had been, he said in his May 1, 1905 report to Alexander Renick and the members of the trustees' committee. Substantial moneys, for instance, had been spent in Dayton because the superintendent did not want to live in Chillicothe, and because the superintendent—the same under whom George Mead had worked in 1897, who was "a hard worker, a great labor driver and economical to a degree, but very autocratic and bullheaded"—had let the property run down when he saw his own resignation impending. Thereafter, an inexperienced and incompetent superintendent had speeded employee demoralization and plant decay, while the sales office had dropped a profitable account in favor of a dubious contract with a jobber who never did deliver sales. All this had happened under the eyes but without the notice of the old second generation management.

But even under poor management the foundation for a profitable enterprise was there. After deliberation, George Mead decided that the Chillicothe operation was inherently profitable. It included the pulp mill, the old No. 1 paper machine, and the No. 2 machine whose removal from Dayton, George Mead himself had effected two years earlier. Sensible management and the removal to Chillicothe of the remaining Dayton machine could resuscitate the Company.

The bankers said yes. The yes was spoken somewhat gingerly: an August 17 letter from Alexander Renick to George Mead spoke of repairs "badly needed in Chillicothe Mill, which to my notion will be much more extensive than I had any conception of until I visited the Mill with you a few days ago. . . . This will delay matters, for which, on your account, I am very sorry, but you must see the necessity of having these matters determined before we can organize." Mr. Mead later reported:

After many lengthy discussions I was finally persuaded to undertake the reorganization of the Mead Paper Company, first because of the desire to protect the Mead name in the communities of Chillicothe and Dayton, and secondly, because my grandfather in a codicil to his will had stated that his estate, which included several equally important investments to the paper company, should consider the paper company first in the protection of its business. The trustees of the estate were, therefore, to use the credit of the entire holding for the benefit of the paper company. He had been a citizen of Dayton throughout his business life, having started the paper company in 1846 with two other partners and having gradually acquired all the interests until he personally owned the entire capital stock. I, therefore, believed he felt the paper business to be a worthwhile undertaking. I was not married, and, therefore, was in a position to take considerable chances in a business venture and agreed to help the banks in the sale of the stock and undertake the management.

A Shaky Start

The Mead Pulp and Paper Company was therefore incorporated September 14, 1905, with a capitalization of $50,000 non-callable 6 per cent preferred stock and $250,000 common. The directors, in addition to George Mead and Charles A. Craighead, a Dayton lawyer and businessman, were the preferred stock purchasers: Harry E. Talbott (George Mead's uncle), the banker Alexander Renick, and three other Chillicothians. The officers, as finally agreed upon, October 21, were Alexander Renick, president and treasurer, George H. Mead, vice president and general manager, and A. L. Rieger—a long-time Mead employee—treasurer.

On November 1, 1905, the Company bravely started business with a discouraging balance sheet:

ASSETS		LIABILITIES	
Plant & Equipment	$320,089	Capital Invested	$250,000
Inventory	46,071		
Bills & Accounts		Bills & Accounts	
Receivable	72,358	Payable	155,906
Cash	291		
Deferred Charges	100	Surplus & Reserve	35,003
	$438,909		$438,909

Somewhere in the reorganization, the boost of fresh working capital had disappeared. The working capital ratio was two-to-one the wrong way; there was only $291 in cash; and except for the hard sum for accounts and bills receivable, the principal figures were somewhat fictitious. Capital had been inflated; many bills and accounts receivable were dubious; surplus and reserve served simply to achieve a paper balance with assets. As for the value of plant and equipment, Mr. Mead admitted later, "Of course, it would have been much better if we had started with a vacant lot and a new mill . . . The Company had $285,000 invested. That is the value that was placed upon the property . . . I don't think the property was worth that amount; in fact, I have my doubts if it was worth $3,000."

The physical condition of the Chillicothe plant was as depressing as the fiscal. Within the first two weeks of operation, George Mead was awakened at two or three in the morning with the news that the plant was shut down for want of power because the boilers were leaking so badly they had put out

The view from the back of Little Woods (top) in the winter; a sleigh was part
of the winter fun for the Mead family. In the sleigh (l. to r.) are Nelson, Katherine,
George, Jr., H.T. and Louise with Elsie and George Mead in the rear.

the fires. The 80-inch paper machine, in top condition when Daniel Mead redid the mill in 1891, was held together by pieces of wire and cord. Bricks were falling out of the boiler room stacks. However, said George Mead, "it was not the physical value of the plant that I was interested in but the personal value, the fact that here was an organization that could do things if it was given a chance."

Obstacles and Dissidents

George Mead took up residence in Chillicothe on November 1, 1905, living for a time at a Paint Street boarding house and later, when his grandmother came once again to keep house for him, in a small house on the same street, from which he went to work and back on a bicycle. Once a week he assayed a trip to Dayton (in those days the 75 miles required three hours in a coach hitched to a freight train) to check over sales and finances at company headquarters in the old U. S. Building. Here he promptly went to work to recapture as much business as he could from the Crowell Publishing Company. The company management consisted of just three men: George Mead; in Dayton, A. L. Rieger, a longtime Mead clerk who had struggled to run the old company during its last dismal years, now in charge of sales and the books; in Chillicothe, Hector McVicker, member of a family with many working generations at the mill, and now a promising superintendent.

Thus began the third generation of Mead management with George Mead acting in somewhat the same role as his grandfather, proprietor of a family concern, even though the company had now become by law a public corporation. Between grandfather and grandson there was one significant difference: George Mead was not only watching the books and determining policy; he was also the on-the-spot operator.

The hours were as long as the task was large, and for more than two years George Mead took time out only for food and sleep, working on the day-to-day technical problems of the mill, acting as its chemist, carrying out tests on paper weight, formation, furnish and strength, and emphasizing quality as vehemently as his grandfather ever did. Working closely with Superintendent McVicker, he launched a program of production and cost controls. Working intimately with the men, he struggled through makeshifts and small repairs to eke the utmost efficiency out of the old machinery. There was only one capital improvement: the erection of a small frame machine shop, built adjacent to the mill to save the loss of time occasioned by sending out broken machinery for repair at the town machine shop.

The first step in the reconstitution of the Company was to be the transfer of the Dayton machinery to Chillicothe. From the very start at Chillicothe, George Mead had been struggling to get the plant ready for it and to establish an operation sound enough that the banks would lend the money needed to make it. The savings from the move were estimated at $5,800 from operation of the Dayton machinery in Chillicothe—where local labor was more dependable, fuel costs lower, and more readily obtainable—and $9,395 from closing down the Dayton plant, for a total saving of $15,195. The need for the move was urgent: the new Mead Pulp and Paper Company could no long bear the burden of trying to operate at a loss in Dayton. But for a company without working capital struggling to bring receivables into parity with payables, it would have taken years to find cash enough for the move, the costs of which were estimated at $32,156. Recourse was made to the First National Bank of Chillicothe for a $25,000 loan.

The risks of not moving were high, but so were the risks of moving. Three Chillicothians, who together had subscribed three-fifths of the stock in the original rescue operation, now backed out, maintaining that the company should earn $50,000 before attempting the move. Alexander Renick disagreed with them and said, "This plant is being well handled . . . I think Mead is going to pull it out, and I am going to stay with him." George Mead, for his part, was able to find three Dayton businessmen to take the place of the dissidents on the board, and the move was authorized. The transfer of machinery began on the first day of July; at the end of ten weeks the Dayton Fourdrinier was turning out paper at its new location. For this time and for weeks before it, Chillicothe production had to be kept going without a shut down, that is, not only during the move, but also during the time the plant was torn up with the construction necessary for installing the Dayton machines. George Mead did the engineering work necessary, leaving space for a fourth machine and giving emphasis to his hope for future expansion by numbering the paper machines 1, 2, and 4, instead of 1, 2, and 3.

Construction for the new machine had to be as economical as possible. In 1941, George Mead recalled:

A later employee said he did not see how that machine stood up—all you had to do was walk up to one of the concrete columns and give it a little push and it would fall over. They are made of ordinary gravel and cement. I did not tell him when he made that remark that I engineered that job. Yes sir, I made the drawings for that job and I superintended putting in those columns and erecting the machine myself. To be honest with you the reason we did not put any reinforcements in the columns was because we did not have enough money to buy the iron—we had just enough to beg the gravel from the Cincinnati, Hamilton & Dayton Railroad. I asked them if they would give us the gravel if we built another paper machine, and they said yes they would get enough freight to pay for the gravel. They brought us all the gravel from the Scioto River free of charge. I don't remember how I got the cement. . . . We did not have any money or any time to put reinforcements in those columns; we put in the gravel and cement and there they were.

And there, it might be added, they stood for 35 years until they had to be torn down for an entirely new machine.

A Timely Sale

For almost a year the risks from the move were still high. George Mead had counted on selling the Dayton real estate to pay off the bank loan. But 1907 turned out to be a year of panic, the effects of which were felt through 1908. "We took a big chance, a long chance," he said, "and the panic [of 1907] was pretty nearly the end of the Mead paper company again." Fortunately, at precisely that depressed time, Myron C. Taylor, later to be chairman of the board of U.S. Steel but then in the textile business, had a contract with a pressing delivery date to make envelopes for the federal government. The Dayton land met his requirements, and he purchased the old property at First and Second Streets for $33,100, almost a thousand more than the moving costs. "That," said George Mead, "saved the little Mead Pulp and Paper Company and permitted us to go forward in Chillicothe until the panic was over with a little more surety or certainty."

George Mead's working concepts were as big as his early plant was small. From the beginning of the new company he appears to have operated according to a concept of pushing for more and more production at prices lower and lower consistent with quality, for George Mead was counting on quality alone for his sales and advertising push. He was already formulating his great paper production idea:

When I took over the little Mead Company in 1905, I found they were making 15 different grades of paper. . . . To make that is just an impossible task from an operating standpoint, because you are constantly changing pulps, formulas, and so on, and we haven't any longer the skilled talent in paper mills who can do the sort of thing they did a hundred years ago. At that time a paper maker was a

A three-goal polo player, George Mead would
practice diligently for a weekend game.

With son, H.T., at Aiken, South Carolina, about 1924—
he helped his family appreciate horses and riding
as much as he did himself.

highly skilled man who did everything for himself, who could make one kind of paper for an hour, then another, and make the changes and still make a living for the company. As the labor situation began to change in the paper world, that was more difficult, and I conceived the idea of following the cotton industry; that if we could get together a dozen mills and say you make this, and you make the next, and have a central force for selling the paper, we could make a complete change in the paper industry. That was [45] years ago, and I still haven't accomplished any of it except in our own plants. If I were 20 years younger, I know that could be accomplished in the next 20 years. We have 11 paper machines in Chillicothe in three mills [1951], and are trying to do that very thing under one roof. Mill #1 makes one paper; Mill #2 all our magazine paper, and Mill #3 writing paper. Every year we make more profit; and once it is cleaned up, the mill will make 50 per cent more profit . . . I do not know of any other mills doing quite that job.

In 1906, when he was working out this concept, he began concentrating on volume production, trying so far as possible to run his three machines full and without changeovers on single grades of paper. In the process he gradually abandoned the manufacture of the varied grades required by the jobber and wholesale market, looking for sales to the big publishers. He depended heavily on the Crowell Publishing Company, which as early as 1907 was taking half the plant's output. George Mead was by no means overlooking the hope of diversification in the future, any more than he was forgetting his plans for capital expansion. But both were dependent on more cash and better prospects for raising it than he had. Diversification, in any case, would have to wait for expansion. He had already picked the spot for a new paper machine and had conceived the idea of erecting a brick structure around the old frame buildings without upsetting production. But even this was an idea for the years yet to come, and the closest he could then come to a capital expenditure was a forestry project, undertaken with the West Virginia Pulp and Paper Company. Figured on a two-thirds one-third basis, Mead capital outlay was just $6,000. As for cooperation between management and employees, the atmosphere was one of working together, whereby every man was dependent on every other man, except that all the men were dependent on George Mead. He provided not only hourly direction and hourly recompense, but also provided out of pocket on an *ad hoc* basis any benefits that the men's circumstances might require. He also instituted an open-door policy that continues today.

Production and sales figures for 1906 and 1907 were encouraging, although hardly sensational. Three hundred tons of paper had been the most produced in a month by the Company's three paper machines during the year prior to

November 1, 1905. The 1906 and 1907 highs for the same machines, after they were located in Chillicothe under George Mead's direct attention, were 500 tons a month and only once, in a bad sales month, did production drop as low as the old 300-ton top. During panic-hit 1907, sales managed to reach a high of more than $500,000, some $40,000 more than during the year before reorganization. The profit figures gave reason for optimism: in 1906, despite the costs of moving from Dayton to Chillicothe, the loss was no more than $3,750, and the next year the gain was $24,898. (The Company, indeed, was not again to operate in the red until the arrival of the Great Depression.) The third generation of Mead management was well launched.

Merchandising Concepts

By 1908, the mill was running smoothly; Hector McVicker had gained two years intense experience as superintendent, and the machines had been coaxed, prodded and repaired into production to the limit of efficient output. George Mead, who expounded the philosophy that "we can make anything we can sell," now discovered that the big problem of the small company was sales. "I found," he said, "that in our Mead company we had spent six months time trying to save 50 cents a ton in the manufacture of paper, and our sales manager would sit at the telephone and give away a dollar a ton in order to get an order. I couldn't quite understand the economics of that. . . . So I decided to learn merchandising."

At this time the sales were in the hands of A. L. Rieger, who had been general manager for the bank trustees and who now, with the title of treasurer, served as a one-man sales and finance staff. He had years of experience with the jobbing trade and felt that the company should look to it for much of its business. George Mead's first step in learning merchandising was to visit, not the jobbers, but the large paper manufacturers with whom he had become friendly during the early years of viscose experimentation, in particular the successful West Virginia Pulp and Paper Company, whose president, John Luke, told him that tonnage was his company's chief sales aim and that the magazine field was its chief market.

George Mead's second step was to take up residence in Dayton at his father's house (Runnymede continued to be a second home), and to make the Company's small new office in the Reibold Building his headquarters. Reports came to him daily from Chillicothe, and once a week he made the trip there by train, usually staying the night in an apartment he kept on the second floor of the Masonic Temple, but when necessary staying on as long as a week. The efficiency of the Chillicothe operation continued to be a primary concern, but sales now had equal urgency. George Mead, however, was a born salesman—he enjoyed selling and was good at it.

The competition which the little Mead Pulp and Paper Company now faced included the West Virginia Company, successful, fast-growing and possessed of no fewer than ten paper machines, the equally large Crocker-Burbank Company, the New York and Pennsylvania Company, third in size, and the Kimberly-Clark Company, big in the West. The Champion Paper Company was in its development stage, but already had ten paper machines, and the Oxford Paper Company, long established in the East, had eight. After examining these lions, George Mead felt that his company should not play the role of the jackal, contenting itself with the lion's left-overs. He continued to eliminate the Company's jobbing business, although he knew he was incurring the displeasure of the trade, and to emphasize tonnage production for big buyers, whom he now began to visit personally, making high quality rather than low price the gist of his sales argument. The Crowell Company in particular found the argument persuasive, took an increasing share of output and signed a substantial contract in 1909. More and more the Chillicothe paper machines were running full on single grades of paper.

The results were gratifying. Tonnage for 1908 was 6,377; for 1909, 7,111; for 1910, 10,675—more than double the tonnage for 1906. Sales for 1908 and 1909 stayed around the $500,000 level but shot up to over $800,000 in 1910. In 1908 the Company began paying dividends on its preferred stock, in 1909 on its common. In 1910, George Mead felt justified in proposing to the board of directors an increase in capitalization to $800,000 ($300,000 preferred, $500,000 common), almost three times the original capitalization of the company. The proceeds from the sales of new stock were to be used throughout the next five years, but a substantial part was to be used immediately for the plant extension he had been planning and for the long-anticipated No. 3 paper machine, which now gave the Company a total of four. The balance sheet figures for 1909 and 1910 were in sharp contrast to those of November 1, 1905:

ASSETS	1905	1909	1910
Net Plant	320,089	414,415	664,815
Current Assets	118,720	141,623	266,193
Other Assets	100	3,813	3,259
LIABILITIES			
Current Liabilities	283,003	144,338	258,925
Other Liabilities	—	2,115	—
Shareholders' Equity	155,906	413,318	675,342

Not only had figures for net plant increased, but they represented solid worth. The outside auditors in 1909 reported: "Equipment and plant are in a high state of efficiency, and many improvements have been made which have been charged off against operations." In 1909 and 1910 current assets had caught up with current liabilities, and, in contrast to 1905's pitiful $291, the company had $18,906 in cash.

Looking back on the occasion of the Company's 20th anniversary, George Mead said:

During the first five years, it was very, very difficult to raise money for the purpose of replacing equipment to give the organization half a chance. The consequence was that for the years 1905 to 1910 the progress of the company was very slow and its growth not very rapid. It always takes a few years, gentlemen, in any business to establish credit because bankers and investors are accustomed to failures. It is a matter of statistics that over 90 per cent of the business ventures started in this or any other country fail: in other words, the percentage of success in business is somewhere between seven and ten. Naturally, men of means and those responsible for other people's money must be most cautious and careful. With a young company, and particularly with a young management that is untried and unproved, and bankers must refuse to give assistance until they are convinced by actual operation that the business that is being offered to them for financing is being properly handled and has a chance of succeeding.

By 1910, the Mead Pulp and Paper Company had convinced the bankers and investors.

Canada and Newsprint Beckon

In the fall of 1910, precisely at this juncture of the Mead company's improved affairs, began George Mead's sensational association with Canadian newsprint. During a 20-year period he was to become salesman of more newsprint than anybody in North America, president and organizer of a series of large modern mills, chairman of the Canadian Newsprint Association, and finally organizer and Chairman of the Board of the largest newsprint company in the world, only to see it fall into trouble and collapse in 1932.

In reflecting about the competition that the little Mead company was facing from the big white-paper producers, George Mead said:

I made up my mind that if I lived long enough I might possibly become a competitor of this large group, but that was a question. So I wondered how I might get into the big leagues, and in looking over the paper of the future I decided that Canada had some real prospects. About that time newsprint was put on the free list, through the chicanery of the news publishers and the Reciprocity Treaty between Canada and United States in 1910, in which there was a rider that said regardless of what happened, newsprint was on the free list. . . .

In 1910, Mr. Talbott, President of the Mead Pulp and Paper Company, whose business was contract engineering through his own company, the H. E. Talbott Company, was building a steel plant at Sault Sainte Marie for a group of Canadian and English capitalists. H. E. Talbott's association with the English and Canadian group was the result of curious coincidence. When his wife, Katharine Houk Talbott (George Mead's aunt), was on her way to England in 1898 to continue her voice studies, she sang at several ship concerts. A Canadian industrialist aboard ship, Mr. F. H. Clergue, was impressed by her voice, made her acquaintance and learned of her husband's engineering abilities. In 1899, as President of the Lake Superior Corporation, Clergue asked him first to build a railroad from Michipicoten on the lake to newly discovered iron mines 150 miles north, and later to undertake dam and canal building at the Sault together with the construction of the new steel mills. While the work was in progress, Mr. Clergue ran out of money, and the Lake Superior Company was put up for receiver's sale, at which time it was purchased by the English and Canadian group.

These same financial interests had acquired, along with a steel plant that had previously been built at the Sault, a groundwood [pulp] mill and a sulphite pulp mill, the latter being new and having never been operated. Mr. Talbott was asked if he had any connections in the States in the paper industry, and as a result requested me to go to the Sault and make a survey of the mills and report to the English and Canadian group as to what might be done with them. After a couple of weeks there I advised they interest the Kimberly-Clark Company of Neenah, Wisconsin, who were manufacturers of newsprint, in building a newsprint mill adjoining the pulp mills to utilize the pulp. . . .

They went to Kimberly-Clark, and Kimberly-Clark investigated carefully and turned it down. These English capitalists had a good deal of money—this was in 1910—at the moment, and they said to Talbott and me that they would like to have us build the mill ourselves and they would put up all the money. . . .

We both felt . . . that the undertaking was a large one for the Mead company and might jeopardize the investment in Ohio. But since the English and Canadian group was willing to supply all of the money necessary for the construction and operation of the plant, we decided to undertake the venture individually, and the Lake Superior Paper Company was organized and built in 1911, with Mr. Talbott as President and myself as Vice President and General Manager. All of this undertaking was, of course, first discussed with the directors of the Mead [Company] and approved by them, as it had been their decision that the Mead should not become involved.

George Mead and Harry Talbott left for England to arrange the finances of the operation and to study newsprint production abroad. Construction of the new mill in Canada began immediately after their return.

George Mead's motives in undertaking the Canadian venture were considerably more complex than his statement about wanting to be in the big leagues suggests. He himself later emphasized on more than one occasion that he took on the venture solely for the purpose of trying to make enough money to promote the Mead company. He was also seeking more experience in merchandising and finance. (He was still smarting from his inexperience in 1905, when he did not catch the mistake of issuing 6 per cent preferred stock without a call date.) What is more, with Mead company affairs beginning to prosper, he had time on his hands, and his drive and enthusiasm wanted a satisfying outlet. Finally, he was putting into practice for the first time a basic concept, which at that time he may not yet have formulated consciously, of decentralizing authority and responsibility.

Long Distance Supervision

His actual division of time worked out much according to a proposal he made in 1910: one-half to Canada, one-half to the Mead Company. This division was facilitated by his setting up a sales office for the Lake Superior Company in the same building in Dayton where the Mead company had its headquarters. During the construction of the paper mill at the Sault, he was actually in residence in Canada for a year, but it can hardly be said that he lived there. He usually came to Dayton twice a month, always once a month, and—including regular side-trips to Chillicothe—typically stayed a week. After a year he moved his place of residence in Dayton and reversed his method of commuting. "I was unmarried, so I could move anywhere quickly," he once commented, "and I made my headquarters in Dayton continuously from the end of 1912 on." Wherever he was, he made such use of the long distance phone and the telegraph cables that to many of his associates he seemed to be everywhere at once.

Of marked help in this simultaneous operation of various ventures was George Mead's ability to select, train and inspire his colleagues. Hector McVicker, for example; had become an able and resourceful superintendent at the Chillicothe mill, and A. L. Rieger, despite his ideas about catering to the jobbing trade, was effectively handling sales and accounts in the Dayton

Two views of the Chillicothe mill (about 1907), just after George Mead took over the reorganization of the company.

office. George Mead was beginning, moreover, the practice he invariably followed thereafter of drawing on the Mead Board of Directors not only to backstop his own ideas but also to benefit from ideas of their own. Policies, plans and projects were circulated among all members for thorough discussion before formal board meetings. Action was never taken unless the directors were in unanimous agreement. This procedure had the effect of more than doubling the numbers of the Mead management without producing any of the confusion that would have resulted had additional managers been actually in location at the mill or the office.

George Mead always wanted his Board of Directors to consist of at least 50 per cent non-company people to provide a system of checks and balances. The board and its officers had undergone some changes since the break with three of the original Chillicothe directors early in 1906. But the changes, made for considerations of convenience, involved changes of titles only. In the spring of 1906, Alexander Renick relinquished the presidency, feeling that since the majority of stockholders were from Dayton the president should be a Daytonian also, and insisted that Harry E. Talbott take the presidency from him. Mr. Renick remained active as a director. Thereafter the officers were H. E. Talbott, president, G. H. Mead, vice-president and general manager, and A. L. Rieger, secretary-treasurer until 1908, when C. A. Craighead, already a director of the company, became secretary to give A. L. Rieger more time for the treasurership. In 1910, Mr. Talbott and George Mead interchanged their posts of president and vice-president. The board of directors was composed of Messrs. Renick, Talbott, Mead, Craighead and another Dayton businessman, E. F. Platt. With these men supplementing his efforts for the Mead Pulp and Paper Company, George Mead now pushed rapidly into his various endeavors.

The Lesson of Chillicothe

Progress at Chillicothe continued with speed and success. During the decade 1911 to 1920, the development of the Chillicothe mill served as a model for future Mead plants, the Canadian newsprint mills with which George Mead was concurrently involved, and for the white-paper industry in general. It is unlikely that this was his conscious purpose at the time; at the beginning of the decade it would have required arrogance as well as optimism to imagine such a role for the little Mead company. But towards the end of the decade, the Chillicothe mill was in fact becoming a model.

Later decades were to see the fruition of George Mead's efforts to make the Chillicothe mill the very best.

There was no change in his basic philosophy of high-quality, high-volume production, but continually throughout the decade of the 1910's there was opportunity for the philosophy to be realized on a wider and wider scale. The decade began with the impetus provided by the 1910 expansion. The impetus was dramatically accelerated by major expansion in 1915 and again in 1920, but was also steadily increased by yearly outlays for additional plant and machinery. It is the nature of papermaking that much of the equipment used is susceptible to continuing modernization, improvement, and refinement. Paper machines, in particular, can be rebuilt repeatedly over periods of decades so that little more than the original framework and anchorage remain. The width of paper produced remains constant, but speed can constantly be increased and quality constantly bettered—granted, of course, the continuing economic health and financial resources of the Company.

In 1911, after the first five years of struggle in launching the Mead Pulp and Paper Company, assets had increased to nearly $1 million, sales to more than $1 million; the working capital ratio was two-to-one, the right way. The foundation had been laid for the program of capital expenditures that was to continue uninterruptedly, subject only to year-to-year variations. Figures for 1911 and 1912 no longer exist; for the years 1913 and 1914 combined, the outlay was about $95,000; for 1915, $54,761.80. Precisely at this time a domestic recession combined with the first impact of World War I led to a demoralized state of business throughout the country—worse even than the panic years of 1907 and 1908. But precisely at this time George Mead chose to carry out a major expansion that, in 1916 alone, added $487,297.83 to the net value of the Chillicothe plant.

On July 15, 1914, he made his proposal formally to the board of directors:

The last extension to the plant was completed in 1910, and the output for the three years following has averaged 48½ tons per day. With the extensions now proposed, the plant will have a capacity of 80 tons per day.

The earnings of the company during these past three years, on the output above mentioned, have amounted on the average to over $1,150,000 annually of gross sales, with an average profit of $77,780 per year. . . .

At the time of the founding of the company in 1905, the following statement was made to investors:

The writer in a most searching and thorough investigation, has failed to find any obstacle whatsoever to the making of a great success of the enterprise.

The writer has since found no reason for changing his view; the operation of the company being consistently profitable since the year 1905, passing through the panic of 1907 and 1908, as well as the more recent depression without the loss of a dollar in bad accounts.

In 1913, he went on to say, sales and profits were crimped by the disastrous Dayton flood, which, while it had no physical effect on the Chillicothe plant, upset business throughout southwestern Ohio. Nonetheless, profits improved from 1910's $5,000 a month to $6,480 a month during the following three years. With the new program of major expansion, he predicted monthly profits of $12,800 or over $150,000 a year, and thereupon proposed an increase in capital from $800,000 to $1,250,000, a sum soon increased to $1,500,000.

One year later, at a time when the business recession was at its nadir, the board minutes record that George Mead stressed the urgency of taking advantage of existing low costs and of beginning the enlargement of the plant.

Price / Production Concepts

During the century's second decade the dynamic of production and price, central to George Mead's production strategy ever since 1905, was put to work forcefully. At the time, this concept had been acted upon by only a handful of businessmen, the most notably successful of whom was Andrew Carnegie. The Carnegie success was based on two fundamental business discoveries, which, despite his outpouring of ideas in some eight books and eighty articles, he never reduced to words, and, indeed, were not discussed in print by anyone until long after George Mead independently put them to work.

The first discovery, succinctly stated, is that rapid economic growth results from the interrelationship between growing expenditures for plant and machinery, increasing production at decreasing prices and mounting wages and profits. The interrelationship is such that each increase in profits provides more expenditure for plant and machinery, which in turn generates more production at lower prices, and which in turn yields increased profits, whereupon, of course, the process is launched all over again, so that plant growth is not only self-sustaining but fast, slowing only at times of general panic or depression.

The second discovery is that times of panic or depression, while they may curb production increases, provide a signal opportunity for multiplying the generative force of investment in plant and machinery, the low level of general prices making possible greater capital expansion than at times when price levels are high.

Even today, it requires boldness and optimism to expand plant at times so depressed that most businessmen confine themselves to husbanding their resources and limiting their activities. Two generations ago, it required not only optimism but marked brilliance of mind to grasp the interconnectedness of production, price, pay and profits. In view of the fact that George Mead and Andrew Carnegie shared these characteristics, together with an aversion to speculation and a concern for blue-collar employees, it is significant that Mr. Mead was not wholly impressed by Mr. Carnegie:

> The United States Steel Company had been formed. I knew Mr. Phipps, personally. I didn't know Carnegie . . . Mr. Phipps was much more responsible, in my judgment, for the success of [the Carnegie Steel Company] than Mr. Carnegie. Mr. Carnegie was a great merchant and publicity man and a very shrewd operator, but Phipps was the fellow who ran the show, and he was a certified accountant and a top man in figures.

Henry Phipps, Jr., was in fact an honest, unobtrusive man with great capacity for finance and for well-reasoned direction of many of the Carnegie company's affairs. Without Phipps, the Carnegie Steel Company could possibly have come apart at the seams. But without Carnegie and the pressure that he exerted precisely on the seams, there would not have been a company nor success on a scale that had never before been achieved by a productive enterprise. A strong light is indeed thrown on the character of George Mead by the fact that he could be more impressed by Henry Phipps than by this man with whom he had so much in common. It is evident that he was apathetic to Carnegie's exuberance, boastfulness, ostentation, unabashed publicity-seeking and extreme absenteeism from his company's affairs, spending time, instead, in a castle in Scotland, in a mansion in New York, or in gatherings of celebrities everywhere instead of on the production floor.

Genuinely modest, averse alike to ostentation and publicity, maturely confident rather than adolescently exuberant, and dedicated for all the multiplicity of his endeavors to constant day-by-day labor in the offices and on the floor of his plants, George Mead could appreciate a man of integrity and unobtrusive kindliness much more readily than he could the man whose economic vision was basically similar to his own. He was not simply a combination of Carnegie and Phipps, with the conscious bearing of the latter and the unconscious drives of the former. His personality, for all its many facets, was all of one piece; its conscious and subliminal aspects were notably integrated; indeed his warmth, his humanness and his modesty were inherent in his optimistic will to create an ever-expanding productive enterprise. Like Carnegie, he was not a man who reacted to economic circumstances but one who created them, not one content to react to his times, but one driven by a vision of shaping them. But his vision involved not the noisy imposition of himself on the environment around him, but a quiet dynamic interaction with it. In this he was a civic and business organizer of an entirely new and even today still-unrecognized order.

The Great War

In the Chillicothe plant, George Mead went on quietly effecting dramatic growth. By 1915, the Company's assets had increased modestly during the preceding two years to reach $1,161,327; sales had grown by 15 per cent to hit $1,268,350; profits had swelled from $44,232 to $79,235. The construction of new plant and the installation of an array of new machinery, including paper machine No. 5, were complete early in 1916, precisely at a time when recovery from depression at home and the demands of war abroad provided a powerful stimulus on business in general and on the demand for paper in particular.

The Company's 1916 performance vindicated George Mead's daring in 1914 and 1915 in a manner considerably more spectacular than he had envisaged. Increases in tonnage from 14,030 to 19,971 and in net plant from $794,240 to $1,236,890 were propheciable, but a doubling of working capital, a tripling of other assets, an increase in sales from $1,268,350 to $2,300,820, and a quadrupling of profits (they reached $365,678) were hardly foreseeable. In that year, net earnings were 15.9 per cent of sales, 37.6 per cent of net worth—a return of phenomenal proportions in the paper industry—and the Mead Pulp and Paper Company almost doubled its dimensions.

The next three years were not propitious for the paper industry. Paper, essential to every business activity and to almost all aspects of a civilized society, is not a directly war-related commodity; it was not understood as essential in World War I and not recognized as such during World War II until paper scarcities actually began to curtail ammunition shipments. In 1917 and 1918, the Mead company was beset with government restrictions

In between his many trips to cover far-flung operations,
George Mead still found time for hunting.
Here he's at Cabin Bluff, Georgia during the thirties.

George Mead was always
able to select, train
and inspire his colleagues
from management to mill.

and labor shortages—in neither of the World Wars did the company request
deferment of any employees– together with sharply increased costs and actual shutdowns under wartime fuel restrictions. Tonnage dipped slightly in
1917, and while higher prices increased dollar sales by 70 per cent, increased costs trimmed profits to a third of 1916's record high. In 1918, sales
were off, tonnage was down a thousand tons and profits were trimmed to
2.4 per cent of net worth.

Then came 1919, a year of post-war readjustment and slump. Business in
general was less than good, and the paper industry again found itself faced
with its characteristic feast-and-famine problems. The addition of one new
paper machine with its ancillary equipment could even then boost the tonnage of a single plant by as much as 5,000 tons a year. The addition of
many machines in many plants in times of prosperity plus the return to production of many other machines in marginal plants let loose a glut of paper
that even a moderately depressed market could not absorb. Consequently,
marginal plants were knocked out of business, and established companies
found their operations abruptly slowed.

During these years, George Mead's business strategy had little in common with typical and commonly accepted industrial practice. He avoided major additions to plant in 1917 and 1918 when the times appeared propitious for expansion to many other businessmen, holding himself to his program of steady improvements, which amounted to $175,000 during the two years, and which were balanced by a comparable addition to depreciation reserves. On December 10, 1917, moreover, he advanced his philosophy of running full so far as possible on single grades of paper by negotiating the Company's first substantial cost-plus arrangement with the Crowell Publishing Company: a five-year contract that called for 75 per cent of Chillicothe's current capacity. The contract required expensive alteration of production and commercial operations, and bound the Company to only a fair return on its investment at a time when many other companies were charging what the traffic would bear. During the first year of the contract, indeed, the Mead company went beyond the contract and diverted additional tonnage to Crowell after several of the latter's other suppliers failed to deliver promised tonnage. In spite of this strategy of concentrating production and limiting profits in 1918, its long-range benefits on sales and profits were almost immediately manifest. During the slow year of 1919, when many paper companies were operating at a loss, the Mead Pulp and Paper Company suffered only a minor drop in sales, pushed profits from $42,387 to $141,484, and increased capital expenditures 27 per cent. During that year, moreover, George Mead perfected a far-reaching program he had been formulating for post-war expansion, and, seizing upon a slump as a time of opportunity, launched the expansion program on January 6, 1920.

CHAPTER 5

The Family Man and the Family

MR. MEAD at work, he was plain "Pops" at home. No man is just a businessman, an abstract individual who can go through the motions of living without ever feeling. And George Mead's business career with all its intensity, advances and retreats, was only possible because of a warm and stable family life. Affection and support were the foundations of his youth; they were the mainstays of his married life. George Mead earned the love and respect of his wife and children. They, in turn, dubbed him Pops. Because he loved to laugh, because he knew when to unbend and when to be stern, his wife and children felt close to him even if he were called out of town for business a week or more at a time. Just as he trusted his business associates to carry out huge responsibilities without him, he trusted his children to follow the example of living set for them. Fortunately, he had an exceptionally strong ally in this task—his wife, Elsie.

George Mead married a girl he had known all 21 years of her life: Elsie Louise Talbott, his first cousin, daughter of his remarkable Aunt Katharine and Uncle Harry. Both George and Elsie were grandchildren of Eliza Thruston Houk, the brisk, bright and devoted Yannie who had such an influence on his life.

Katharine Talbott, who made regular entries in the birthday books she kept for each of her nine children, is a good source of information about George and Elsie's growing attachment through the years.

Age 3—"September 3, 1896. Elsie has so much character in her face that George thinks she will be the handsomest of all."

Age 7—"September 3, 1900. George is especially fond of her and thinks she has the makings of a fine girl."

Age 17—"September 3, 1910. She is as devoted as ever to George Mead and he to her. From the time she was a tiny thing she has been George's special 'Set' as he has always called her. And it is such a joy to me that she has his devoted care as well as my own. He is keenly interested in every-thing for her and she is devoted to him."

Age 19—"September 3, 1912. Her nature is quite as it has always been, serious, sincere, unselfish . . . So much reserved force and so much reserve that very few people think they really know her. She is very popular with the boys . . ."

Age 21—"September 3, 1914. Elsie grows handsomer all the time . . . she is extremely popular, but as for loves, she will have none of them. Her devo-tion seems all centered in George Mead, and while she sees a lot of the boys, it seems almost a certainty that no one else can ever mean anything to her. Just how we will adjust ourselves to meet so unusual a situation we do not know, but of one thing we are certain that is—as our dear mother has always felt—it will be settled in the right and happiest way."

How right the birthday book was—it was settled in the right and happiest way. Elsie Louise Talbott and George Houk Mead were married November 22, 1914 in the chapel at Westover School in Connecticut; Elsie was a graduate of the school. Elsie's brother, Nelson, was captain of the Yale foot-ball team at that time, and many of the couple's friends and relatives were in Connecticut for the Saturday game between Harvard and Yale. Sunday afternoon seemed the perfect time and place to have the wedding. Their honeymoon was short and, after a few days on the coast of New Jersey, was actually a business trip through Canada.

The couple set up housekeeping in Dayton and rented a bungalow in Hills and Dales (outside the city of Dayton) where their first child, Elsie Louise, was born September 6, 1915. Just a year later, in 1916, George, Elsie, along with little Louise, packed their belongings and moved to Cher-ry Angle, closer to the Talbott's Runnymede residence. Three new Meads were added in quick succession: George Jr. came along on August 3, 1917; Harry Talbott was born October 16, 1918; and Nelson Strobridge joined the family on October 28, 1921. A baby boy, born in 1920, died in infancy.

During this time, George Mead was at work building up the Mead paper enterprises and developed four new Canadian newsprint mills. But at home, he and Elsie were planning and building their own home—The Little Woods. It was completed in 1922 just after Nelson was born. The Little Woods, only a short distance from the Runnymede house and farm, man-aged to recreate the warm atmosphere of Runnymede hospitality that George and Elsie Mead had found so meaningful and important. Set in the rolling southern Ohio countryside, The Little Woods was the place where the Mead children grew up—the only place they called home until they set up their own homes with their own families.

A Housewarming Party

To celebrate their housewarming, the Meads gave what they considered their best party. They invited all the people who had worked on the home, including their families, set up a huge buffet, and George Mead gave a small speech warmly welcoming everyone and thanking all the men for their various jobs well done.

George and Elsie Mead put a lot more stock in their family and friends than in high society. They loved nothing more than having their children bring friends to enjoy The Little Woods' squash court, swimming pool, tennis court and stables. George's childhood friends were among his special golfing friends. And The Little Woods was always the center of activity, whether it was for dinner with business colleagues and their wives or entertaining of family and friends. All found cordiality, warmth and substance at The Little Woods and among the Mead family.

The fact that stables were part of the plan for The Little Woods is indicative of George Mead's great interest in riding and the sport of polo. He began playing polo in 1913, just before his marriage. Some years later, he founded the Miami Valley Hunt and Polo Club and served as treasurer of the U. S. Polo Association and as a member of the committee to select the U. S. International Polo Team. The Polo Club was active in the Midwest Polo League, a rich source of friends and entertaining for the Meads. The teams did not travel alone; for instance, the Chicago, Cleveland and Buffalo players always brought their wives to Dayton, and Dayton wives also went to the out-of-town games, making the weekends a round of parties and, in the words of Elsie Mead, "really great fun." George Mead was serious about polo—he would practice all week long to prepare for a weekend game. The practice paid off; George Mead was rated a three-goal player. When George Jr. took up the game, George Sr. stopped playing—he recognized a better player and decided to leave the heroics to his son, who eventually was rated a five-goal player.

Their interest in horses and the pleasant climate soon led the Mead family to Aiken, South Carolina, a very horse-conscious community. In 1932, a home was purchased to serve as school and winter headquarters. All six of George

The most imaginative and unique
Christmas gift George Mead ever got
from his family, a gypsy wagon,
was refurbished inside and out
by his wife and children.

A favorite pastime for the Meads was
listening to their father play the piano
and sing some of his own compositions.

and Elsie's children, including Katherine (born October 12, 1924) and Marianna (March 28, 1930), went to school in Aiken at one time or another. Kay and Marianna attended a day school their mother started. The sons attended Aiken Prep School. George Mead took a keen interest in the boys' school and eventually served as a trustee; later, his son, Nelson, took his place as a trustee. Aiken, being a resort community, had a condensed school year—late fall to early spring—leaving a lot of time for the family to enjoy their home, family and friends in Dayton during Ohio's pleasant seasons. Actually, Aiken was just as much "home" as Dayton and in many ways the family life was closer because "Pops" was vacationing and free to join in on the tennis, golf, quail hunts, Drag Hunts and picnicking in the woods.

While the children were young, the Meads usually alternated Christmas holidays between Dayton and Aiken. Every year, Mrs. Mead and the children looked for a suitable gift for their husband and father, and usually came up with an imaginative and unique surprise. By far the most unique gift was a gypsy wagon Mrs. Mead located during a trip to her alma mater, Westover. The old wagon had seen better days, but Mrs. Mead thought it would be a perfect place for George to take naps during quail hunts in Aiken. She procured the wagon, had it shipped by flat car to Aiken, and she and the children plunged into feverish work to rejuvenate it. The wagon's ornate beveled glass and stained glass windows were washed and cleaned, the slightly weathered oil paintings of hunting dogs on the sides were left intact, and a new coat of paint made it shine. It was wrapped in clear cellophane with a big red cellophane Christmas bow and a sign that read "Merry Christmas to Pops." The final touch was a team of mules driven by the boys to pull the wagon in the driveway close to the house for presentation to George. But he was so wrapped up in another of his gifts, a golf putting game, that Mrs. Mead and the children had to forcibly push him, shout and ask him to look up. They were so excited about it that they put up the picnic tables and had Christmas dinner, turkey and all the trimmings, right in the wagon—all eight of them.

Christmas was a time for parties, whether in Aiken or Dayton. Even the horses were allowed to party—the Meads set up Christmas trees decorated with carrots, sugar and apples in the stable yard for the horses. Neighbors brought over their horses to join the festivities. One Christmas, George Mead received a motorized golf cart from the family. He drove it around the room for awhile, until one of his sons decided to show Pops how to back the thing up, backing right into a table and scattering lamps, pictures and trays, resulting in merriment the whole family, especially George Mead, enjoyed.

A Love for Music

Those were noisy good times, and George Mead joined in to make noise and have a wonderful time. Often the children would persuade him to play the piano and sing the songs he wrote. Though not an accomplished musician, George Mead had always loved music—especially opera. When he was young and in Boston, he bought the cheapest tickets to the opera, contenting himself with the "peanut gallery" because he could afford no better. He even took occasional bit parts at the Boston opera, carried a spear around and had one of the best seats in the house. He learned to play the violin and guitar, but it was the piano he enjoyed most. Old-fashioned sing-a-longs were part of the fun at the Mead household. But George's solos stole the show. Elsie Mead refers to her husband's songs as "silly songs" because they were stuff and nonsense and made people laugh—songs like "You Drive Me Mad My Madagascar Maid," "Handle Me with Love, Bill," and "John James Brown."

These were light, affectionate and humorous moments in the Mead family life. But the health and well-being of his family was of paramount importance to George Mead. So when his second son, H. T., developed a serious case of bronchitis, there was no question but to follow doctor's orders and seek a temporary home in a warm, dry climate. That meant somewhere in the West —a long way from the Mead enterprises. When H. T. suffered an especially severe attack one night, Elsie called George, who was in New York at the time, and said she was leaving that day for Phoenix with H. T. and a nurse. But the family was not to be separated. On her own, Elsie was to find a suitable house for the entire family. The original idea was to find a house in either Phoenix or Tucson. After looking there unsuccessfully, Elsie ended up in Riverside, California, at a home owned by Bud Pinkerton of detective fame. But Mr. Pinkerton had no intention of renting the place to anyone.

The house had been built for visiting polo teams and was complete with stables (a good selling point where the Meads were concerned because George wanted to bring his horses). Elsie Mead was unable to negotiate rental of the house, and she asked George to intervene with Pinkerton. He immediately contacted Pinkerton, who still wouldn't budge from his "no renting" stand, saying that the house wasn't big enough for the family and, anyway, Mrs. Mead wouldn't like it. George Mead countered with, "My wife says it *is* big enough—and you don't know my wife!"

Pinkerton said he'd think it over; the result was a change of heart and even some quick improvements in living space. The Meads consider the time spent in Riverside as probably one of the closest in their lives. Having the horses meant family rides through beautiful California landscape, and a togetherness that wasn't a popular slogan but a real family bond for Pops, his wife and their children.

At Aiken, Riverside, Dayton and elsewhere, George Mead was an enthusiastic horseman. Since he rode a pony to school in his youth, he developed his riding ability. He was always enthusiastic about any sport he practiced. Long walks were part of his self-imposed health program. The program included playing golf, tennis, polo, canoeing, daily setting up exercises and a daily nap after lunch. This was no hour or hour and a half nap, though, as he would frequently lie down on the sofa in his office and hold a set of keys in his hand. When he relaxed into sleep, the keys would fall to the ground and he'd awaken—completely refreshed and ready to go on with the day's activities.

Golf was one of George Mead's favorite ways to get exercise. Frequently playing in the Ohio State championships, he garnered a whole rack full of trophies and cups. During those Ohio championships when he was young, he played against a tall, slim young man—Prescott Bush. The next time he saw Bush was many years later when his oldest daughter, Louise, married Dr. John M. Walker. Dr. Walker's brother-in-law was the same golf-playing Prescott Bush, later a senator from Connecticut.

When he no longer rode, George Mead was still playing golf, traversing the links well into his seventies. He made his first and only hole-in-one when he was 72 years old.

At Aiken and in the family's month to six-week summer vacations, George Mead was always on the go. While the family took up residence for the summer or winter, George Mead commuted between his family and work. One Christmas he counted up that he had spent 21 nights in sleeping cars during the month of December. It was not an easy way to live, but George Mead loved both his work and his family and found plenty of time for both. Travel played a big part in all their lives. Occasional trips to Europe with the children were taken—George taking the boys, Elsie taking the girls. For many summers George and Elsie got away from everyone by taking canoe trips into Canada and camping out along the route. George considered these trips his "honeymoons." For several years their summer vacations were spent in a different place each summer. In the twenties the Meads started spending summers on Cape Cod at Hyannis and continued this for some 30 years. It was here that George Jr. and the Meads got to know the Kennedy family. The same age as the older Kennedy children, young George Mead partied with the Kennedys in Aiken and at the Cape. Mrs. Mead still has a silver tray given her after a house party in Aiken, just at the start of the war that was to change the lives of both families. The inscription on the tray reads:

FOR MRS. MEAD
In recognition of her hospitality above and beyond the line
of duty during the great spring offensive of '42 at Aiken.

Kick Kennedy (Kathleen)
Betty Cox
Jack Kennedy
Chuck Spalding
Johnny Coleman

During the Depression and World War II, the Meads were a close and happy family. The paper business, being a family enterprise, was talked about and dissected at home. George and Elsie Mead entertained his business colleagues at home, and the whole family got to know them. George Mead's sons came to understand and appreciate the paper business as their father had. In addition to taking the boys bird-shooting and to hockey games, George Mead brought his sons to foremen's meetings and talked about the family business while at play. Everyone who remembers George Mead recalls his generosity, kindness and understanding of people. He was so well-liked as a man, for instance, that a train was held for him when he was detained at a doctor's: the trainmen knew him and when they saw his secretary waiting on the platform, they paid back his many favors to them by holding the train for the few minutes Mr. Mead needed to arrive.

His laughter, which came so easily, and his love for people, which came just as naturally, made him the kind of man people didn't forget.

Resuscitating the family paper mills was the means by which George Mead provided for his family financially; a healthy dose of love from "Pops" provided for them in all other ways.

CHAPTER 6

Growth and Growing Pains

EVEN BEFORE THE 1920 EXPANSION, the Mead Pulp and Paper Company had come a long way in the short time since it began over again in 1905 with its dilapidated plant and run-down machinery, its deficiency in working capital and its paucity of cash, and with its purely nominal asset value of $438,909. During the much longer period between 1880 and 1919, the Chillicothe operation had covered an even more impressive distance:

	1880	1919
Coal Consumed Per Day	28 tons	150 tons
Wood Used Per Year	1,500 cords	12,000 cords
Lime Used Per Year	18,000 bushels	100,000 bushels
Soda Ash Used Per Year	240 tons	1,000 tons
Employees	50	425
Pounds Paper Made Per Day	6,000 pounds	150,000 pounds

Improvement in efficiency was even more marked than increase in size. In 1919, using roughly five times as much coal and chemicals, eight times as much wood, and eight and a half times as many employees, Chillicothe was producing 25 times as much paper as it did 39 years earlier.

In 1920, Chillicothe jumped a very great distance both in efficiency and size. For a medium-size company with assets the previous year of $2,202,788, the scale of the expansion program was mammoth. Capitalization was raised from $1,500,000 all the way to $6,300,000 ($3,000,000 common, $300,000 preferred, $3,000,000 special preferred). Capital expenditures in that single year totaled $2,841,741.58. At the end of the year, net plant had increased three and one-half times to reach $3,917,951; at $5,930,660 assets were nearly three times the year before; sales jumped to $3,869,303; profits were $277,750, a solid 7 per cent on net worth, and net worth itself more than doubled to reach $3,942,000.

At an employees' dinner on Saturday, January 4, two days before the start of construction of a large building, George Mead announced that the expansion program would include two big 152-inch paper machines (numbers 6 and 7), other pulp and paper equipment in large quantities, an increase in capacity from 75 to 150 tons per day, a major shift from steam to electric power, a chemical recovery system and four new buildings. "If cooperation and quality continue during the period of planned expansion during the coming years," he said, "the Chillicothe plant will be the biggest book-paper mill in the world."

By the end of 1920, the plant was already one of the largest. A conception of its size is suggested by the amount of water consumed per year: 3.5 billion gallons. The plant now covered ten acres, consisted of 50 buildings, and included two miles of railroad track over which a switch engine handled 6,000 carloads of incoming and outgoing freight a year, exclusive of the freight that arrived either by horse and cart or by the two and one-half ton trucks of the day. There was no provision for new office space, although the old 1909 building was jammed. "We'll spend money for machinery," said George Mead to William Ludwig, then in the shipping department, "but office is overhead. No."

Steam engines of 985 rated horsepower still drove the 15 beaters, two of the older paper machines, and a few small pieces of auxiliary equipment, but now there were two new steam-driven turbo-generators of 3,500 rated horsepower, producing 3,450 kilowatts of electricity for some 250 other machines, among them the chippers, four bleachers, the washers, seven Jordans, the five other paper machines and twelve supercalenders, the largest of which weighed 75 tons and was powerful enough to handle a paper width of 140 inches. The two big new paper machines were 200 feet long by 13 feet wide and moved at speeds from 250 to 450 feet per minute. One of them could produce 20 tons of paper a day: almost as much paper as the entire plant was producing at the beginning of the decade.

"No Man Is Expendable"

No remark better describes George Mead's approach to organization than his flat statement, "No man is expendable." His practice and the unstated policy of the company was to seek out the best men to be found: not conformists, not anything resembling company men, but men of strong personalities and of diverse temperaments, experiences and backgrounds. George Mead once said that he looked for and preferred men who were only 80 per cent efficient but 100 per cent loyal to men 100 per cent efficient and only

80 per cent loyal. Once a man was hired, Mr. Mead felt it was his and the company's responsibility to find the right place for him, bring out the best in him and stick by him. Trial period for the new employee and the company was one year. If everyone was satisfied after that, the man was considered permanent. Even today, most of the principal executives of the company were hired personally by him. Before 1947 all of them were so hired, together with many blue-collar workers.

Told in 1930 by bankers who were arranging a bond issue that he had good executives but perhaps too many of them, he replied, "It is easy to get machines, it is hard to get good men." During subsequent depressions, there were no discharges, no layoffs. Cuts in salaries and wages—at first confined to executives—were handled like a progressive income tax. One evening at home, George Mead actually became angry over the news of Eugene Grace's million-dollar bonus, and he personally sought to convince Walter Chrysler that mass layoffs in the auto industry were both inhuman and bad business.

George Mead insisted upon a democratic process in his business. He thought of democracy as a system in which every man has a chance to express himself. For convenience he used the terms labor or management or company or industry or government, but he saw them not as impersonal and static groups, but as active and vital gatherings of people. Fully aware of the differences between people, he was not aware of any distinction between them, and his concern for executives did not differ from his concern for blue-collar men. "Men of one position," he once said, "are not the natural superiors of men in other positions." His emphasis was always upon the person, no matter income or rank, as the unit of accomplishment.

By the early 1920's, the Company had a full system of employee benefits of a sort that did not become common in industry until more than 20 years later: an active mill council that engaged in collective bargaining, an advancement from the ranks policy, paid vacations, accident and health insurance and a stock plan so attractive that by 1923 one-third of the men had become Mead shareholders, together with such things as employee direction of the company restaurant and its recreation facilities. Company policy held that wages and working conditions must be the best in the industry; bonuses were once offered for finding better ones. The safety program had as its chief protagonist George Mead himself, who repeatedly declared in public that its success meant more to him than the company's profits. It was not simply that he put men above capital; he put nothing above them. Free communication with his men was the basis of his organizing their efforts. George Mead always had an "open-door" policy in business, but as the company grew, it became a physical impossibility to get everyone through his still open door. By that time, however, he had opened doors throughout the Company to the degree that free interchange had become not simply a policy, but the unspoken and established way of doing Mead business. These egalitarian sentiments were suggested by George Mead in a 1922 talk, when it was still possible to get all the men in the same room: "There is no reason why the Mill Council should not be made as familiar with the policies of the company as are the directors. There is no reason why the Mill Council should not take to the employees these policies. . . . The men who are working at the machines should know exactly what they are working for."

Policies, Procedures and Benefits

With the Chillicothe plant expanding so dynamically, the number of employees increased constantly—between 1916 and 1920 there were 300 to 400 men—so that the early *ad hoc* practice of George Mead's ideas of cooperation and mutual benefits had to be buttressed with set policies and procedures. In 1916, the plant changed to three shifts a day from the ancient and onerous two-shift system; the Mead company wanted to be first in the industry to make the move, but had to settle for second when Crocker-Burbank moved first. In the same year, the board of directors and the stockholders gave formal approval to an employee stock purchase plan (preferred stock only: George Mead felt common stock involved too much risk for men dependent on wages). A mill council, which had been operating in effect but without name since 1905 was formalized in 1920 into a 16-man group, eight chosen from management, eight elected by employees, empowered to handle grievances and set working conditions.

Bonuses proportionate to earnings were formally introduced in 1916: in that good year they amounted to 5 per cent of each man's wages, in the less-than-good year of 1919, to 2 per cent. During World War I, wages were pegged to the cost of living; wage levels were defined by a chart posted on the plant walls showing the gradation of opportunities and wages for each job; a policy of promotion from within, in operation since 1905, was officially declared. Vacations with pay were formalized in 1919; a retirement plan was set up in 1920; in the same year sickness and accident insurance supplementary to workmen's compensation was arranged through a group policy with the Travelers' Insurance Company. For some years, a full-time nurse and a part-time physician had been on duty in the plant; during the 1919 expansion, a factory hospital was installed, and the nurse was provided with a car for home visits when requested. About the same time, a cafeteria and an athletic field were constructed, their operation being put entirely in the hands of employees. In 1920 the Company contributed $5,000 for a mutual benefits funds, set up to meet special needs and thereafter to be maintained through dollar-for-dollar additions by the company and the men.

In 1916, the men themselves formalized George Mead's practice of talking to them individually about company plans and policies and industry conditions. A group came to him saying that they didn't get out of town and he did, and would he talk to everyone at once? The first of many extemporaneous speeches—they evolved into president's dinners and then foremen's dinners as the number of employees became too great for any meeting place in Chillicothe—was delivered from an up-ended box in the finishing room. An employee magazine, *Mead Co-Operation*, began publication in July, 1919. It communicated employees and company news notes, short articles on the war effort, safety in the shop and at home, mutual relations and quality.

Formalization of employee relations did not supplant George Mead's informal practice of dealing on the spot with special situations as they occurred. One day in 1920, he learned from George Sutton, driver of the company horse-driven pick-up wagon and a former slave, that he wanted to see his old home and his old master in Virginia before he died. A leave of absence and a $50 bill were immediately provided, and the trip became an annual occurrence.

In 1919 or 1920, an attempt was made to unionize the plant. George Mead had never been opposed to unions and had, indeed, been working with them smoothly for some time in his Canadian operations. Several years later, he reported:

I have always thought it was proper for men to form an organization to combat . . . the grasping hand of the capitalist who is trying to crush labor. When people can come together as we do, and have our own cooperative spirit, our own union of thought, and our own shoulder-to-shoulder idea of discussing matters, there is no necessity to pay out money to a group of men in New York, Chicago, or Cleveland to keep them engaged throughout the year to come down and negotiate with us for our own welfare. We can do that between ourselves and save that money. . . .

A situation arose . . . several years ago when a union organizer came here and said our labor conditions were not as good as in union mills. Mr. Carruth [then general manager at Chillicothe] asked me what answer should be given to the men, some of whom really believed the statement. I said: "You go back and tell the men we will pay the expenses of any three men in our company that they may select to travel about the country and visit all union mills. If they come back and tell me of any plant in this country that is paying any better wages or that has any better working conditions than our plant, I will give them a bonus. That is the information I'm looking for." That statement was given to the union organizers, and we did not hear anything more from them. They did not want the committee appointed and an investigation made. That, gentlemen, is my attitude today. If I can find any plant in the United States that can afford to do anything more than we can for our men, I want to know it and how they do it, and it will not be a month until we will be doing the same. I want the position of this company, although we are in a highly competitive business and manufacturing paper for the Crowell Company, to be that we pay the best wages and have the best working conditions in the entire paper industry and yet have the lowest production cost.

First of All, Men

George Mead categorized people as management and employees only to the extent required for the running of the plant, later on for the functioning of such bodies as the War Labor Board. In fact, the term "employee" was one he was inclined to dislike and used infrequently, preferring to speak of "men," by which he meant, depending on circumstances, everybody in the plant including himself or everybody receiving hourly wages. To his mind, everyone—everyone without exception—should know exactly what is going on and what is being planned, everyone should advance any ideas he has about any program, plan, or policy; everyone should be able to have a sense of purpose in what he is doing, and everyone should be treated not simply well but like a man. The idea that labor should be induced to cooperate with management or that management should be benign enough to cooperate with labor was foreign to his values, whereby men were first of all men and not integers graded by set concepts of rank. Mutual benefits were not, therefore, company benefits; they were benefits derived from everyone in the plant working together first for the benefit of everyone in the plant, second for the benefit of everyone's family, and then for the benefit of customers and stockholders who made the working together possible.

Cooperation, thus, included quality, for it was quality that sold paper and provided earnings as well as contributed to meaningfulness of work. Quality was not simply a value George Mead inherited from his grandfather; it was a reality around which revolved a good deal of his business philosophy. In the paper business, the interrelationship of production, price, pay and profit is possible only if orders come in increasing quantity from big publishers who are also big printers and as such are rightly conscious of how smoothly paper runs on high-speed presses, how well it takes ink, how attractive it looks in the hands of the final consumer. Press breakdowns or involved press adjustments because of poor quality paper are enormously costly in money and time; poor appearance eventually hurts subscription and news-stand sales. Quality, moreover, is inherent in the one-machine one-paper-grade idea. After a visit to Europe with Harry Talbott and David Luke in 1919, visiting paper mills and seeing first-hand the consequences of the war, he commented on a Scandinavian mill that was making as many as 15 changes in grades of paper in as many hours: "They have attempted to take a mass production machine and apply to it custom production." His objection to this mismatch was its inevitable consequence of decreased output and impaired quality. In actual production, high output and high quality are interdependent; moreover, they are difficult enough to maintain with one grade of paper; with many grades the problem is not simply that output plummets but that quality collapses.

Establishing Quality Standards

A Mead paper machine running day after day, week after week—as it did for Crowell paper—demanded the establishment of a standardized technique of controlling quality, constantly under development in Chillicothe throughout the 1910's. There was unceasing pressure not only from George Mead but also from Crowell to improve the various characteristics of the finished paper—press runability, printing surface, ink receptivity, opacity, strength and some hundred other considerations, all of which figured in constant interchanges of letters and phone calls between the Chillicothe office, the Dayton headquarters and the Crowell plant in Springfield, Ohio. Men and technologists alike had to be alert to produce paper of proper flatness, trim, strength, smoothness, levelness, cushion, coverage, ink receptivity and general mechanical perfection, which in turn required precise measurement and exact controls. Controls included laboratory tests for basis weight, bursting strength, tensile strength, thickness and density, internal tearing resistance, folding endurance, smoothness, porosity, water resist-

Horse-lovers all—the Mead family in Aiken. From l. are George, Elsie, Louise, George Jr., H.T., Nelson, Katherine and Marianna.

ance, internal bond strength, stiffness, dimensional stability, compressibility and the like. Also watched for were defects, such as curl, cuts, uneven caliper, poor splices, cracked edges, wrinkles, improper moisture, pin holes, draw marks, surface lint, scale, buckles and welts, ropes, calender spots, ridges, overcrush, shadow mark, dirt, bug spots, dryer smudge, dye spots, felt-seam marks, color lumps, shaft marks, feathering, stiffness, show-through, wire marks, two-sidedness and so on. In 1916, for instance, chemist James O'Conner from the lab and John Graves, boss of No. 3 machine, spent months trying to eliminate wire marks by taking photographs of series after series of samples of finished paper, blowing them up, studying the indentations left by the Fourdrinier wire, and then making small carefully measured alterations to the controls on the suction boxes that draw water from the matting pulp as it moves over the wet end of the machine.

Quality problems were further complicated during World War I by an order of the War Production Board during the summer of 1918 that magazine publishers could use no more paper tonnage than that used the previous year. Crowell circulation for the *Woman's Home Companion,* the *American Magazine,* and *Farm and Fireside,* was swelling; advertising was skyrocketing. All Crowell paper was supercalendered to an exact finish—coated papers were not yet used—and had a basis of weight of 56 pounds. Experiments at first showed that a 48 pound sheet was the lightest that could be produced and supercalendered, but this reduction in weight and gain in quantity by no means met Crowell demand. Further experimentation finally produced a usable but far-from-satisfactory sheet with a basis weight of 24 pounds. Immediately, the Chillicothe plant launched a long-continued attempt to improve the quality of this admittedly make-do product, leading in time to an entirely new series of operating standards and machine improvements, the recovery and use in the pulp mixture of the pulp-mill sludge that had previously been considered waste, together with the use of old paper in the making of new.

The net impress of George Mead's policies, speeches and conversations on the men working with him was simply what he had on his own mind, cooperation and quality. For all his constant concern with the mechanical perfection of the mill, he seldom talked about worker efficiency. Here as elsewhere, he proceeded with typical and successful indirection: George Mead believed and proved that efficiency can be encouraged by talking quality.

New Ideas and New Processes

In 1920, the Mead Pulp and Paper Company with its $6 million assets had increased enormously in its dimensions, but it still had years to grow before it would become a large corporation. Well before 1920, however, George Mead was acting on the basis of large enterprise procedures, such as long-term advanced planning, research and development, product diversification and organizational structuring, that did not become an accepted part of large corporation activity until the 1940's. Even then, these procedures were accepted bit-by-bit rather than as a logically connected whole.

In the 1920's, for instance, Owen Young of General Electric was to develop his concept of a corporation's balance of responsibilities to employees, customers and stockholders. Du Pont was already developing its program of diversification and its pioneer system of decentralized management. In comparison with these giants, the Mead company was not much bigger than a gnat—at the time General Electric, for instance, had 100,000 employees, and 100,000 stockholders, and millions of consumers—but the Mead company was big enough for George Mead not only to make pioneer discoveries on his own but also to link them together.

Between 1910 and 1920 he was planning Company activities ten-to-twenty years ahead in a manner that baffled those of his contemporaries who knew of it. Tied to one product, magazine paper, even to one customer, Crowell, and to an industrial process whose basic shape was as old as the Industrial Revolution, his mind was probing forward, searching for new processes, new products, new markets, new plants. In 1950—30-odd years after the fact—he was presented with a medal by the paper industry for, among other things, his discovery of three new processes, the basic ideas for which came to him during World War I. One of these was the use of the chemicals in the pulp-mills sludge, later known as Raffold, a filler that added opacity to paper and overcame in some part the problem of two-sidedness. A second was utilization of chestnut chips, a waste product in the manufacture of tannic acid, in the production of brown paper or paperboard. The first mention of this idea appears in a letter dated September 5, 1918, before George Mead had any experience in the brown paper field. After a decade of research, development and pilot plant operation, this idea took shape in the form of five chestnut-chip plants operating throughout the

South. The third idea led to a series of pioneer developments over a period of almost two decades in on-the-machine coating of paper. Coating, a process that improves the color, smoothness, opacity and printing quality of paper by treating its surface, was then a complex and costly process applied to paper after it had been produced; i.e., off-the-machine. The development of on-the-machine coating led the way to the high-gloss paper used today in almost all magazines.

Coating procedures probably began revolving in George Mead's mind sometime around 1915. No written record remains. The earliest verbal mention of it was made several years before the 1920 expansion to shipping clerk William Ludwig. He came to George Mead to ask whether space in back of the office building could be used to store paper and was told that that was the space where the coating operation would be, and the paper should be stored temporarily on the street. "Sometime when you come to Dayton," George Mead added, "I'll show you a plan I have on my desk." The next time William Ludwig was in Dayton he saw, under the glass top of the desk, the layout of the existing Chillicothe plant and—amid dots indicating the future expansion that would double the size of the operation—an area labeled "coating."

All during 1918 and 1919, the year before the expansion, George Mead kept discussing coating problems with his colleagues. Crowell then required coated stock for covers and special inserts, and George Mead, adverse to the then-universal method of brush coating and festoon drying, was hopeful that a coating contrivance could be devised to fit into the mid-section of the paper machine dryers, so that paper making, coating and drying could be one continuous process. The immediate result of the discussions was the inauguration of a research program at Chillicothe, which chemical engineer John Traquair was hired to direct. Up to that time, the Chillicothe laboratory had confined its activities to quality control tests, and George Mead himself had functioned as the research staff. Technologically trained and, unlike most executives of the time, technologically oriented, he now established one of the pioneer research laboratories. Roll-coating, an improvement over the regular coating process, was one of the laboratory's earliest achievements. On-the-machine coating became a reality during the twenties, and the process was further perfected during the thirties and forties. "Probably they will come up with dozens of ideas that are no good," George Mead explained to the men at the plant, "but they will probably come up with one that will offset all the bad ones."

A Policy of Continued Growth

Meanwhile, he had been seeking out and evaluating opportunities to expand and diversify outside the Chillicothe plant. A few faded notes and the balance sheet of the Friend Paper Company indicate that he was considering acquiring that organization in 1912, although it was then twice the size of the Mead company. No acquisition resulted, but within the next several years he formed the Mead Investment Company to protect the company and to aid in future acquisitions. He said later:

> Having taken over this little Mead Company for the purpose of trying to preserve the name and family tradition, I thought the smart thing to do was to immediately put all the stock I had and what I had given my wife, if it was worth anything, into an investment company, and get two or three men associated with me in that company also by giving them stock which they could purchase over the years, so that they would be around in case anything happened to me, as a nucleus of stock to try to perpetuate this little Mead Company.
>
> I hadn't the same interest in the Canadian company. I had gone into that as a temporary venture in order to try to make enough money to build the Mead Company faster, because I didn't think I could ever build it fast enough if I kept to the book business.

A principal and unpublicized purpose of the Mead Investment Company was to assist in the financing of the growth of the Mead Company itself. The portfolio included, of course, substantial holdings in Canadian newsprint, but, at the time of the investment company's inception, George Mead conceived for it the role that it later assumed: a locus for carrying part of the burden of plant expansion and for assuming the risks of new enterprises and acquisitions until they were sufficiently established for transfer to the Mead Company itself. Regular improvements in the Chillicothe plant, for example, were roughly equal to the amount of profit retained in the business ($465,000 of a total of $1,215,000 from 1910 to 1920), but the extraordinary expansions of the decade were financed by the sale of additional stock, which the investment company purchased as heavily as its resources permitted, thus increasing the total amount of capital available for outside undertakings.

George Mead's mind was full of ideas for new operations. In 1915, just four years after the first successful Kraft mill had been built, he had already started planning for the establishment of such a mill in the South, possibly in Florida. An immediate move to realize this plan would have been highly dramatic—and probably highly imprudent. As it turned out, the Kraft undertaking was long in incubation: it was not until 31 years later that the mill was actually built, and then in the state of Georgia. Indeed, the first steps of the Mead Pulp and Paper Company toward outside acquisitions consisted of an apparently timid investment in a new venture in Tennessee, initiated and carried out by others, and in an apparently prosaic purchase of a distressed paper-making operation in Dayton. The primary purpose of the investment was to secure adequate soda-pulp supplies in anticipation of war shortages and the dwindling sources of wood for pulp near Chillicothe; the aim of the purchase was to supply small-order customers whose demands could not be met by Chillicothe mass-production techniques, and, incidentally, to satisfy in some measure the long-standing devotion of Treasurer A. L. Rieger to the jobbing business.

It was more than ten years later that the new pulp operation—the Kingsport Pulp Company—made any money, and then only under direct Mead ownership. The small acquisition in Dayton—the Peerless Paper Company— became profitable only after sundry vicissitudes, and eventually it proved advisable to dismantle the plant altogether and move the machinery to Chillicothe. Yet, during the long course of apparently unexciting labor in patient rescue work with losing operations, George Mead revealed a dramatic inventiveness in new ways of papermaking, gave spectacular evidence of concern for his co-workers and worked out an extraordinary system of decentralized organization for coping with his company's increasing size.

The Model Industrial City

The Kingsport Pulp Company was one of a number of industries planned for a new city in Tennessee that was itself planned, literally from the bare ground up. In 1910, the Clinchfield Railroad first penetrated the area between the Blue Ridge and the Great Smoky Mountains and—under the leadership of its presidents, George L. Carter and John B. Dennis, aided by local investors, the New York investment house of Blair and Company, and such diverse bodies as Columbia University, the Rockefeller Foundation and the Department of Architecture at M.I.T.—conceived the idea of expanding freight by creating a model industrial city. Blair and Company invited George Mead to examine the potentialities of the area in company with the railroad's directors. Already planned for construction was an extract plant that would derive tannic acid from chestnut wood.

Front view of the Mead Kingsport, Tennessee mill, one of the long-range and
important expansions of the company.

George Mead found both his civic and professional sensibilities stirred. At that time, the chestnut blight, which had come into the United States with shipments of Oriental chestnut in 1906, was already making marked inroads in timber stands of the South. The question was how to make full use of a valuable and vanishing natural resource, which was then used only to produce an agent in the tanning of leather, with no profitable employment of the spent chips, not even as fuel. George Mead knew that efforts were being made by at least one paper company to convert such spent chips into soda pulp, the same pulp that was the chief ingredient of papermaking in the Mead plant at Chillicothe. He saw possible business opportunity in locating a pulp mill beside the extract plant; he saw possible civic opportunity not only in the use of raw material but also in the creation of a new town; and he was active in both business and civic counsel.

But he did not counsel a Mead Company investment greater than $100,000—approved in April, 1916, by the Mead Board of Directors—even though the company was to take practically all of Kingsport's production. Construction of the plant was in other hands, and George Mead's initial caution soon appeared to be sound foresight. The plant was being built at a time when construction costs were unbelievably higher than they had ever been. The promotors compounded the cost problem by changing construction plans when the plant was half built. It turned out, moreover, that chestnut chips did not lend themselves satisfactorily to the soda-pulp process: no amount of bleaching could get the pulp clean enough for high quality book paper, and regular woods had to be purchased at prices far higher than those for used chestnut chips. Management problems set in, and in 1919 George Mead was asked by the principal owners of the company to step in and manage it. A year later, the rescue work had assumed such proportions that it was found necessary to accede to persuasion ("somewhat against our will," remarked George Mead) and to buy the company outright for $700,000.

George Mead undertook these responsibilities essentially because the unlikelihood of immediate profits did not dim his vision of future viable enterprise and his determination to see difficult problems to a satisfactory conclusion. The entire Mead organization labored for years on a multiplicity of technical and production difficulties, added paper machines to the pulp mills, even encouraged the development of a book-printing business in Kingsport to use the paper being manufactured and make the most profitable use of the pulp.

Eventually the problem of chestnut pulp was solved, solved indeed so successfully that an entire new semi-chemical procedure of making pulp was invented, five new factories were erected and an entire new dimension was given to the Mead undertakings.

As for the structuring of this new enterprise, George Mead at once applied his system of extreme decentralization. When he was asked in 1919 to manage the business without owning it, he promptly formed a new company staffed by engineers who had been working on construction projects in Canada and Chillicothe. Not the Mead Pulp and Paper Company but this separate entity (named the Mead Engineering and Development Company, or M.E.A.D. for short), ran the Kingsport operation and at the same time assumed autonomous control of construction programs elsewhere. When Mead eventually purchased Kingsport, the active agent was not the Company but a new autonomous group called the Mead Fibre Company. In these two separate organizations, a third—the Mead Investment Company— took almost half the financial interest. Kingsport, indeed, was in effect under its wing for nine years. In such manner the Mead Pulp and Paper Company was insulated against risk by George Mead's risking the bulk of his private means. More important, a new part of the Mead organization was not submerged in the older part. It was given concrete and individual existence, and the men involved in it were encouraged to think of the operation as their company. By whatever means he could, George Mead was resolved to limit the number of men in any work unit so that each employee could feel that he was part of a particular working community and not simply an integer in a large corporate entity.

Peerless Changes Hands

The application of this resolution at Kingsport was perhaps the more rigorous because of difficulties encountered at the Peerless Paper Company acquisition in Dayton. The plant had been purchased outright by the Mead Pulp and Paper Company at the urging of local bankers and had been established as a forthright subsidiary, although it was being operated as a separate entity. In this case, however, A. L. Rieger, employee of Mead family companies since 1892, acted simultaneously as treasurer and sales manager of the parent company and as treasurer and general manager of the subsidiary. The sales price of Peerless was not high—$70,000 and 100 shares of Mead common stock—although renovations and improvements brought the total costs to over $1,100,000, which had to be borrowed from the banks. Here the immediate problem was not one of profits—losses for the first eight months of $14,000 were quickly swallowed up by subsequent gains—but of personnel. The account of how this problem was dealt with is best left to the words of George Mead himself:

Mr. Rieger was of the old school, very set in his ways, very stubborn in his own point of view. He had no elasticity in him. He could not bend. He could not see anybody else's point of view, and after many years of close work with him in the paper company he found himself in a very unhappy frame of mind. He said to me one day that he would like to have a small mill of his own; that he didn't agree with my policies and I didn't agree with him, and while I had always been very friendly about it, he thought if he had a small mill to run his own way that he could build up a business for himself and his sons. (Mr. Rieger later reported, "I couldn't die happy until I had a mill of my own.") I said "All right, that is fine and I will be delighted to help you. Now, how can we do it?" And one or the other thought of the Peerless Paper Company which we had taken over a year or so before on account of one of the banks in Dayton having a substantial amount of money tied up in it that they wanted to get out, and because at that particular time we needed some additional tonnage in the Mead Paper Company.

So an arrangement was made [at the end of 1918] with Mr. Rieger whereby he was to take over the control of the company, the capital stock to be paid for through a ten-year period, which he thought would be an easy matter. He asked, however, that I remain in the company as an equal stockholder with himself, and the first year he asked that I be president of the company, which I did. However, I told him I would fall out at the end of the year and thereafter he should have the company and be president and run it his own way. Well, he was very successful, of course, the year following the war as everybody was in business, because it was an extraordinary year . . . however, the next year was the year of the crash in business, 1921, and along with a great many other concerns, Mr. Rieger found himself in serious difficulty. He had large inventories with goods on hand at very high prices and he couldn't work out of it. So in the next year he probably lost all the money that he had made the year before.

Then the question of his future faced him and he came down to see me, and I would tell him what I thought of the policy he and his company should pursue, and he would always tell me that I was wrong, that I really didn't know exactly what his problem was; that I could see my own problem, but I couldn't see his. I said, "You have been telling me that ever since I was knee high. You told me that when I used to work on the paper machine, and there is no use of my talking to you any more because you won't pay any attention to what I say." This all in good humor. But it is a fact that Rieger would come down and spend a couple of hours with me, and when he left the office he would still have his own ideas, and all the suggestions that I made were worthless from his viewpoint.

Mr. Rieger . . . made a serious mistake in not having a fixed policy for his company. He could not make up his own mind what he wanted to do. In the second place, he had the notion, from a salesman's standpoint, that a paper mill could make anything that the salesmen could sell, and consequently he tried to make all the grades and kinds of paper that there were in the book field; and you men who have been working around the mill . . . know that you were asked one day to make hard paper in the form of "Peerless" or "Idlewild Writing," and the next day or two after that to make a soft paper in the form of some sort of bulking book, or anything that might come along that looked like it had a proper price to it. And consequently, Mr. Rieger was asking of you men and he was asking of his equipment, he was asking of the organization, an impossibility. . . .

Before Mr. Rieger died [in 1924] he asked me, and his doctor came to me and asked me, if there was some way that we could take the plant back. He said that the losses were . . . largely responsible for Mr. Rieger's health, and he thought if we would relieve him of the mill—the doctor thought it might prolong his life. So we took the mill back at a considerable financial loss to ourselves. Obviously Mr. Rieger had but a few months to live. If we had waited until his death we would have profited by it. But I told the directors of the Mead Pulp & Paper Company that I personally was willing to sacrifice a considerable amount—in fact I would gladly contribute any amount if possible to save Mr. Rieger's life and certainly to prolong it. And, therefore, we agreed to take back the Peerless.

To this account it is necessary to add only that the principal source of A. L. Rieger's capital in the purchase of Peerless was George Mead, that Rieger remained a director of the Mead Pulp and Paper Company even though he had resigned as an executive, and that—after making possible this personal venture into the jobbing business—George Mead soon found it necessary to reconvert it to the mass production of magazine paper.

Search For Talent

The Mead system of doing business was, in reality, not a system at all. Rather, it was something more human. Mr. Mead employed no paradoxes to explain his non-systematic system of organization. But he did like the story told him by one of his colleagues about a mid-western university that planted grass but installed no walks on a newly built campus so that the walks could be installed later over the paths the students had made for themselves.

Mead was not, of course, impressed by the book—the rule book that he held likely to be wrong—and in the same way he was not impressed by commonly accepted ideas about business and its organization. He opposed autocratic rule in business; on the other hand, he was not impressed by formal committee systems of organization. He directed barbs at General Motors' and others' formalisms (as regards Lindbergh's solo flight across the Atlantic: "It would have been more marvelous if he had done it with a committee!"), sometimes till the barb stuck.

Authority in the Company was not sharply defined. In the 1920's, one executive received word of new responsibilities during a taxi ride between a hotel and a bank, in the course of which Mr. Mead said, "I think you had better take over the paperboard development. Go over to the bank and borrow a million or a million and a half and get started." Authority granted in so casual a manner was bound to seem less like policy than a hunch—only George Mead's hunches were long considered and actually very minutely thought out.

When in 1918 A. L. Rieger left Mead for a mill of his own, he did not leave the Dayton headquarters unmanned. As the Company had grown in size, George Mead had been seeking new talent. In 1913, he induced his maternal uncle, R. T. Houk, to serve as general factotum with the title first of secretary and later of vice-president, and with duties that paralleled but did not cross those of Mr. Rieger. In 1917, he hired away from the Canadian operation a young man, Speed Warren, who had a keen and analytical capacity that shortly led him to the treasurership of the Company. Towards the end of 1919, his eye lit upon another young man, Sydney Ferguson, a trained auditor who later succeeded his employer in the posts of president and chairman of the Company, and who had a searching logicality that related small details to large propositions. To Sydney Ferguson, George Mead indicated that he was not interested in employing world-beaters, by which he meant men who went into business simply to show how big they could act or how much they could make. He might have added that he was seeking men who could act for themselves and whose interactions with him and with one another could shape, but not upset, the organizational structure of the Mead company.

An Appointment Generates Friction

An appointment he had made in the spring of the previous year did, however, generate friction. Indeed, it led to developments quite as dramatic as the departure of A. L. Rieger for a mill of his own. Involved was H. P. Carruth, a promising young chemist at the Holyoke Writing Paper Company, who was hired in the course of a breakfast conversation at the Vanderbilt Hotel in New York, which George Mead concluded with the following words: "In the office adjoining mine there is a desk and a chair which you can occupy. Just what your job will be, I don't know, but there is plenty of work to be done. As to salary, just pick out what you want between your present salary and double that amount, keeping in mind that the higher the figure the more will be expected of you."

Installed in Dayton as assistant to the president, Carruth found himself gravitating toward Chillicothe, and commented one day that he regretted losing some of the momentum he built up during the week by commuting back to Dayton. Instantly, George Mead inquired, "Do you mean you would be willing to go to Chillicothe to live? If so, we will really make something of the Mead Pulp and Paper Company." Within 30 days, Carruth was in residence in Chillicothe with the title of general manager of the company, a post from which George Mead had promptly resigned.

In this event, Carruth was impressed, even overwhelmed by the speed with which George Mead arrived at decisions on matters of far-reaching import. A decision seemed to follow instantly upon a suggestion. Throughout his life, indeed, George Mead was notorious among his executives for his alacrity; it puzzled many of them who could not reconcile such spontaneity with sound sense until they realized that he had foreseen a variety of alternatives, weighed them, made up his mind about various possibilities and had then waited until someone else verbalized a suitable conclusion. At this point, Carruth was not aware that a series of apparently troublesome problems was about to arise, but, in retrospect, it seems entirely conceivable that George Mead had anticipated, not perhaps the eventuality, but at least the possibility of all of them.

Long-time employee Hector McVicker, who had emerged after 1905 as superintendent, was now manager at Chillicothe; indeed, the announcement of Carruth's appointment, dated April, 1919, emphasized that McVicker would remain in direct charge of the mill. McVicker, however, felt that his authority was being diluted, and he now began to look for a mill of his own together with men to staff it, among them Austin P. Story, a promising laboratory worker who, at George Mead's encouragement, had taken his degree in chemistry.

Hearing rumors that McVicker was raising money among Chillicothe residents, bank president and Mead Director Alex Renick telephoned the news to George Mead, on vacation in South Carolina, and urged his immediate return. George Mead replied, "We have an organization to handle such matters. I will return in two weeks as planned."

When he did return, McVicker's plans had matured and the new Chillicothe Paper Company was about to be formed, but costs had been underestimated, and McVicker now found himself stymied by want of capital.

Thereupon, George Mead subscribed personally to a substantial block of stock, helped secure other funds, appointed McVicker consultant to the Mead Company and arranged to supply the projected mill with all its pulp needs on 90-day credit. "Mr. McVicker," George Mead explained later, "was a man of integrity, a first-class papermaker and a lifelong friend. He had been of such loyal assistance to the Mead Corporation that I volunteered to help him establish his own business."

(Hector McVicker's own business did succeed. At the time of his death in 1943 at the age of 76, however, he counselled his colleague, Austin Story, to sell the Chillicothe Paper Company to Mead whenever he got the chance. The sale eventually took place in 1955, when Story wished to retire. At that time, he returned to the Mead Company as a member of the board of directors.)

When defections are rewarded with such munificence, it might seem that would-be defectors would multiply. Such was not the case, basically because the defectors were treated not as defectors but as human beings and friends. It was obvious that George Mead looked after his own, and the loyalty of his executives not only remained intense but also continued unbroken.

All the while, however, George Mead had been gradually transforming a small operation that had come into being as an extension of a family company into a medium-size version of the new sort of large corporation. The dimensions of the company had, of course, greatly increased. In the decade from 1910 to 1920, assets had swelled from $934,267 to $5,930,660, and the company was in the midst of a construction program amounting to $2,800,000. Sales had increased six times, from $830,179 to $3,869,303; net earnings had gone from $30,640 to $277,750; in August of 1920 capital was increased to $6,800,000, a jump of $1,200,000. Most important, an organization of professional managers was coming into being without being forced into a mold.

The secret of this transformation was not simply the forethought of George Mead. He did indeed think ahead, but, humanely, he let the human organization evolve as if of itself. The consequence was a remarkable esprit.

H. P. Carruth later recorded:

During this period, I was privileged to spend many hours with him, both in formal conferences and in very informal talks at his home or mine. These meetings, especially those which were informal, resulted in my becoming greatly attached to him and acquiring a great respect and affection toward him.

He demonstrated an attitude which aroused the greatest response of loyalty because he was always willing to listen to ideas and to make his associates feel significant. When he laid out policy, he had the happy faculty of making you feel that you were a part of that decision, and in its execution he gave a great measure of responsibility to his associates. It was a team activity where the juniors could and were encouraged to feel that they were important.

This attitude made for the building of character in the entire executive personnel on a personal basis. Among ourselves, he was never "the boss" but rather "the chief"—the head of the clan, so to speak. We felt that we were not so much his subordinates as his friends. He made us feel that our work was important and that we were responsible for it, and he deputized authority in such a way as to give each man the feeling that he was looked upon as a person, not just as a cog in a machine.

CHAPTER 7

The Canadian Venture

T HROUGHOUT THE DECADE of strenuous expansion of the Mead
Pulp and Paper Company between 1910 and 1920, George Mead managed to pursue even more strenuously his Canadian enterprise. The Canadian career was almost immediately and all but inordinately successful. Not
only was George Mead selling more newsprint than any other person or
company in the world by the time he was barely out of his thirties, but also,
during his forties, he was already occupying the role of a senior statesman
of the paper industry. He was skilled in production, sales and finance of
the rarefied sort that creates large corporate entities. Jobs and emoluments
were urged upon him; his counsel was sought; and his paper was purchased
in such quantities as to suggest that he had found a means of perpetuating
a merchandising miracle.

His attitude, however, to all this stir and success may have been somewhat mixed. The Canadian venture consisted to some extent of a series of
tentative advances through the doorway to glittering success, interspersed
with a series of definite retreats, and when he finally closed the door on the
venture in 1932, it was as if he had never walked through it.

His motive for opening the door at all, as he said himself, was to win the
capital for his Mead Pulp and Paper Company that no small enterprise in a
long established branch of industry could hope to gain for itself. Clearly
this was his goal. His mind, constantly active and extremely acute, could
not be content with dealing with the problems of one small company; it
seemed to need the stimulus of those of a dozen larger ones. To be sure, his
manner of business was precisely the same in Montreal, New York, Chicago
and Toronto as it was in Chillicothe. He was as always the courteous,
humane man of strict integrity. His newsprint operations were conducted
according to the same firm convictions as his operations in white paper. He
was, in short, in no way a changed man, but, amidst the bright glare of success, he may conceivably have felt that he was not entirely the same man.

The plant that George Mead and his uncle Harry Talbott constructed for the Lake Superior Paper Company in 1911 at Sault Sainte Marie was then the most modern and one of the largest on the continent. Shortly after it was completed, George Mead decided that the principal spot for him as general manager in charge of the entire operation was not the Sault itself but Dayton, where he would be nearer the newsprint market. From Dayton he promptly moved out on sales campaigns all over the Middle West.

"We were surprisingly successful in selling the output of the Lake Superior Paper Company," he reported later. Three reasons accounted for this. It was the best mill in the country at the moment, built and designed by the best engineers. George Mead was able to get a good organization together. And the company made the best paper, a reputation which grew quickly. He said:

> While newsprint wasn't tight at that time, after I proved we could get freight cars across the Strait every day in the year—they had icebreakers, you know—those fellows in the Middle West became quite enthusiastic and good supporters of ours.
>
> And we did another thing at that particular moment that we felt was good business. We went to the publishers of this part of the country and to the paper merchants who supplied all the small papers . . . I thought it would be a good thing to have them get a first class paper, and in a couple of years we had made quite a reputation among the small publishers for this service and good quality. And we became in time the largest supplier of merchant paper for newsprint that there was in the country in just a few years.

This backdoor approach to the market succeeded so well—large companies, in this case followed the example of small ones—that within two years output was oversold, and the British owners of the Sault mill decided to consolidate it with two other mills at Espanola and Sturgeon Falls, Ontario, whose output was heavily undersold. Hopefully, these weaker operations could benefit from the sales organization of the Lake Superior company. Accordingly, the mills were merged into a company known as Spanish River Pulp and Paper, but at this juncture George Mead decided to back out.

George Mead and Harry Talbott put up their Spanish River equity securities for sale in Toronto, "expecting," as George Mead said, "to get out. But this president of the Spanish River Company who (we won't say falsified, but who had been responsible for the misstatements in the inventory situation) was a banker in Toronto at that time, also started to sell his stock in Spanish River, and he sold faster than we did. I don't know whether you know the Canadian Stock Exchange, but we know a great deal of its goings on, and they sold his stock and none of ours. If we would wire up a lower price to sell ours, the market had already hit that and gone below it, and we never sold a share." Not able to retire, George Mead retained a branch sales office in Dayton located in offices adjoining those of the Mead Pulp and Paper Company.

Problems Crop Up

The new Spanish River company almost immediately fell into difficulties. The sales organization did not function as well from its new headquarters in Toronto as it had from Dayton, and before long the auditors discovered a $2 million shortage in the assets, arising from loose calculation of the wood stockpile and other raw materials. The British investors demanded a receivership, threw out the management and Canadian investors began trying to argue George Mead into taking charge. Finally he replied, "I will accept the vice-presidency of sales for one year . . . But I won't take any salary for it . . . I don't want it to be known what I am doing." The next year, however, when World War I broke out and the new Spanish River president was called to London, George Mead was induced to accept temporarily the presidency of the mill. Actually, this temporary employment was to last until 1928.

Meanwhile, the Chicago bankers of the Abitibi Company, which had just built a new low-cost mill at Iroquois Falls, Ontario, near the Spanish River timberlands, had been urging George Mead to sell the output of this mill as well as that of the Spanish River company, and with the approval of the Spanish River directors, he agreed. "Otherwise," he observed, "they would have raided our market."

At this time, his lawyers objected to his assuming too great a personal liability by selling so much paper under his own name, and a new legal entity, the G. H. Mead Company, was formed for the purpose. Sales swelled, and it became one of the most active and powerful organizations in the entire newsprint industry. Under the tax laws both of Canada and the U. S. during World War I, it became necessary for it to function as an import company and thus to have adequate capital. So profitable had newsprint already proved that George Mead was able to put up about half a million dollars—"all that I had at that time, but they were good securities and marketable securities." Once possessed of capital, the sales company attracted

Canadian canoe trips meant relaxation and a chance to be
with his family for George Mead.
Top picture shows him with son, H.T.; bottom picture has George Mead and
his daughter, Louise, enjoying a trip at Pancake Lake, Ontario about 1926.

more capital and before long it was functioning not only as a merchandise organization but an investment house as well, in which role it was joined by the Mead Investment Company.

From this base, the Mead newsprint organization enlarged suddenly and vigorously. As early as 1916, ten full years before the peak of his newsprint activities, George Mead was responsible, as the new president of the Spanish River company, for some $20 million assets, more than 20 times the assets of the Mead Pulp and Paper Company at that time. During the year 1916, he sold through his G. H. Mead Company 47,400 tons of Abitibi newsprint and 110,739 tons from Spanish River's three mills. He was not only the youngest man on the executive board of the Canadian News-Print Manufacturers Association—others on the board were principal executives of International Paper, Laurentide, Gould and Abitibi—but also its president.

To be sure, George Mead went into Canadian newsprint at a singularly propitious time. The size and circulations of newspapers were increasing at a time when production of newsprint in the U. S. could no longer be increased. The vast additional tonnage needed could come only from Canada, which prior to 1904 had exported practically no paper, and as late as 1909 was shipping only 19,000 tons to the United States. By 1913, that figure had increased to 220,000 tons, by 1916 to 468,000, of which George Mead was selling more than one-fourth. (Ten years later, when the figure had reached 1,852,000 he was selling one-third.) Never before had any one facet of the paper industry shown such rapid growth.

The market was there—a wildly active one. But why was George Mead— a controlled and temperate man deeply concerned with humane enterprise and profoundly opposed to wildcat schemes—to prove so successful in an area that was attracting get-rich-quickers of every variety? A possible answer lies in his attraction to orderly, rationalized enterprise and in his understanding of the opportunity to bring a well-directed sales agency to the chaotic Canadian scene. Such an agency could bring pressure to bear both on production and distribution methods, resulting in more sense and order in the newsprint business, which would benefit both the newsprint and publishing businesses.

It is doubtful whether sense and order could have been introduced in a more persuasive way. Effectively expressing the clamor of publishers for high quality paper, for example, was actually a much more decisive means of directing and improving production than any amount of on-the-spot supervision could have been. In Canada as in Chillicothe, quality remained the key to George Mead's basic management philosophy. And it produced impressive results. During the feverish years between 1916 and 1920, for example, Spanish River production averaged 96 per cent of full-rated capacity, about as high a rate as possible in a paper mill. Yet when the sharp depression of 1921 hit and production dropped to 75 per cent of capacity, the company was one of only two paper companies in Canada able to pay dividends on both preferred and common stock. Such success in directing the company's affairs was, in all probability, effected more through George Mead's privately owned sales company than through his actual position as chief executive of the company. His *de facto* influence on the affairs of Abitibi, with which he had no connection other than that of a sales agent, was incalculable but undoubtedly great. Again, comparable influence on the newsprint industry at that time could not have been had in any other way.

But it is doubtful whether comparable influence could have been exercised by any one other than George Mead. In areas of dramatic business expansion that seem to present unlimited opportunities, an atmosphere of getting advantage by taking it from someone else often prevails. Distrust of and dissimulation with competitors and customers can be rife. In such an atmosphere, George Mead remained the same man he was in Dayton and Chillicothe: he was considerate of others and helpful to them. His integrity was beyond question, and even though his power was feared in some circles—in the twenties he was sometimes called the little Caesar of the newsprint industry—he was to be trusted completely. As a go-between that linked the mill-builders in Canada and the publishers in the U.S., he was ideal: he already knew many of the publishers, and in the Crowell company he had been dealing every day directly and personally with one of the biggest. Moreover, his formidable powers of remembering, assimilating and linking together thousands of pertinent facts made it possible to bring the full weight of customer pressure to bear on precise solutions of problems and not on exhortations to solve them. One time, for instance, when Spanish River customers were complaining of overweight paper (it not only reduced printing surfaces but sometimes jammed the presses), George Mead walked through the Espanola mill, pointing out the precise technical errors that required correction.

Timetable of Success

Besides these personal qualities—the net effect of which proved to be that he gained personal advantage by refusing to take personal advantage—he brought to his Canadian adventure an unfettered energy that seemed to be limitless. A partial record can be recreated of his comings and goings during the year 1916 which, although it is necessarily incomplete and omits many of his trips, conferences and phone calls, still gives a glimpse of the almost inordinate intensity with which he worked.

The first entry for the year, January 13, finds him in Dayton. Six days later he is at the Ritz Carlton Hotel in Montreal. On the 21st he is back at Dayton headquarters, writing a letter of acceptance of the presidency of the Spanish River company. A letter dealing with newsprint problems reaches him on January 25 in Chillicothe. On the 31st, he is planning a trip to New York, from which he writes the first of a series of polite and politic letters to British stockholders of the Spanish River company. (They do not know him and are not entirely ready to accept the judgment of the Canadian stockholders and papermakers who had urged his appointment. At this time, P. B. Wilson, vice-president of Spanish River and a man considerably older than George Mead, wrote to London as follows: "Owing to Mr. Mead's energy in the sales end of the business, the mills are now fully supplied with orders, and will probably be so for several months . . . Owing, I believe, to his personal influence, he has prevented the slaughter of the market when the Abitibi Company recently had occasion to find outlet for 200 tons of paper per day. He was responsible for the layout of the very efficient plant at the Soo after visiting the principal mills of Europe.")

On January 24, George Mead wires Dayton, "LEAVING TONIGHT FOR TORONTO KING EDWARD HOTEL THEN TOMORROW SATURDAY ESPANOLA SUDBURY MONDAY AND TUESDAY SOO . . . NOTIFY FAMILY." On the 7th he is still at the Sault, answering memos from Dayton on a variety of newsprint problems. February 14th, his office dispatches a telegram to him about tonnage and price developments and addresses it to "DRAWING ROOM A CAR 7 BIG FOUR TRAIN NO. 6 CLEVELAND OHIO." The office in turn receives a memo from him proposing the abandonment of job-lot business at Espanola. The next day, the 15th, he is back in New York.

Shortly thereafter, he proceeds to Aiken, South Carolina, on vacation, but this year (as on several other occasions during the period of the Canadian venture) it looks less like a vacation, more like a recuperation from near col-

The house at Aiken, winter home for the Mead family.

lapse. Indeed, on February 27, he wrote by hand to his cousin, Henry S. Mead, one of his principal assistants in the G. H. Mead Company:

I am already feeling greatly rested although just beginning to take things a little more slowly and get some sound sleep. Another week will, I am sure, put me in shape to at least begin some work, so I shall send for Hendrickson [his personal secretary] to be here a week from tomorrow morning, Monday the 6th . . . The G. H. Mead Company books must start clear and clean, not carrying over the G. H. M. Agent's accounts at all. We can then gradually close up the G. H. M. agency books in the next 30 to 60 days . . . From March 1st on, I shall give the mornings to work and expect everything from the office for that week of March 6th. If I can hold out and not become too restless, I want to stay here until the middle of March.[*]

On March 3, even before secretary E. C. Hendrickson has arrived, correspondence is again flowing; after his arrival, it becomes a flood. On March 10, George Mead writes to a colleague in Canada that he has "eliminated all correspondence from my vacation for a couple of weeks," but he is now definitely restless and on the same day he wires Dayton: "I AM CONSIDERING LEAVING HERE TOMORROW NOON ARRIVING NY SUNDAY NOON TO MEET ALEXANDER SMITH [president of Abitibi] . . . I SHALL RETURN AIKEN FROM NY MONDAY OR TUESDAY NOON TO SPEND BALANCE WEEK THEN GO TO NY AND MONTREAL AS PER LETTER." The next day he changes his mind, wires that he will not leave before Sunday noon, possibly Monday noon. But now the pace picks up again. On the 14th he is in New York and writing about groundwood pulp problems. Back in Aiken on the 17th, he receives a wire from Henry Mead arranging a conference with a publisher who has tonnage problems: Henry Mead's wire concludes, "AM PLANNING MEETING YOU BALTIMORE TRAIN 152 AT 8:35 MONDAY MORNING." Presumably this conference takes place in New York, but by the 22nd of the month, George Mead is in Montreal, writing to ask a Spanish River executive to meet him in Dayton the coming Monday.

April 4 and 6 find him again in New York, the 19th in Dayton, the 26th at the St. Regis in New York, the 28th again in Dayton. On May 2 he is at the Blackstone in Chicago reading a long memo on tonnage figures and contract commitments. At this point gaps appear in the record—possibly because he is in Chillicothe and easily reachable by telephone. May 29 finds him at the

---

[*]A letter from George Mead, dated March 20, 1924, to a Spanish River colleague suggests similar exhaustion that year: "I am already feeling a distinct benefit from my rest here and even able to do a little more each day by way of exercise. I am beginning to feel anxious at getting back to work, but propose to follow my instructions to the letter and not rush the situation."

Fort Pitt Hotel in Pittsburgh, May 31 at the Vanderbilt in New York, June 10 in Dayton, June 22 in Toronto, and June 23 again in New York.

He then left for a protracted stay at the Sault plant, where he received a flood of office correspondence on July 24. In one answering communication dated July 28, after mentioning a short but pleasant visit to a fishing camp, he argues against too strongly worded contracts with publishers and concludes, "The smartest way to bring about your results is to have the customer following your wishes without realizing he is doing so." Trouble, unspecified, meanwhile is building at the Sault, for an August 7 telegraph to Henry Mead states: "PLANT WILL PROBABLY BE DOWN SEVERAL WEEKS ADVISE CUSTOMERS NECESSITY TAKE ADVANTAGE CONTINGENCY CLAUSE IN CONTRACT AND UNABLE TO DELIVER PAPER FROM ABITIBI MILL ALSO SEND SIMILAR MESSAGE LAKE SUPERIOR CONTRACTS." "CRITICAL TIMES," he wires the next day, "I CANNOT COME DOWN TO TALK WITH YOU UNTIL NEXT WEEK."

On August 17 he reports that he is leaving the Sault Monday afternoon and arriving Thousand Islands Tuesday afternoon, but by the 20th he is back, only however to take off for Alexandria Bay, N.Y., where he stays almost a week, appearing in Chillicothe on September 11 and proceeding thence by sleeper to New York that night. On the 16th he is at the Layfayette Hotel, Portland, Maine; on the 18th he is indicating by telegram: "RITZ CARLTON MONTREAL TODAY TUESDAY WALDORF ASTORIA NY ARRIVE DAYTON WEDNESDAY EVENING."

And so the year continues, with constant visits to customers, trips to mills, conferences with colleagues, discussions with fellow newsprint manufacturers and an endless flow of communications dealing with, among others, the following matters: power, production, water, pulp, fuel, inventories, sales orders, improvements, repairs, expense authorizations, storage, cost efficiencies, freight car movements, a host of mechanical and engineering matters and quality considerations of every nature and degree.

The only unusual trip of the year is to Washington towards the year end. Here he remains from December 12 to 28 for reasons unrecorded, returning to Dayton for Christmas and New Year's to prepare himself for another year quite as fevered as the one past.

Mead's Pullman Cavalry

The record of George Mead's labors during any year is highly incomplete: it includes only such letters, memoranda and telegrams as were preserved, excludes, of course, the phone calls and personal talks that were his favorite means of doing business, not to mention documents that got lost or chits and notes that were thrown away. In the year 1916, for example, he may well have visited close to twice as many places as the existing records indicate, probably threw himself into his labors with greater intensity than any recounting can suggest. In times of crisis, as in the fall of 1929, he was capable of taking on a schedule that called for 21 consecutive nights in sleeping cars, and of dismissing the attendant discomforts with the remark that he was made the size he was so that he could fit into a Pullman berth. In fact, he used to travel so much he eventually referred to himself and his traveling associates as Mead's Pullman Cavalry.

The extent of his travels would not be remarkable for a salesman, and it is not to be forgotten that George Mead was indeed a salesman. But he was a salesman with principal executive responsibilities, and those in a large number of enterprises. In 1921, for instance, he was president of the Mead Pulp and Paper Company, the Spanish River Pulp and Paper Company, the Escanaba Paper Company, the G. H. Mead Company, the Mead Investment Company, M.E.A.D. Company, Mead Fibre Company and the City National Bank in Dayton. Actually, his responsibilities centered sharply around three of these organizations—the Mead Company itself, Spanish River and the G. H. Mead Company—to which the others were subsidiary in practice even if not in fact. But each of these three undertakings were taxing and none was routine. Why then did he choose to travel so endlessly about the country?

For one thing, travel gave him an excellent opportunity for thorough reflection upon all his ventures. His eye difficulty made it impossible for him to read on trains. His thoughtfulness toward colleagues prevented him from requesting them to accompany him so that he might enjoy the ride. He formed the habit, consequently, of sitting in silence and of framing and reviewing his business ideas, and thus found his time well used. Moreover, he was thoroughly comfortable at this time in what he was doing. During a period of more than a dozen years from the time he got out of the Spanish River company in 1913, the ambivalence he apparently felt at that time toward his Canadian venture did not assert itself. It did not, indeed, reappear until the time of the merger of the Abitibi and Spanish River companies into one huge company.

During this period the G. H. Mead Company kept setting sales records each succeeding year. In 1926, for instance, newsprint tonnage sold amounted to 1,525 tons a day. The Spanish River company increased its assets from

$14,809,411 in 1913 to $45,983,000 in 1927. Various Mead companies—sales, engineering and investment—were responsible for the planning of construction of four new mills in Canada: the Fort William Paper Company, Fort William, Ontario; the St. Anne Paper Company, St. Anne, Quebec; the Murray Bay Paper Company, Murray Bay, Quebec; and the Manitoba Paper Company of Winnipeg, Manitoba.

These projects were a response to the still expanding opportunities in newsprint and to a need to preserve the Abitibi and Spanish River timberland areas from possible inroads of competition. All of the mills were included in the Spanish River/Abitibi merger. In addition, a new organization, the Mead Sales Company, was created to deal specifically and expertly in the buying and selling of pulp (The G. H. Mead Company had performed brilliantly in keeping Abitibi supplied with pulp at a time when its pulping operation had been severely limited by drought—and then dismally found itself, after the emergency was over, with a heavy oversupply that could be sold only at a loss.)

What is more, George Mead was assuming responsibility for an increasing number of independent paper mills. Sales of Escanaba newsprint led to discussions of the problems of the company, a high-cost American company located on the north shore of Lake Michigan and to George Mead's becoming president, investing money and changing the mill over to the better profit-margin manufacture of wallpaper. A comparable realtionship developed with the nearby Manistique Pulp and Paper Company. The management of the Deerfield Paper Company asked for and received Mead supervision. At the request of the Royal Bank of Canada, which frequently sought counsel and advice from George Mead, he put the M.E.A.D. Company to work on the design, construction, operation and sales of a book paper plant for the Frazer Paper Company of Edmundston, New Brunswick, just across the St. John River from the State of Maine, and conceived the idea of putting the pulp mill on the Canadian side and of pumping the pulp across the river to a Fourdrinier mill on the American side, thus avoiding a heavy duty on book paper.

All of these various projects required not only strenuous management and sales effort, but also heavy participation in the complex financial arrangements that prevail in the newsprint industry, in which publishers, newsprint makers, investment houses and syndicates made up of a variety of partners are constantly joining together—particularly when newsprint supplies are tight—to underwrite new plants or enlargements of old ones. After World

War I, George Mead, with the resources of the G. H. Mead Company and the Mead Investment Company, and in combination with other groups in which he had temporary interests, moved freely and comfortably in the atmosphere of high and complex finance that surrounded each transaction.

The greatest financial maneuver was, of course, the combination of the Spanish River and Abitibi companies under a single name—the Indian name was selected because it was more suggestive of Canadian newsprint—and a single management into the biggest newsprint corporation in the world. (Daily capacity was 1,873 tons compared with International Paper's 1,041 tons.) The chief instigator of this merger was Abitibi's president, Alexander Smith. George Mead's private views about the merger are not known, but he was as active as Smith in bringing it about.

Change of Heart

Precisely at the time of this master stroke, George Mead began to show signs of uneasiness about his Canadian venture and to begin a partial disengagement from it. First of all, he was concerned about the optimism of Canadian newsprint makers toward the price levels of 1926—a year when demand actually outstripped supply. They were convinced unitedly that price levels would continue to rise. George Mead, only too well acquainted with the characteristic feast and famine cycles that had long beset the paper industry, tried repeatedly to advise lower prices, but on this matter his counsel went unheeded. Undoubtedly he was also concerned about the overcapitalization of the new Abitibi company. His own computation of the combined assets of the two constituent companies was $94,000,000, whereas Abitibi in 1928 claimed assets of $177,919,211. In any event, he was even willing in 1927 to let his G. H. Mead Company be disposed of as a nucleus for a new industry-wide sales organization, which was of course to include Abitibi itself. The sales price was $1,750,000, to be paid over a ten-year period, but within a year the new sales organization failed and George Mead had to take it back, reconstitute it and rebuild it. His tours through Canada became less frequent. Most significant of all, he refused any position of authority in the new Abitibi management and agreed to serve only as chairman of the board.

In 1932, when Abitibi was declared bankrupt, when he himself lost $8 million by refusing to take the easy way of compromising his stock, and when he took additional losses in going to the rescue of personal friends, his disengagement with the Canadian venture was practically complete. Several

A giant in the paper industry,
George Mead could also
enjoy the rugged
Canadian landscape
like an original *voyageur*.

years later, he sold the sales company to the Abitibi receiver—the price had
by then dropped to $750,000—to help the company get back on its feet, and
for the remainder of his life he remained in Abitibi employ as a consultant.
But, while he by no means closed the door on the experience he had gained
in Canada, he closed it tight on the Abitibi merger and collapse. He spoke
of the bankruptcy only once in public, and then he spoke laconically in the
course of a legal hearing:

> Shortly thereafter [i.e., the taking back of the sales company], the Abitibi com-
> pany was put in receivership, along with several other of the large Canadian
> companies. However, the reason for the Abitibi receivership was not, like the
> rest of the companies, for lack of funds, but because the president of the Abitibi
> company, without consultation with his directors, had purchased a competing
> company for $12,000,000, and also built a power plant on which he had guaran-
> teed payments on the bonds, again without knowledge of his directors, in con-
> junction with the Ontario Government. Therefore, the Abitibi company found it-
> self with an obligation of some $15,000,000 which it did not have.

The question insistently puts itself as to why George Mead—experienced,
honest, sagacious, and at once widely successful and widely respected—
could not somehow have forestalled the Abitibi collapse. Any answers to the
question can be no more than surmises: George Mead, who believed it fruit-
less to dwell on past mistakes, never answered the question aloud. An im-

portant key to his character, however, is how he may have answered the question to himself.

Why did he feel he should not be the chief executive officer of the merged organization? Why did he not raise violent opposition to the overcapitalization of the company, even to the extent of trying to block the merger altogether? Why, from his post of board chairman, did he not try to influence the affairs of the company? While he did not foresee the depression of the thirties, he did foresee hard times for the newsprint industry. Why did he not act?

It should be noted first that George Mead was not a man to insinuate himself forward. He was personally so disinterested as to be disinclined to push or be pushed into high places. Moreover, his business effectiveness depended not on solitary direction or imposition of his will, but on a mutually effective realtionship with the men with whom he worked. He had not had the chance to imbue his Abitibi associates with his way of business as with his colleagues in the various Mead companies. It is possible, of course, that he did not know his associates in the merger negotiations well enough to see their weaknesses —and indeed he was a man who looked for the best in others—but it seems more likely that he knew them only too well, that he knew that his counsel on Abitibi affairs would, had it been offered, been received with no more notice than his counsel on newsprint prices. In short, he may well have known that under the circumstances there was no way at all of combatting the speculative urge, the blindly self-seeking interest, and the semi-innocent lack of comprehension that often grip men at the height of a speculative boom.

A man's wisdom arises very often from awareness of what he cannot do, and it is very possible that George Mead knew exactly what he could not do. The likelihood is that he had decided that he must close his personal door on Abitibi some years before the door was closed on Abitibi itself. He disengaged himself, concentrating more heavily on the affairs of the Mead Pulp and Paper Company, whose solid growth and unspectacular consolidation were at the time in marked contrast to Abitibi's showy manipulations. He took his losses when they came and did not weep over them. It is to be recalled that he had long had a distaste of bigness for the sake of bigness and of money for the sake of money. It may be that a disenchantment with the world glittering financial maneuvers, the world of spectacular business coups, the world of big deals lacking in greatness—it may be that this disenchantment was the answer he derived at the end of his Canadian venture. Thereafter he adhered strictly to his own way of business.

CHAPTER 8

Consolidating A Corporation

WHATEVER THE DEGREE of George Mead's engagement and disengagement in his Canadian venture, his involvement with the Mead Pulp and Paper Company and its offshoots was total. The pattern of this involvement is suggested even by the office layout in the early 1920's at Dayton headquarters, which then occupied the top five floors of the City National Bank Building, located at the corner of Third and Main Streets. Floors eleven and twelve were strictly reserved for the business of the Mead Pulp and Paper Company, while space on floors eight, nine, and ten was assigned as need required for the G. H. Mead Company, the Management, Engineering and Development Company, and the Mead Sales Company. A common switchboard and a common reception room served all these enterprises, but the U. S. company and those involved primarily in Canadian operations remained distinct, not only in regard to space but particularly in regard to personnel. In 1922, to be sure, W. N. Hurlbut, together with Henry S. Mead, the right hand man in the Canadian operation and for a time resident assistant manager at the Spanish River mills, served on the Executive Committee of the Mead Pulp and Paper Company; and later during the decade, Sydney Ferguson assisted in some of the planning of the Abitibi merger. Each man, however, crossed the line that separated the Canadian and U. S. premises as an officer of the Mead Investment Company, not as an employee of his respective organization. Moreover, they were almost the only men who crossed lines in any way.

Line-crossing was left almost altogether to George Mead himself, but the wonder is that he found time for it. When he was at headquarters, his days were full, but by no means overwhelmingly so. At 8:30 or 9:00 in the morning he was at his desk. (It was of mahogany with a surface neither empty of paper nor littered, and located on one side of a white fireplace in a large, dark-panelled room, across from a mahogany conference table with chairs for five.) At 12:30 he took lunch, which he invariably followed with a nap until 2:30 in the afternoon. When he left the office at 6:00, he usually took no paper work home with him. He enjoyed dinner with the family and an evening of talk, relaxation and laughter, suitably mixed.

While he was in Dayton as frequently as his traveling schedule allowed, his family was in Dayton for only some four months of the year. The children's health dictated a stay at Aiken roughly from November first to March first. The Dayton heat made necessary an escape during June, July and August to a succession of places in the mountains and at the shore, until in the late twenties a rambling Cape Cod cottage near Hyannis became the family's regular summer locale.

Obviously, George Mead drove himself. He left to others the question of the pace they would set for themselves. But he also left to others large and increasing areas of authority. It was his unique method of delegation that made it possible for him to be so effective in absentia in the numerous locations of the Canadian and U. S. operations. He wasn't, in any sense, an absentee manager. His mind retained so much and he entered so whole-heartedly into all the concerns, business and personal, of his colleagues that he seemed ever-present to many of them. In fact, they were not always aware of the continually increasing authority that each one of them was carrying during the 1920's.

The period was one of marked growth. In a formal sense, the growth was from a series of highly decentralized operations that centered around the Mead Pulp and Paper Company without being a legal part of it. A new centralized organization, the Mead Corporation, created in 1930, brought together the Mead Pulp and Paper Company, which had already taken to itself the Peerless Paper Company and the Mead Fibre Company, along with the Management, Engineering and Development Company, and the Mead Paperboard Company. The latter involved a whole series of new mills erected during the 20's to operate in a new field with a new process on a new raw material.

Between 1921 and 1926 assets and sales doubled; profits and tonnage tripled. By 1929, assets had increased more than three times, sales almost four times, profits and tonnage almost five times. The 1930 consolidation increased the assets, sales and profit figures more than five times, more than doubled the tonnage that had already increased five times during the decade.

The degree of growth and the size of the consolidation are indicated in the year end figures:

	The Mead Pulp & Paper Co. The Mead Corp.			
	1921	1926	1929	1930
Current Assets	$1,363,270	$2,256,296	$3,291,500	$5,591,759
Net Plant	4,200,909	6,299,351	14,873,710	23,123,051
Total Assets	5,887,451	11,090,854	18,961,000	30,819,521
Current Liabilities	669,576	1,076,215	1,784,953	835,218
Long-term Debt	1,100,000	2,922,500	2,362,500	9,500,000
Shareholder Equity	4,060,374	7,011,777	8,791,135	12,755,023
Total Liabilities	5,887,451	11,090,854	18,961,000	30,819,521
Net Sales	3,271,054	6,854,618	12,889,396	16,707,101
Net Profit	226,862	401,575	1,151,210	1,215,984
Tonnage	18,384	63,818	98,500	238,890

The Staff Expands

Given an expansion of these dimensions, and given a roughly 50-50 division of George Mead's time between the Canadian and the U. S. enterprises, there had to be, of course, an increase in the numbers of workers and managers. In 1921, the headquarters staff of the Mead Pulp and Paper Company consisted basically of George Mead; Vice-President R. T. Houk, who had served since 1913 as a sort of general factotum, Treasurer Speed Warren, Auditor Sydney Ferguson, together with recently employed Henry G. Meyer, comptroller, and John S. Davis, assistant secretary. Robert E. Cowden, secretary, worked out of his own law office. At Chillicothe, H. P. Carruth was backed by John Traquair, research; Michael Ludwig, Jr., a second-generation Mead employee who had started in the mill as a cutter-boy and become superintendent, and by a new employee, W. H. Kettra, a cost accountant who served with the title of assistant treasurer.

A key characteristic of the various new employees was their solid experience in auditing and accounting. Despite his ability to keep in mind myriad facts of his various enterprises, George Mead had an aversion to running any one of them from the top of his head. "Facts and facts only," he emphasized in a 1926 talk to employees, "not guesswork." He was able to let the organizational structure of his companies take form loosely and freely in response to patterns of work that the men themselves developed, largely because every aspect of every company from sales and costs to quality and productivity was studied and analyzed in clear and detailed figures. He was attracted by the type of fiscal expert who seeks to know as exactly as possible what is going on as a means of determining the feasibility of various business strategies, not the fiscal busybody who is impelled to use account data simply to keep down all costs, irrespective of their importance.

His aim was enterprise of a humane sort, but he never imagined that such enterprise could exist unless it was thoroughly rationalized. Operating and research men like H. P. Carruth and John Traquair quickly learned their figures. Legal men like Robert Cowden and his many colleagues and successors, were called upon frequently, not to keep the companies out of legal difficulties but to give assistance in logical analyses of each company's basic business performance and outlook. During the twenties, George Mead even undertook, in a number of talks to foremen and mill council representatives, to give short courses on how to understand balance sheets and profit and loss accounts.

Upon a solid foundation of factual report and analysis, the organizational superstructure developed as if by itself. The duties of the headquarters staff, aside from precise understandings as to who was keeping what books, were vague. Very probably they were purposefully vague. Almost everyone functioned in fact and some indeed by title as assistant to the president. George Mead, particularly during the push-ahead twenties, let various men undertake the projects, duties and responsibilities to which they themselves were drawn. He was looking for the sort of men who were not seeking status but developing stature.

1921 Recession Hits Hard

The first critical test of this method of management was the sharp quick recession of 1921, which hit the paper business with unusual impact. After operating at 90.5 per cent capacity in the U. S. in 1920, it suddenly fell to 61 per cent. In Canada, as it has been noted, Spanish River was one of only two companies to pay dividends on common and preferred stock. In both Canada and the U. S., sulphite pulp sales were abruptly cut in half; with only one exception, the sulphite mills in Canada went into receivership. Book paper was even more depressed than newsprint, and severe losses throughout the U. S. were general.

"In perhaps 50 years of industrial life in America," George Mead reported at the time, "perhaps in the entire history of the country, there has never been a year quite so severe in industrial and financial affairs as the year past. At such a time the unfortunate executive of a company is called upon to do many things that do not ordinarily come into the regular routine of his duties . . . I have been compelled to spend many nights and many days travelling in an effort to do my part toward keeping the wheels down at the end of Paint Street [Chillicothe] turning." The Company, he noted, made a profit for the year—a respectable $226,862 on sales of $3,271,034—"at a time, when, to my particular knowledge, no other paper company in the United States has been able to operate without some loss." He noted that many bankruptcies resulted from "some slight carelessness in management or financial undertakings," and attributed the remarkable showing of the Mead company to the cooperative spirit that existed in the Company and to the cooperative relationship that existed with the Crowell Publishing Company.

The strength of this relationship had indeed been reinforced during the year immediately preceding the recession. The circulation of the various Crowell magazines was increasing so rapidly that paper needs were greatly in excess of contract requirements. Prices in 1920 were high, and the Mead Pulp and Paper Company could have sold all the paper in excess of the contract tonnage at prices much higher than contract. But George Mead, alert to the duties as well as the benefits of being a customer's single supplier, refused to consider cashing in on the market and fulfilled Crowell's excess needs at the contract price. The consequence was, of course, that Crowell was anxious to help Mead in every way possible in 1921, and in 1922, when depression turned almost overnight into boom, Crowell orders poured into the Chillicothe plant.

Meanwhile, however, the bottom of the market and the completion of new machines No. 6 and No. 7 had practically coincided, and the Company found itself with doubled capacity and almost no outlet other than Crowell. The paper itself had been developed especially for Crowell: it was high in quality, printed excellently on high-speed presses. But in its unprinted form it looked a trifle dirty, largely because of the old paper used in its manufacture. Relations with potential customers other than Crowell were limited, and one jobber who took some of the paper promptly rejected it; he could evaluate his shipment only in terms of the unprinted sheet and found it too dirty. Generally almost all jobbers were unaware of the improvements in printing quality that the Company had developed with great effort. It was the basic Crowell contract together with the sound business foundation of the Company that brought it through 1921 profitably.

George Mead had long been seeking means of diversifying output, and the experiences of 1921 strengthened his desire to broaden his search. He had concentrated on Crowell production to secure the advantages of running paper machines full on large orders, and, forced to choose between business for jobbers and business for big publishers, he had unhesitatingly chosen the latter with full knowledge of the risks that accrue from having one principal product and one principal customer. He was not inclined to re-enter the jobber business until he could do so on a rationalized basis with sufficient volume to run paper machines full. It was not until 12 years later that he found such a basis. But he could and did seek out other publishers, among them Time, Inc., which bought its first carload of paper—enough for the first four issues of *Time*—in 1922. Thereafter, Time, Inc. became a regular customer, along with McCall's magazine in 1925.

How this latter contract got into the Mead fold illustrates several facets of George Mead's way of doing business. In the course of the negotiations with Marvin Pierce, assistant to the president of McCall's, according to the report of General Manager Carruth, "We juniors had been wrangling with Pierce for a couple of hours. Just before lunch time, George Mead stuck his head in the door and inquired how we were progressing. On being informed that little progress had resulted, he said to Pierce, 'I have the greatest confidence in the fairness of the McCall management. We will just leave it to you to tell us what is fair, and that will be the price.' Later, Pierce said, he had never been put on such a spot."

Mead Paper Passes The Test

Meanwhile George Mead undertook to put the Crowell relationship on a somewhat less exclusive basis. This undertaking, as he commented more than 20 years later, proceeded with apparent indirection to kill two birds with one stone:

The Crowell Company used to say to the Mead Company, "We think that West Virginia and Oxford (the two other largest manufacturers in the trade)—we think their product is better." So we would say, "All right, go ahead and buy a few carloads of paper and run it against ours," and the paper would be very good. Not very much better than ours but a little better, and not enough to disturb the Crowell Company very much. They'd say, "We'll let it go for a while."

Finally, I got tired of that sort of thing, and I said to the Crowell Company one day as we were reviewing this contract, or making certain changes, "I want to supply you with only 80 per cent of your requirements," and they said, "Why?" I said, "I am sick and tired of hearing how much better than ours the other paper is, so you buy 10 per cent of your requirements from Oxford and 10 per cent from West Virginia, and we'll supply 80 percent, and we'll run these papers every day in the year and find out who has the best paper."

That is substantially the way the contract stands now. These other two manufacturers supply them regularly and they rate the paper every month, and about eight months out of the twelve, Mead is number one and the others alternate between two and three. We get down to number two every now and then for a month, and one of the other fellows gets up to number one; then we are back in number one place. We've never been in number three place in 20 years, according to my recollection, and I have maintained a policy in other contracts that we have taken in the future, similar to that. For instance, *Time*. We originally furnished all the paper for *Time* Magazine from the day it started for ten years, and they ran trials. However, that was annual contract, and they ran trials every year and always gave us the order. When they started printing *Life*, we made the first paper, a special kind of coated paper, and we took care of them for a couple of years. But they grew so fast that we couldn't keep up with them, and I didn't think it was proper for us to spend so much money to install machines.

This decision had, of course, double consequences. It made possible increased customer diversification, but it also created within the Mead Pulp and Paper Company a powerful stimulus for quality production of the sort that George Mead was forever seeking. However, he by no means gave the Crowell Company any less attention. In the midst of the 1921 difficulties, he took Sydney Ferguson with him on a trip from Dayton to New York, talked Crowell the whole way, and on his return to Dayton wrote a letter appointing Ferguson—company auditor by title and assistant to the president by function—his personal assistant in all matters relating to the Crowell contract. Up to this time, George Mead had handled personally all contacts, telephone calls and correspondence.

Meanwhile, developments in Canada led to setting up another new organization—the Mead Sales Company. This company was to undertake the sales effort of the decentralization drive, although founded for an entirely different purpose. In 1920, the Abitibi company suffered critical water shortages and had to depend on outside sources for its large supplies of ground wood pulp. It turned, in some desperation, to its sales organization, the G. H. Mead Company, with orders to buy pulp; purchases were so large that they were made all over Canada and the United States. Suddenly the recession hit, and, as George Mead said later:

Things went to pieces very quickly. We had a lot of pulp bought on the word of the Abitibi company that they wanted it . . . telegraphic communication and so forth to keep on buying. Then they took the position—the president of the company did—that the G. H. Mead Company had gone way beyond their orders, and we found ourselves with a lot of pulp on our hands. The Abitibi company wouldn't take it and wiped out a considerable amount of profit we had made in that period. As a result, I decided very promptly that we had to have a different setup for our pulp and paper in the newsprint game.

This decision resulted, typically, in a separate new corporation. It is indicative of George Mead's thinking that he planned it from the beginning as an organization that could at once begin to take over such sales of Mead book paper as were not handled directly with customers. The sales were initially small—they amounted to only $750,000 in 1922—but by 1924, when the organization was selling paper from Kingsport's new machines, they had increased to $2 million and by 1930 to $5,800,000, 36 per cent of the newly consolidated Mead Corporation's sales. Eventually, in the 1940's and into the 1950's when the Mead Sales Company became a part of the parent company, it was responsible for up to two-thirds of all company merchandising.

Almost every decision of George Mead concerning decentralization of product and sales efforts during the twenties brought with it steps to decentralize responsibility and, apparently, to dilute his own authority—to such a degree, indeed, that it is impossible to know which type of decentralization had priority in his mind. The Kingsport operation illustrates this point.

Losses Prompt Stern Letter

Kingsport was the only one of the Mead companies to operate at a loss during 1921, but it had not made money even in the big year of 1920 and was not going to make any for years to come. Operating as a soda pulp mill, it suffered from a sharp and continuing decline in soda pulp prices that followed the earlier dip in sulphite and ground wood prices. Even when two paper machines were added to the plant to provide a use for the pulp—an expense that taxed Mead resources—problems multiplied and costs rose. Losses for 1922, the year before the addition of the new machines, came to nearly $100,000 on sales of $860,000. The next year, despite a new customer—a book publishing concern George Mead induced to settle in Kingsport—losses doubled even though total sales rose to nearly $2 million. John H. Thickens, one of the founders of the Management, Engineering, and Development Company, had the thankless and frantic job of plant manager, and every expert from Chillicothe came to give assistance and advice: manager H. P. Carruth, superintendent Michael Ludwig, Jr., Howard Teter, now superintendent of Production Methods. As soon as one critical problem seemed to be solved, another equally critical appeared.

Just after the close of the year 1926, George Mead summarized his own views in a talk to the Kingsport men:

The net result of the five-year period in this plant, gentlemen, has been that we have been able only to make the interest on the bonds that we sold to put in the paper mill, and carry ourselves without any particular loss, but without any possible profit. In order to properly show a profit in any business, you must charge depreciation from your earnings before figuring profits. This company has been unable to earn a proper depreciation on its plant. I have felt seriously to blame personally for this situation, but try as I would, I could seem to find no solution to our problem unless we were able to finance a much larger undertaking and build a much larger paper mill here. That, in turn, brought up a most serious problem in the merchandising of the paper . . . To anyone who has been in the paper industry for a period of years it is manifestly poor business to ever enlarge a plant unless your product being made at the time is well sold, and unless you have substantial prospects for selling the increased production. To date our plant here has not reached that position.

Noteworthy in this situation is the fact that there was a possible solution to Kingsport's problem that George Mead apparently did not even consider: namely, his personal intervention in it. His own financial interests could have prompted such intervention, since during the years of the worst losses—1919 to 1926—the only pocketbook that was seriously affected was his own, by reason of the Mead Investment Company's major ownership of Kingsport stock. By this time, moreover, he was widely considered the most knowledgeable man in the industry, and he had the practical experience of putting on its feet not only the Chillicothe operation, but also the operation at Lake Superior and at Spanish River. He did indeed visit Kingsport regularly, and he was always available and eager for consideration of its problems. But he did not increase the frequency of his visits, and he did not take to issuing orders. His attitude might be described as one of benevolent non-interference, a sort of watchful waiting for his men to work out the right decisions themselves. These he strongly encouraged and warmly ratified. He would not, however, take over. He wanted his colleagues to take over. Witness his letter of August 8, 1928, to H. P. Carruth, one of the strongest in tone that he ever wrote:

I have just received copy of the first six months result, and am very much pleased with the showing Chillicothe has made. However, I am terribly discouraged at the Kingsport showing, and can hardly believe my eyes when I note that the broke for the month of June was 50 per cent of production.

I remember when the Peerless operation was turned over to you and the

Chillicothe organization, it was a number of months before the seriousness of the situation seemed to be realized, and I feel certain that the same applies to Kingsport. I firmly believe that if you had gone to Kingsport personally and stayed there for six or eight weeks continuously the operation would long since have cleared up, and that it is due to your personal absence that we have lost so much money.

On your return I hope you will go vigorously after the situation. . . .

He was not only urging Carruth to get busy; without saying so, he was also urging Carruth to delegate enough of his Chillicothe duties to accept other responsibilities.

Mead's "Pilot Plant"

It was the Chillicothe plant itself, however, that remained the center of George Mead's interest. He referred to it from time to time during the decade as a pilot plant, used it as a model for operations at Kingsport, at Peerless, and at the Spanish River Company so long as he remained its chief executive. It was at Chillicothe that he had worked out his ideas of cooperation and mutuality of interest among employees, customers and stockholders. Here he had applied his belief that industry could find lasting viability in an organizational atmosphere that met human needs and pursued humane ends, and within an operational framework in which constantly improving quality and productivity—directly stimulated by the organizational atmosphere—would make for continuing growth. Size, he continued to insist, was not a goal in itself, but his expansive enthusiasm welcomed growth as a basic factor in excellence.

And Chillicothe was indeed growing, growing to such an extent that by the early twenties its dimensions were far larger than those of most pilot operations. It was, in fact, already one of the biggest white paper mills in the country, and it was now serving George Mead as a place to experiment with the problems of organizing a sizeable endeavor. By 1922, it had more than 500 employees, a number George Mead was then inclined to consider optimum for one plant. The production of its seven machines amounted to 104.5 tons per day in 1922, increased steadily during the next five years, reached 170 tons a day in 1927—a 70 per cent increase. No new machines were added until 1929, although improvements and expansions kept the plant in a constant state of construction during a great part of the decade, particularly during 1926.

George Mead directed this growth according to the system of indirection typical of him. He was indeed determined to give good men their heads, whether hired from the outside or developed on the inside. With blue-collar workers, emphasis was strongly on inside development. In 1922, for instance, when production increased 20 per cent over the preceding year and 100 new employees were added, 139 old employees received promotions, roughly one out of three of the existing force, and it was necessary to look outside the Company for only six skilled men. In his numerous talks to the men during the twenties, George Mead discussed time and again the program of mutual relations he had worked out during the preceding decade and this theme was reiterated by Manager Carruth and his principal assistants. Strongly emphasized was the team approach based on the division of operations into 17 departments, each one big enough to field a baseball team in the intra-Mead league. Responsibility was diffused as broadly as possible, and when size necessitated the building of a cafeteria, its operation as well as that of the baseball park was divorced entirely from management and given to the men.

One topic, plant safety, did receive new emphasis. As size increased, so did accidents. In 1926, on the occasion of the 20th anniversary of the Mead Pulp and Paper Company, George Mead said:

I think the record of accidents in the Mead Pulp and Paper Company plant indicates more clearly than any other how by giving thought and attention to our fellow workmen we can reduce suffering and save the greatest of all things—the life of other men. I am particularly pleased with this endeavor and want to express to the men who have been working on the safety program the delight I feel in the progress made along this line. In the last four years the accidents have been reduced from fifty to seven. That is a greater performance, gentlemen, than paying the dividends which have been paid to our stockholders.

As for executive workers, George Mead continued to let them work out their jobs for themselves, displaying an unusual degree of permissiveness that was feasible, basically, because he was able to select unusual men. His four principal appointees to the Chillicothe staff in the mid-twenties were all young men with a high degree of technical education, of definite though as yet unproved abilities, of strong personal conviction combined with the sort of cooperative spirit that George Mead admired, and of marked readiness to accept responsibility. Responsibility was quickly given, given indeed with unusual quickness. For example, Russell H. Savage, who later became director and then vice-president of Research and of Planning, joined the Chillicothe force during the winter of 1924-1925, within a few months expressed doubts that a new grade of machine finished paper would print well, promptly found himself setting up a new sales-service program of which he was soon put in full charge. Future President D. F. Morris, a young chemistry major from Washington and Jefferson College, went to work about the same time for the company, his first and only employer, joined the laboratory staff as its fourth member, found himself defining the technical standards of the new sales-service organization, went next to Peerless and then to Kingsport to troubleshoot quality problems.

(Typical of the development of the Mead organizational system was the evolution of sales service. After being attached to the Mead Sales Company for several years, it was made an integral part of the manufacturing operation—for the obvious purpose of bringing customer experience most effectively to bear on quality problems—without anyone knowing precisely who proposed the change and who ordered it.)

Employed in 1925 was future president and chairman, Howard E. Whitaker, an M.I.T. graduate in civil engineering. He was dispatched almost as soon as he was hired to serve as superintendent of the troublesome Kingsport pulp mill. Future President George H. Pringle, who came to the company in 1927 with a graduate degree in mechanical engineering from McGill and nine months' experience installing a paper machine for another company, was immediately given major responsibility for getting more paper out of the Chillicothe machines without sacrificing quality.

George Mead was looking for scientific and engineering men for the paper mill while he continued to look for bright young financial men for the Dayton headquarters. In 1923 he found Alan G. Goldsmith, who had graduated from college at the age of 18, had gone to work with the Hoover relief commissions, and had followed Hoover into the Department of Commerce. He was dispatched almost immediately to Europe—George Mead had not been there since 1919—for a thorough study of European papermaking methods, and on his return became another of George Mead's right-hand men. Two years later came future Treasurer George Robinson, whose first assignment was to take over the books of the Management, Engineering and Development Company from Sydney Ferguson, who needed more time for his Crowell work. Allan Macbeth, comptroller until his death in 1939, came in as a cost accountant in 1927, and Al. H. Mahrt, who was to serve later as treasurer and vice-president, was hired in 1928 from the company's outside auditors, Allan R. Smart and Company, as still another right-hand man. He was immediately named assistant treasurer, but there is no indication that he or any other executive was hired during this period to fit into a particular job opening.

The third and fourth generations of Mead management:
top row l. to r. are Ford T. Shepherd, A. Rodney Boren, J. H. Cunningham,
George Robinson, Al. H. Mahrt and R. H. Savage;
front row l. to r. are L. R. Growdon, Sydney Ferguson, George H. Mead,
H. E. Whittaker, D. F. Morris and George H. Pringle.
This photo was taken in 1953.

Everyday Occurrences

This system of organization was so flexible that, while there was in fact notable decentralization of authority there was no such thing as formal delegation of it. The board of directors represented obvious and final authority. George Mead himself appeared at first sight to be executive authority of an equally obvious and all-but-final sort. This appearance resulted not so much from his making decisions as from George Mead's insistence on being informed on all the facts and figures of the business. This information could and did involve everything from details of laboratory techniques and precise accounts of the compositions of pulps to the accident rate and the turnover of labor. It appears to have been George Mead's conviction that if he could be assured that the facts of each enterprise were known—known demonstrably to him by reason of their being dispatched to him wherever he might be—then each enterprise was being well run. In personal and telephone conversations and in letters he talked over everything that happened, advancing his own suggestions, considering other suggestions, adding his own observations, soliciting other observations, and thus led his company through a process of personal interchange with his executives.

From time to time he made very large decisions, particularly in areas that required planning ahead over very long periods of time about major expansions or important new products and processes. But the record of his existing correspondence reveals no effort to impose his will on others, not even to the extent of indulging in the habit of *ex cathedra* utterances commonly practiced by U. S. executives. His somewhat dramatic intervention in the McCall contract negotiations (by giving McCall freedom to write its own ticket, he in effect forced McCall also to write the Mead ticket) was one of few instances of decision-making of the ordinary sort; its rarity as well as its keenness delighted his colleagues, and the story was repeated for years.

What is more, he was a man personally allergic to publicity, who liked to distribute credit to others. He specifically disclaimed, for instance, his own role in securing such customers as *Time, Life,* or Sears, Roebuck in favor of that of his sales executive. The consequence, of course, was added esprit for the Mead Sales Company. This company had been created as an independent organization to encourage such esprit. John G. Sutherland, who headed it during most of the twenties, and his successor, Rufus I. Worrell, found that so long as they kept George Mead fully informed they were subjected to no form of dictation.

George Mead maintained this same attitude of involvement and detachment toward technological advances during the twenties that he had personally launched during the preceding decade. Raffold, the pulp-mill waste reconstituted to make the best paper filler yet found, came into use in 1927. Coating of paper by machine (although not yet on-the-machine coating as an operation integrated into the dry end of a Fourdrinier mill) was proving so successful that in 1926 the coating plant had to be doubled in size. Super-calendered paper (produced under pressure on a series of special and separate rolls to yield special finishes) was winning new customers for the company. Moreover, the subject of quality, so close to George Mead's heart, was constantly under critical study. Concerning each of these matters, George Mead knew all details and regularly discussed them, but the record reveals simply his participation in the discussions and not his utterance of decisions.

The Way to Sell Paper

He was, however, a ready spokesman on all matters he felt vital to the health of the company. Addressing the Chillicothe men in 1923, for instance, he said:

I am not as interested in production records as I am in quality records. If every man in this room can take back to the mill with him the solemn resolve to try to turn out A-1 quality, and to teach each and every man in the mill the same thing, and if the quality is not right to give to the management of the company suggestions and advice that will help to make it right . . . we will have the information that the products of the Mead Pulp and Paper Company cannot be equalled in this country. That is the way to sell paper.

George Mead limited himself here to exhortation. Actual description of quality procedures was given not by him, although he was entirely familiar with them, but by Howard Teter, superintendent of Production Methods.

There was nothing indefinite about these procedures. For the year 1924, they involved a new and precise set of standards for the inspection department, power and water studies undertaken to reduce the number of breakdowns, a reformulation of wash-up procedures at the end of paper-machine runs whereby lost time was reduced from eight hours to 60 minutes or less, the regrinding of paper machine rolls to a tolerance of one-half of a thousandth of an inch, compared with tolerances of three to ten thousandths when the rolls were delivered brand new, a continuing series of studies of all possible variables in the composition of pulps, and researches into mechanical variables affecting the paper stock as it came out on the Fourdrinier machine. The data on all these and many other considerations went to George Mead, but how the specific procedures came about or who first thought of them is undiscoverable. It would seem that George Mead was primarily concerned with abandoning the old traditional way of doing certain things and expecting certain results in favor of a new attitude of, in Teter's words, "ask and reason out why."

A surviving file of correspondence between General Manager Harry Carruth and George Mead reveals how very detailed were the reports he received and how few the orders he issued. Among a host of data, ranging from the technical to the personal, appear such items as the following: a report that 34½-inch paper required by Crowell is having to be run on a 48-inch machine, since a smaller machine cannot produce the desired quantity; the chemical make-up of sodium sulphate pulps; tests of English clay; compositions of pulps other than sulphate; labor turnover rates; the employment of a coating mill superintendent; the use of liquid chlorine as a bleach; the purchase of waste papers; the possibilities of making pulp from straw; production schedules in detail; coating improvements; construction proposals and blueprints; test runs on straw pulp; quality considerations; the death of an employee. There are, in addition, long reports on expenditures and repairs sizeable enough to require board of directors approval.

George Mead's answers to this latter type of report were prompt and brief; they usually consisted of a few words of approval written on the margin of the original report: e.g., 7/4/1922, "HPC—Chillicothe. You may proceed with the work." Many of the other reports were not answered at all. When he did answer, his letters were brief and almost unvaryingly approving: 2/6/1922, "I am very pleased with your letter of the third regarding the results of your clay test." 5/24/1922, "I have your letter 24th regarding labor situation, which is most satisfactory, and I think along excellent lines." 4/4/1923, "INTEREST IN STRAW MILL AS GREAT AS EVER LEAVING HERE 16TH OR 17TH FEW DAYS DAYTON AND CHILLICOTHE." Carruth's letter concerning the employment of a coating mill superintendent elicits the suggestion that the man be asked why he left his last job. The notification of the death of the employee, who had been long with the company, brings a detailed letter from George Mead on how the estate should be arranged to make the widow financially comfortable.

On February 14, 1924, he wrote to give Carruth authority for repairs up to

$500, to reiterate Carruth's authority for more expensive and more urgent repairs to paper machine wires and felts, and to indicate a system of procedure whereby R. T. Houk, Speed Warren and Sydney Ferguson are to pass upon the requests that formerly went directly to George Mead himself. Four years later, there is approval of Carruth's request for authority to spend up to $5,000 for any repair or expenditure. On March 15, 1925, George Mead sent Carruth a copy of a courtesy letter turning down a friend who wanted to sell coal to Chillicothe: "I do not take part in the details of our purchasing and even the entire management of the company is left with the local management, which has full responsibility." A decision to build a straw pulp mill is referred to on June 26, 1928, as a joint decision, and in the same letter George Mead advances purely as a suggestion the possible need for buying straw at the end of the harvest season.

Any one of these notes from George Mead, whether dealing with the most homey or the most involved considerations, could be thought to reflect a sort of formalistic politeness, but the tone of the entire Carruth-Mead correspondence belies this possibility. In all the correspondence, and in all the references in it to personal and telephone conversations, there are only two instances in which there is so much as a hint of George Mead issuing orders. The first was his letter, already quoted, expressing the belief that Carruth's personal presence at Kingsport would have helped straighten out the problems at that plant. The second was a letter of February 8, 1929, regarding difficulties in producing Raffold in the special plant erected for the purpose in Chillicothe: "I think," wrote George Mead, "this plant should be given vigorous handling for a few weeks, and that the management should be severely shaken up . . ."

The Company That Can Improve . . .

Long-term planning was a principal concern of George Mead and one to which he brought an uncanny skill. Yet even in this area of business his methods remained flexible and permissive. For instance, chemical experimentation at Chillicothe led to paper of increasingly high quality and to new products, such as Raffold and machine-coated paper. However, the paper machines were running at a slower speed than George Mead's experience in high-speed newsprint mills led him to think was feasible, and produced more broke—paper literally broken in the production process. In this situation

George Mead did not intervene personally. Rather, he moved indirectly toward altering the chemical-mechanical balance of talents in the Chillicothe plant only after years of preparation.

His views, as he expressed them privately and publicly during the twenties, had balance and restraint. In two talks to the Chillicothe men in 1923, he said, "I believe the most important part of our future development will be in paper machines. I liken a paper machine at the present time to an automobile of a few years ago . . . We are not holding our own with other lines of industry . . . we are making almost no changes and we are suffering about as many breaks as we did ten years ago . . . The automobile has outdistanced us in refinement."

Later in the same talk he looked to the future when book paper machines would be running at 1,000 feet per minute like newsprint machines. In his next talk, constructive praise and constructive criticism were expressed:

Processes that have been in use for the past generation, the methods of manufacture, the way of doing this, that, and the other thing, will soon be forgotten . . . The companies that insist upon following old methods . . . will one by one fall by the wayside and lose their identity and finally their lives. The company that can devise new methods, that can foresee the necessity of improved processes for materially reducing the costs of production and such like will have possibilities such as never before. . . .

The Mead Pulp and Paper Company seldom shuts down. We have a splendid record in that direction . . . The only way we can continue that record is by the quality of our product. We must, in spite of the increased production, maintain a uniform quality of paper. I am encouraged each year by the improvement made in this regard. If you go over the samples of ten years, seven years, or five years ago, you will see the gradual improvement in the quality of our production. We still have a long way to go . . . a quality product is the one thing that will ensure continued operations.

George Mead sought to create an atmosphere that would encourage improved mechanical performance. He saw wisdom in waiting until the atmosphere was right before making any definite move in this direction. It was not until 1931 that he did move, and then in the only manner in which he was accustomed to move—directly, by hiring another executive. In this case, the man was a mechanical engineer, Charles R. Van de Carr, Jr., whose abilities had impressed George Mead in Canada. Van de Carr was first hired in 1926 to run the Fraser plant in Madawaska, Maine, then under Mead management. Three years later, he was hired directly by the Mead Pulp and Paper Company, but his first area of work was not even directly related to the production of white paper. Finally, in 1931, when the company had become big enough for chemistry-minded H. P. Carruth to take the new job of

Three-goal polo player George Mead with other members of
the Miami Valley Hunt & Polo Club (Dayton):
(l. to r.) George Mead, Nelson Talbott, Harold Talbott and Colin Gardner
about 1926.

At Aiken about 1927 are (l. to r.) Nelson, H.T., George Jr. and George Sr.

executive vice-president, Van de Carr filled Carruth's old job as general manager (by formal title, vice-president in Charge of Operations) and took up
residence in Chillicothe.

Ups and Downs At Peerless

During the mid-twenties the newly reacquired Peerless plant fell into difficulties, losing $170,987.27 the first year, 1925, and in the month of August
suffering the humiliation of having the McCall Company reject a large
tonnage of paper. How did George Mead deal with this situation? He was
the man who decided to sell the plant to A. L. Rieger back in 1917, and who
decided to buy it back again at the end of 1924. He was also fully informed
about everything that concerned the Peerless. He later commented, "In
taking the plant back into The Mead Pulp & Paper Company we immediately
suffered the same losses that he [Mr. Rieger] did, because it was a question
of what to do with the plant. We gave it a lot of thought. It took months of
serious consideration." The outcome of this deliberation was the decision to
manufacture magazine paper for the McCall Publishing Company. Cooperation of the McCall people was needed in this project—and it came. Mr. Mead
recalled:

> We immediately started to rebuild the small machine to make it large enough to
> make the McCall paper. That cost us some $50,000. We found one instance after
> another through the mill where the equipment was inferior, where to our surprise
> we could not accomplish what we started to accomplish, and before we realized it
> we had spent $150,000 on that mill one way or another, just getting it in proper
> condition to run. . . .

In spite of this large expenditure and subsequent loss at that plant, George
Mead stuck to his policy. He felt that he was right and that it was bound to
work out:

> Finally, we began to see daylight. The losses began to disappear, and we have
> reached the point where the company is no longer losing money. The Peerless paper
> mill will always be a somewhat expensive mill to operate. As you men know, fuel is
> much more expensive in Dayton than in Chillicothe, and it is more expensive in
> Chillicothe than in some other mill towns. We also know a small organization is
> more expensive to operate than a larger one.
> However, there is always an advantage to a plant in manufacturing one article.
> Mr. Henry Ford has proven that to our complete satisfaction, and in that some of
> the disadvantages are compensated. Another thing which impressed us all was
> that to make a very high-class product you not only require first class equipment,
> but you require a first class organization. And Mr. Carruth and Mr. Benson [Peerless

manager] and all of us were convinced that we had a first class organization in the Peerless Company.

If we make a bad roll of paper, which we will always—I hope I won't be sent to my grave with the inscription, "He stopped making bad paper," because we will always be doing that. But we will make it less often, and when we do, it is going to be so rare that I think we should all be gathered together and a man would say "Here is a bad roll of paper I made yesterday and I want you to see it; and this is the reason. Mr. Benson bought a bad carload of pulp. But also I think something happened to the machine, and I believe this was the trouble, boys, and you fellows watch out for it, because I got myself into trouble."

I probably make more mistakes than anybody in the organization, but I always try to call in all the men that are near me when I make a serious mistake, and say "Look here, I have just made this mistake. For heaven's sake, you fellows stop doing this! This is one thing we want to avoid" . . . . And that accomplishes two things: it teaches the other fellow and gives him the edge of advantage in his experience, and it also makes your own conscience just a little bit better and clearer.

General Manager Carruth's responsibilities were extended to include the Peerless as well as the Chillicothe plant. George Mead obviously approved the decision. The Peerless operation continued profitable until 1929, when the McCall Company decided to shift over to super-calendered paper, which could be made only at Chillicothe. Cost calculations indicated the wisdom of moving out all the Peerless equipment and leasing the property, and Chillicothe received paper machines No. 9 and No. 10 and a new stimulus to increased production.

Looking back at this period of the company's history, Board Chairman Howard E. Whitaker later said:

If you picture Mead's organization system of those days as a systematic absence of system with lines of communication running in every direction, you will picture the system with some exactness, but you may miss the tone of the organization which made the system—or rather lack of it—work.

Obviously, direct relations between Mr. Mead and the [new] generation of Mead managers, unfettered by formalistic organization, made for a fruitful interchange of principles, policies, plans, and projects. I would describe the system as highly flexible and voluntaristic, since it depended on the will of each man to keep in touch with others under circumstances of his own choosing.

Creating Mead Paperboard

In the twenties George Mead led the company into a new field in which neither he nor his colleagues had any experience: brown paper, used in packaging and in making containers. Since the field was indeed new, he was soon participating in a variety of decisions in somewhat the way he made them in the early days of Chillicothe's growth. But since the company was older, larger and better staffed, these decisions were essentially decisions of strategy; he left tactics to his associates. While he kept himself informed of operations, he never became involved to the degree he was in the white paper field.

During World War I paperboard containers suddenly began to replace crates and barrels as packaging materials. Thus, a period of rapid change evolved in transporting industrial goods and in ways of selling consumer products in retail stores. Originally the walls or liners of the new containers were made from jute fiber and enclosed an inner layer of chipboard. Before long, corrugated paperboard proved superior to chipboard, and jute liners were superseded by liners made from sulphate pulps. This opened up a large new market for Kraft papermaking, a relatively new process.

While George Mead had indeed been considering entry into the Kraft paper field as early as 1915, he had made no immediate moves to do so. However, the defeating experience at Kingsport of trying to turn chestnut chips into soda pulp pushed him toward the manufacture of container board.* Here were combined the challenge of rescue work, of discovering uses for a valuable raw material progressively going to waste. By 1918, before Kingsport finally abandoned chestnut as a possible raw material for white paper pulp, George Mead was studying the suitability of chestnut chips for brown paper pulp.

It was not until the early twenties that formal research began. John E. Oberne, president of the Southern Extract Company of Knoxville, Tennessee, joined in the research. Oberne had been a stockholder in the original Kingsport venture, and after chestnut chips proved unusable for soda pulp, he retained his hope that some use could be found for them. To that end, he entered warmly into partnership with George Mead. Research was carried out under the direction of Dr. John D. Rue and under the aegis first of the Mead Engineering and Development Company, then of the Mead Research Company, a corporation founded for the purpose, and, finally, by special arrangement, by the Forest Products Laboratory of the Department of Agriculture. The result was the development of the new semi-chemical pulp process, in which wood chips—from chestnut or from other trees—are only partially reduced in digesters and thereafter mechanically disintegrated into brown paper pulp. By 1925 an experimental machine was producing small rolls of nine-point corrugating board. Tests by box manufacturers indicated

*Also known as paperboard and as brown paper.

the new process yielded the most rigid corrugating material yet known, and George Mead made ready to go at once into commercial production.

Production began in September of 1925 at John Oberne's Knoxville plant. George Mead provided capital for installing and operating the newly designed equipment. An independent organization, the LaBoiteaux Company, marketed the material, a manifestation of George Mead's attraction to separate enterprises for special functions. Manufacturing problems were not so easy to overcome. "The sheet was so rigid," a Mead executive later recalled, "that it cracked in the corrugating machine. The stock was something no experienced operator apparently had encountered before. Some claimed it was too free and others claimed it was too slow. The wild formation meant different calipers all over the sheet. Endless other problems had to be overcome." Costs necessarily mounted. George Mead's bill for the original research was not in excess of $25,000. The costs of adding a board mill to Oberne's Knoxville plant came to $500,000, and the losses before a uniform commercial sheet could be produced amounted to about one million dollars.

At this point, John Oberne and the principal stockholders of his company believed that the purpose of the research venture had been fulfilled; but George Mead saw opportunities for further expansion. There were many tannin extract plants scattered throughout the southern states. Most of them were marginal operations since the price of chestnut extract more often than not was lower than the cost of production. The Mead idea was that a series of small mills using an extremely low-cost raw material could compete effectively with the big kraft plants that were being built throughout the South. The Mead plan was to study each company in the business, survey all timber resources, and then determine where and how to build and operate board mills in connection with the extract plants.

Look and Report

George Mead thereupon assembled an array of talent from his various U.S. enterprises. The men were instructed simply to go out, look and report. T. R. H. Murphy, consulting engineer for Mead, and John H. Thickens, transferred from his job as manager of the Kingsport plant, studied locations. J. Harrison Allen, who had worked as a timber cruiser for Mead companies from Canada to the Gulf of Mexico, studied chestnut wood resources. And in 1927, Alan Goldsmith received the almost casual suggestion from George Mead to borrow two or two and a half million dollars and get the paperboard operation started. Goldsmith served as principal negotiator for George Mead in dealings with other companies and as general coordinator of the various studies and plans. He was joined a year later by new assistant treasurer A. H. Mahrt, who kept a particular eye on sales and finances, which previously had been receiving the attention of John G. Sutherland, president of the Mead Sales Company. Goldsmith and Mahrt both reported daily to Sydney Ferguson, now headquartered in New York and formally titled assistant to the president.

All this activity led to decisions to buy and operate the extract mills adjacent to the sites proposed for the new board mills, to establish a holding company known as the Mead Paperboard Corporation and through that company to purchase controlling interests in five subsidiary organizations: companies at Sylva, North Carolina; Lynchburg, Virginia; Harriman, Tennessee; Chilhowee County in Tennessee, near Knoxville, and a new Southern Extract Company to take care of the original Knoxville operation. All of these companies were founded between December 30, 1927 and May 14, 1929. By July 4, 1929, board mills using cylinder-type paper machines had been completed and put in operation at all except Chilhowee, which was used only to produce extract and spent chestnut chips. By the end of 1929, each board mill had met and overcome most of the proliferating problems that beset novice operations in new areas of enterprise.

The problems were formidable. Sylva's extract operation was yielding only 750 pounds of tannic acid per unit of 150 cubic feet of wood, compared with 1200 pounds secured elsewhere. The solution was central technical control of all extract operations. At Lynchburg, the water of the James River was badly polluted and an experimental semi-chemical sulphite recovery process had to be invented, while the various arguments of residents objecting to refuse in the river had to be reconciled with those of residents objecting to smoke in the air. Then, once the plant was in operation, it ran into complicated technical problems arising from the fact that it had been built to produce liner board, not the corrugating medium for which the other plants were designed. An immediate solution was found in adding Kraft pulp to chestnut pulp. This yielded the best but also the most costly liner board on the market. A long-term solution was found by installing new equipment to transform the pulp into a variety of new laminate specialties, used originally for such things as cigar boxes and loading pallets, later for such things as automobile panels and liquid containers.

The Mead family at Little Woods in 1927:
(l. to r.) Louise, Katherine, Elsie, Nelson, George Jr., George Sr. and H.T.

Meanwhile, the plant at Harriman was beset with problems of too much and too little water. Since the Harriman area was subjected to flood, the plant was set well back from the Emory River and deep wells were dug to serve the plant. But as each new well was dug, it simply drew water from previous wells. Time passed and costs mounted until George Mead declared flatly, "Build a pipe line down to the river." This expensive project had only recently been completed and the plant was within ten days of its scheduled start-up on March 23, 1929 when the river flooded drastically and sent 15 feet of water into the paper machine room. Alan Goldsmith gave George Mead the bad news by telephone, received the startled reply, "Why did you build a plant in that location?" Informed that the flooding habits of the Emory River had been described in one of the reports sent regularly to him, George Mead abruptly exploded in self-anger. (The eventual and lucky solution to this problem was made not by Mead but by the Tennessee Valley Authority, whose dams ended the threat of floods.)

The creation and financing of half a dozen corporations, the erection of four board mills using the new raw material of chestnut chips and a new papermaking process, the consolidation and rationalization of the greater part of the tannic acid extract business in the country, the creation of sales organizations both for extract and for paperboard, and the production of over 50,000 tons of corrugating material a year, 30,000 tons of liner board, and 400,000 barrels of tannic acid—the accomplishment of all this between the beginning of 1928 and the end of 1929—was a feat as striking as the discovery of the semi-chemical process itself. What precisely was George Mead's role in all this?

Interaction for Results

Here, as elsewhere, George Mead worked by interaction with others. Every one of his associates saw him as the center of the Mead paperboard activity, but not one of them could describe his specific acts of creation. One of his contributions did not become evident until many years later. The locations of the new board mills, it had been agreed, would be determined only after there was certainty that the chestnut supply would last for at least the 20 years necessary to make a satisfactory profit on each operation. When the 20 years and more were over, each of the board plants was discovered to be close to large stands of other hardwood suitable for processing by the machinery that had been built for chestnut. It was then recalled that back when plant locations were being discussed, George Mead had regularly and unaccountably been asking questions about the accessibility of pulp wood other than chestnut. Yet there is nothing in the Mead files on any recollection in the memory of Mead men of George Mead saying, directly or indirectly, that the future availability of other hardwoods should be a factor in determining plant locations.

There is, however, record and memory of the way he delegated authority to his colleagues. He himself was present at only a few of the numerous negotiations involved in the paperboard development. When one of the negotiators appealed directly to George Mead for his personal intervention, he was told by George Mead himself that he did not want to make any decision about paperboard in Alan Goldsmith's absence.

While the progress of negotiations was reported daily to George Mead, the subsequent day-to-day operations of the paperboard and extract plants were reported daily by Goldsmith and Mahrt to one another and then to Sydney Ferguson in New York. Reports were made directly to George Mead when the men had occasion to come to Dayton. Organizational channels, however, were far from defined. It is clear, however, that George Mead spent more time at the white paper mills than at the brown paper plants—and not simply because he lacked time. The Abitibi merger had been arranged, and he was less involved in Canada than he had been for more than a decade.* The reason, in part, was that he did not know the brown paper industry, including the various persons active in it, as intimately as he knew and was personally interested in the white paper industry. He was, therefore, content to let Alan Goldsmith and Al Mahrt run paperboard under Sydney Ferguson's watching. Yet he was active in the field almost as early as anyone in the country—much earlier than the men to whom he entrusted responsibility. It may well be that his comparative inaction was the reasoned consequence of an awareness that his principal task was the organization of his Company through the encouragement of his colleagues in it. But at no time did he stop asking questions and reading reports.

---

*Colleagues noted a new concentration of interest in the U. S. operation. Director N. S. Talbott remarked in 1927, "I am sure that the hundred and some millions of dollars of companies he is putting over is just to get that business off his hands so that he can rest up and come back and concentrate his interest on the Mead Pulp and Paper Company, because I know it is in this company that he is most interested and in which his heart lies."

Combining the Various Parts

By the end of the 1920's the compartmentalization of the Mead structure was becoming somewhat onerous. There was duplication of certain headquarters activities; there was extra time, effort, and expense involved in fulfilling simply the legal requirements of a variety of corporations, and there were complications in financing numerous separate undertakings. In 1930 George Mead effected the transformation of a private family business with numerous offshoots in a single public company, the Mead Corporation, and he was elected president of the Corporation.

The consolidation was by no means just another merger of the typical 1920 over-capitalized sort. It was preceded by careful and conservative studies of all aspects of the companies involved: the Mead Pulp and Paper Company, which in 1926 had taken unto itself the Mead Fibre Company at Kingsport; the Mead Paperboard Company; the Management, Engineering and Development Company; and even the Mead Strawboard Company, organized only a year before the merger.* Excluded only were the sales organizations, which remained separate entities for years to come.

In effecting the consolidation, George Mead acted with considerable determination. He pushed ahead until the September, 1929 stock market crash made it impossible to get the preferred stock financing originally planned. Then he sat tight and waited until the bond market picked up in May, 1930 at which time he promptly arranged with the National City Bank for $9,500,000 of first mortgage 6 per cent gold bonds.

Sales of the new corporation were $16,707,101 in 1930, profits $1,215,984. The following year the balance sheet remained essentially unchanged, but as the depression became more severe sales dropped to $12,899,596, profits to $439,837.

George Mead's role in this transformation of his company undoubtedly arose in large part from an obvious desire to simplify and rationalize its structure. In the past, he had tied new ventures such as Peerless and Kingsport directly into the Mead Pulp and Paper Company just as soon as they gave unmistakable signs of future success. Despite the initial complications of the paperboard ventures, their future success was already evident. The Management, Engineering and Development Company had recently been withdrawn from Canadian operations, and it too was a success.

*The strawboard product was excellent but its price was high, and several years after the consolidation had to be abandoned.

Given George Mead's urge to rationalize business operations, his motives seem obvious.

But they may have been less obvious than they seem. One additional motive, to which he himself later referred, was a desire to enlarge and strengthen the Mead Board of Directors, upon whom George Mead had depended from the start for continuing discussion of all company plans and procedures of any consequence. It was not simply a matter of propriety and principle that made him keep his board informed and led him to insist that no action be taken without unanimous approval. It was his way of doing business; his intensely conversational manner of reaching solutions by talking things over. During the twenties, conversations on the board level paralleled those on the management level, and George Mead was eager to have about him men with whom he could converse confidently. During the twenties his cousin, N. S. Talbott, had come on the board after the death of Harry E. Talbott, joining brother Harold E. Talbott and George Mead himself as representatives of the family interest. Chillicothe banker John A. Poland took the place of founding director Alex Rennick, also a Chillicothe banker. H. P. Carruth had been added to represent management. Important additions in 1925 and 1927 were George Mead's personal friends and the co-founders of Delco, E. A. Deeds and C. F. Kettering. Now the opportunity arose to invite on the board John E. Oberne, of the Southern Extract Company; E. H. Reynolds, a Chicago financier who had been active in underwriting the Mead Paperboard Company; R. G. Coburn, executive vice-president of General Foods, and E. T. Gardner, head of his own container company, an intimate friend since childhood, and a man whose advice, given before he was on any Mead board, helped—among other things—to solve the production problems at the Lynchburg plant.

Probably basic to all these considerations, however, was a sense that the time was right to set the scene for the emergence of the fourth generation of Mead managers—George Mead's younger colleagues who had become active during the twenties and who were to assume increasing responsibility thereafter. In his own person, George Mead constituted the third generation; and he had obviously been giving constant attention to the upbringing of a new generation. These were matters about which he was disinclined to talk: talk would simply have upset his strategy of letting the structure of the organization take form naturally rather than to be formed by conscious design.

At the time of the consolidation, he did give some inkling of his thoughts to his younger colleagues. There were, he said, three types of companies in the paper industry: one type was very large, very widely owned and somewhat amorphous—International Paper, for example. A second type was the family-controlled and family-run company like West Virginia Pulp and Paper. The third was an in-between type of organization which George Mead felt that the Mead company should resemble, an organization in which there is family interest, exercised without family domination, to perpetuate the company's policies and procedures—its way of doing business.

Apparently, George Mead had become convinced that the time was right to adapt the form of his Company to the shape he hoped it would assume.

CHAPTER 9

The Depression and Mead Expansion

WITH THE CHANGE from a private to a public company effected, George Mead was planning the orderly shift from third-generation management to fourth that he had begun in the twenties. Probably he imagined entering fairly soon into a new role, basically that of a consultant. He had, indeed, publicly stated his desire for such a role several times during the past five years. This desire, however, collided abruptly with the depression. A company headed by the acknowledged senior statesman of the industry, and one besides with experience of the pre-World War I panics and the post-war recession, is not going to let that head become less active in a period of crisis.

The sincerity of George Mead's desire to play a less conspicuous role in the Mead Corporation is beyond question. He had for years given emphasis to the theme that industry needed young blood. He had established 60 as the age when Mead executives were formally to be translated to senior consultant status, unless specifically requested by the board of directors to continue in their old posts. He knew that new talent was essential to the longevity of the Company, and as he himself entered upon his middle years, the healthy future existence of his creation became a primary concern. When he himself reached the age of 60 in 1937, he tendered his resignation from his executive post to his board of directors, probably not with much certainty that it would be accepted at that time, but with strong insistence that it be accepted soon. The minutes of the November 5, 1937, meeting of the board read as follows:

In concluding the meeting, Mr. Mead stated that he had reached the age of 60 years and that, pursuant to the settled policy of the Company in requiring executives to relinquish a part of their executive duties it was in order for him to submit his resignation as President of the Company. Considerable discussion ensued, and Mr. Mead was prevailed upon to withdraw the tender of his resignation at this time. Mr. Mead stated that he desired that no exception be made in his case, and that he would submit the same at the annual meeting of Directors following the next annual meeting of stockholders, at which time he would expect it to be accepted.

It was not until 1942 that he was able to relinquish his title as president, not until 1947 his title as chairman of the board. Throughout most of the period of fourth generation management, therefore, he remained titular head. In the Mead situation, of course, titles were not nearly as important as functions; and George Mead functioning in the capacity of consultant could hardly be removed from the head of the table unless he himself gradually left the table without those present being entirely aware of it. This he was trying to do, but the depression was not a time for the attempt to succeed. During the thirties, to be sure, he ran the Company much as he had in the late twenties—by receiving reports and engaging in conversation. But, in common with every company in the country, the Mead Corporation's problems had become acute. Moreover, since he had withdrawn from the Canadian venture, George Mead had more time than he had had since 1911 to concentrate his energies upon the Mead Corporation.

Much of this time was given to education of the new fourth generation in the Mead way of business, the nurture of the fifth generation and the enlistment of members of a sixth generation to come. The fourth generation itself was already headed, informally, by Sydney Ferguson, who in his original post as auditor and his later post as interlocutor with Crowell, had remained George Mead's principal right-hand man. Wise, genial, reflective, he possessed a highly developed talent in finance, a strong attachment to the Mead way of business and a capacity to keep in mind the Company's many-faceted undertakings. Concerned with paperboard, and to a definite but undefined degree responsible for it, were Alan Goldsmith and A. H. Mahrt. Responsibility for white paper operations, again definite but undefined, rested with Executive Vice President Carruth and Operating Vice President Van de Carr for the first half of the new decade. At that time Carruth desired to move to the East, where he became manager of a newly acquired Mead property, Dill & Collins. Imported from Canada to work with Van de Carr, therefore, was J. O. Mason, an experienced and mature newsprint operator, with strong skills in production.

Research was the province of Dr. Francis G. Rawlings, one of the inventors of the semi-chemical process, together with Russel H. Savage. Financial matters, cost-accounting, budgets and the like were under the strong headquarters group headed by Speed Warren and including George Robinson and Alan Macbeth, while the Mead Sales Company was under the direction of

Rufus J. Worrell. All these men and their colleagues, together with such late-twenties arrivals as Herbert Kidd, an experienced papermaker who at once began managing brown paper plants, and L. N. Growdon, who became assistant to Operations Manager Van de Carr—all representing George Mead's effort to build a defense in depth for the Company's future—were soon serving as front-line troops in Mead's battle with the Great Depression.

George Mead's specific contribution to this battle is discernible essentially from the style of action that had become typical of him. There is, of course, no record of his generalship or, indeed, of his ever acting like a general. His style of interaction with his colleagues is suggested by his remarks to the Chillicothe Foreman's Club in May, 1939, when he was discussing the problems involved in certain new types of paper:

You men all have probably wondered in your own minds why the company management would permit the taking of certain orders of paper and manufacturing them here in the coating mill, or on No. 11 machine or on No. 5 machine, when it was perfectly obvious to you that it was a losing order. Then, we make the paper and have a terrible time and after turning it out and sending it to the customer, you get another order of the same sort and the question comes into your mind, "What in the world is this management thinking of? . . . some fellow at the top must have slipped badly." I decided that I had slipped and, therefore, we now have an operating committee composed of Mr. Van de Carr, Mr. Ferguson, and Mr. Mead instead of just Mr. Mead, and it was two to one against me, and I am hoping for improvement.* But there are, in business, times when you have to do things that seem perfectly ridiculous in order to accomplish an end.

George Mead was that rare type of man who is perfectly comfortable taking the blame but slightly edgy about taking the credit. Despite the agility of his mind and the breadth of his experience, he was entirely aware of his fallibility and alert to errors of judgment and mistakes of memory. He believed, indeed, that he had made more errors than anyone in the Company by reason of the fact that he had more occasion to make them, and felt no loss of face or threat to ego in admitting as much to himself or anybody. This healthy attachment to the factual reality of life strongly discouraged yes-men and me-first men; it even more strongly encouraged men at once mature enough to recognize their own fallibility and strong enough to speak their own minds. This unusual departure from the normal procedures of much of U. S. business, wherein facts are often made to serve ego desires and status images, sprang

---

*This committee, approved by the board of directors on April 26, 1938, was formally entitled the Management Committee. It appears to have been the immediate consequence of George Mead's first insistence upon his relinquishing the presidency of the Company.

from George Mead's deep inward convictions about the nature of man and the relationship of one human being to another. But its consequences in the business life of the Mead Corporation were remarkably fruitful. Few established companies in the country grew as solidly as did Mead during the depression, and few laid so sound a footing for subsequent advances.

Strategy During Depression

As early as 1926, George Mead foresaw a time of business troubles, based on his observation of overproduction in the paper business ("about 15 per cent," he said) and of the behavior of newsprint prices. He did not foresee the severity of the depression, its extent, or the suddenness of its onset. His initial reaction to the stock market crash of 1929 was to search even more eagerly for the capital needed for the 1930 consolidation, apparently from the conviction that a united organization could survive the buffetings to come more vigorously than a series of quasi-independent companies. He came into the New York office on one of the black days after the crash, and said to Sydney Ferguson, "Well, Sydney, as long as we have our reputation and our health, we will get through by hard work." Whereupon he took off his coat and sat down at his desk.

Several years later, when the depression was approaching its depth, he spoke with somewhat grim determination to the Chillicothe men:

This is our plant and we are going to keep it. We have worked hard to make it what it is today and nobody is going to get it away from us, if we will but follow the dictates of common sense during the next twelve or twenty-four months.

As I have told you many times before, this Company is not being built with the idea of disposing of it, or selling it to some other corporation, or of its consolidation with some other corporation. I was alarmed a few years ago because I thought I could see from the tendencies then prevailing that we might be forced into a consolidation. It looked to me for quite some time as if the successful industry of the future would be the consolidated industry, representative of a very much larger corporation than anything we could visualize from our own developments, at least during my lifetime.

He now felt that the largest corporations had become too large, too liable to inefficiencies, too burdened by internal politics, and too amorphous, so that they were beginning to lose their personalities. Actually it was during the depression that the Mead Corporation laid the basis for becoming one of the larger corporations during George Mead's lifetime, although by no means the amorphous and discordant entity that he disliked.

At the start of the depression, it was his view that international events, the U. S. gold policy, high tariffs and overproduction were, in that order, the major economic forces responsible for the disaster. While he was to revise that view, he did not alter the conviction that during the twenties there had been too much absentee management or, at least, absent-minded management, that industrial leaders had been giving too much time and attention to their personal financial and social affairs and not enough to serious business. A personal reaction of his own was to adopt the more austere style of living that was characteristic of him during the rest of his life—although his previous style had never been as expansive as that of most persons of his means—and the minor social exuberances he had recently enjoyed disappeared entirely from his life.

Austerity had long been the style of his Company. In addition to the headquarters and sales office in Dayton, there were, besides the paper mills themselves, only two small sales branches in Chicago and New York. The one suitable retrenchment he could find in administrative overhead was shifting the headquarters bodily to Chillicothe, leaving only a branch sales force in Dayton. This step may have had value as a token of serious intentions. But, viewed in retrospect, it probably cost more than it saved in terms of efficient operations at Chillicothe, where local management, now headed by Howard Teter, found its authority markedly diluted by the presence of all the senior officers of the Company. (Headquarters were moved back to Dayton in 1944.)

The rest of his strategy was basically expansive. True, in the wretched year of 1932, Mead mills were operating at only 52 per cent of capacity, and he had to use every means available—including reduction of weekly work hours by share-the-work schemes that he fundamentally disliked—to hold onto his work force. He was determined on grounds of simple humanity to avoid layoffs so far as he could, to keep his men occupied, and to pay them as well as the times permitted, but it must be remembered that he never saw a dichotomy between humaneness and good business: business, in his thinking, gained viability through humanity. On June 26, 1931, the board of directors ordered a 10 per cent cut in salaries, held off a cut in wages until the next August, when wages went down 10 per cent, salaries an additional 5 per cent. At times the mills were kept running although there was no foreseeable market for their production: all his life George Mead had held to the conviction that it was best to keep running as full as possible in slow times and to sell off the shelf when times turned better.

Expansion at Critical Times

Basically he reacted to the calamity of the Great Depression as he had to the depressions of the past. He took advantage of the low levels of everything from construction costs to the price tag for entire papermaking companies, and by undertaking expansion as broad as company finances permitted. The corollary to his proposition that the time to build and buy is when other people need money was his proposition that the time to get money is not when you need it but when you can get it. (He applied this philosophy to his personal affairs as well as those of the Corporation. This is exemplified by his building of "Little Woods," the Mead's gracious family home, in the depths of the Depression.) The 1930 consolidation had brought in $9,500,000. The new Mead Corporation had been financed with extreme conservatism, undercapitalization being more to George Mead's taste than its opposite, which had been so prevalent throughout industry during the twenties. The Company's cash position was strong at the time of the crash, and it remained so through the long reaches of years so desperate that many industrialists, unlike George Mead, despaired of recovery, despaired of the economic system, despaired even of hope itself. When in the mid-thirties business began to stabilize, albeit at low levels, the Company promptly paid off in common stock the arrearage on its cumulative preferred; when business turned up in 1937, it just as promptly sold 50,000 shares of convertible preferred through Lehman Brothers for $4 million and in 1940, again with Lehman underwriting, sold $6 million first-mortgage bonds.

The Company expanded so strongly that people in the industry thought George Mead and his bright young men had lost their minds. At the Mead Corporation there was even hiring of new executive talent, like J. O. Mason, whose abilities as an operating man were needed for the present, and men who would be needed in the future. Three hires in 1934 are typical of Mead's building for the future—James W. McSwiney, Dr. George S. Sheets and H. Warren Kampf. Mr. McSwiney was hired as a lab technician and shipping clerk in Nashville; later moved to the Harriman, Rockport, Kingsport and Brunswick operations; came to Dayton in 1954 as an assistant to H. W. Whitaker; moved up the ladder to vice-president in 1957 and executive vice-president in 1963, and was named president in 1969. Meanwhile, Dr. Sheets started both in Research and Operations, later became vice-president for Research and then senior vice-president. Mr. Kampf was hired into the sales company, given production experience and became head of the sales company in 1948. George Mead admitted that he was somewhat amused when bankers, who in 1929 had questioned the size of his talent pool, tried to persuade him several years later to take on some of their talent they now found surplus.

The course of the Mead struggle to expand during the depression is indicated in part by the table of year-end results in the appendix. But the extremely low dollar prices that prevailed during the thirties make all figures look so small in current values that the scope of the Mead achievement is not immediately seen. Thus while net plant was no bigger dollarwise in 1941 than it was in 1930, yearly tonnage shipped increased from 238,789 to 440,602, the number of employees from 2,298 to 4,402 and capacity more than doubled. This growth was possible only because the cash and current asset positions of the Company were extraordinarily sound, and because the company's depreciation policy alone provided a cash flow of over a million dollars each year, including that worst of all years, 1932. Conservative practice held down current liabilities all the way through 1935, but in 1936 policy toward them was eased in correct anticipation of the improved year of 1936 and the first really good year of 1937. When recovery from the depression suddenly ran out of momentum in 1938, creating near-hysteria in many business circles, Mead sustained an operating loss of over $100,000. But confidence was not shaken, and the Company remained as sound as ever financially and shortly became not only much larger but also more profitable than it had ever been.

Productive Capacity Aids Mills

Some of the problems of this decade, as they affected existing plants, were touched upon by George Mead retrospectively in the course of a talk at Chillicothe in the mid-forties:

In the spring of 1930, this company had just completed the installation of No. 10 paper machine and, in order to install that machine, we had thought it best, as is the usual practice, to build a two-machine room, and we found it necessary to build a new power plant and an additional pulp mill which, at the time, was to manufacture straw pulp. Because our main customer, the Crowell Publishing Company, offered its first criticism to us, one which was important to them, namely, that we were dependent entirely upon one mill and if anything happened to the power plant of that mill they might find themselves seriously distressed for paper. Therefore, we told them that No. 10 paper machine, which was for the purpose of manufacturing *Collier's Weekly* exclusively, would be put in a room ready for another machine identical to No. 10 paper machine which would again manufacture nothing but *Collier's Weekly*. It seems that they anticipated a new machine every year, or every other year, for the next ten years, and we felt that we must prepare at least four machines for them. We agreed, in putting in this first machine, to build a separate power plant so that we would not be dependent upon the one, and we also thought this good judgment.

In 1928-1929 there was a tremendous demand for paper and prospects for the future looked good. The new paper machine was started on approximately the first of January, 1930, and ran at full capacity through the first six months. Mr. Mead continued:

Then we found ourselves in the predicament of having orders for only part of the time for the machine and the first thing we knew the machine was shut down and the entire No. 3 mill closed up and, if I remember correctly, there was a period of 18 months when that mill did not turn out one ton of production.

At this time, two separate obligations were introduced in connection with the manufacture of nine-point and tannic acid. We had acquired the Heald Company at Lynchburg and eventually found that we had absolutely no orders for the Lynchburg machine. In that location, we had invested another several million dollars, again building a two-machine mill with one machine installed, and it was a matter for constant discussion for a number of months as to whether it would be cheaper for us to shut down that mill . . . but we felt that it was imperative to continue operation, for if we shut down we would lose what progress we had made. So the Lynchburg mill operated on a three-day a week basis for many months.

The net result of shutting down the Chillicothe mill and operating the Lynchburg properly at so low a productive figure was a loss of $250,000 to $300,000 in each of these locations, that is, here and there, and this was a tremendous burden for our Corporation to carry. Of course, it was very easy to say in 1931, 1932, and 1933, "Why were the officers and directors of the Company so foolish to go ahead with all this construction and get themselves in such a mess and get the Company into such a predicament." But, as I look back, we all know that the years from 1920 to 1930 were years when the judgment of men in most instances semed to be rather poor. We thought we were expanding in this country at a rate the world had never heard of and, as we had most of the money of the world, our future was unlimited and we could go on for another 40-50 years at the speed we had acquired during the twenties. I don't know that it is fair to criticize too severely the judgment our own Corporation used, but it is a fact that, in spite of these seeming mistakes, the management and the directors were able to keep the Corporation in a sound financial position at all times. After the very severe depression years of 1931, 1932 and 1933 were passed, we were able, due to careful operation and saving and better and better judgment, to put in the second machine at Lynchburg and the second machine in our No. 3 mill here and do what we call 'balance' those operations and turn them from losses to gains.

But the Kingsport operation was still the fly in the ointment. As soon as opportunity permitted by sale of additional stock, the Company financed that development. At the same time they were building a mill in Brunswick, Georgia which resulted in the production of the strong pulp the Company so badly needed in the forties.

In effect, the Mead Corporation got itself out of its depression problems by adding more productive capacity.

The rationale behind his move, a radical one for the times, was presented by Mr. Mead, again to the men at Chillicothe, just before No. 11 machine was installed in 1936:

The order has recently been placed for this equipment, and it has been made necessary, not because of the increased business given to us but because we find that we cannot manufacture waxing paper on smaller machines, which happen to be the wrong size for the customers who are doing the waxing, and because the expense of operation of those machines on that grade of paper makes it impossible for us to continue in the business. Therefore, we have to go into our financial reserve and erect a new paper machine, of a particular design very carefully specified in every detail. . . . In other words, gentlemen, instead of taking equipment we have had for many years and manufacturing any kind of paper on it, as in the past . . . every bit of equipment in every plant of this country that is going to be successful will have to be specially designed, carefully designed, and carefully thought out . . . and any company that does not appreciate this necessity is doomed to disaster. Therefore, we have not only our current problems . . . but we have the even greater problem of anticipating . . . the improvements and the changes that are necessary to keep us in advance of the art in which we are working.

Technological Advances Continue

Mead was now well in advance of the art mechanically. C. R. Van de Carr, Jr., and J. O. Mason had successfully applied newsprint production principles to the manufacture of white paper and brown paper alike, achieving great increases in machine speeds and effecting large savings in costs. ("Their associating themselves with you and with me," said George Mead, "has made it possible for us to accomplish the things we have, and without them, I am perfectly frank to say that I do not think we should have been able to do the job.") The emphasis was no longer on the chemistry of paper—indeed the chemical and mechanical aspects of papermaking were not to be in full balance at Mead until the entrance of the fifth generation of management in 1952—but precisely at the critical period of the slump, the sudden stimulus of advanced production methods on the entire Mead organization produced a galvanic reaction when combined with the Company's radical expansion program.

Research was not slighted. In 1930 it became a function separate from

production and received from the board of directors its first separate appro-
priations: $5,540 for developing a pressure-type cylinder paper machine
and for constructing an experimental eight-inch coating machine. The budget
was increased regularly during the thirties. On-the-machine coating became
a commercial reality in 1938 after years of research and experimental development including the founding of a second of George Mead's numerous cooperative relationships, a pooling agreement with Kimberly-Clark covering
coating research and patents. By becoming the first company to turn out
truly mass-produced coated paper, Mead enjoyed a marked and additional
impetus to production in the late thirties.

From the beginning of the depression on, the Mead board of directors
regularly approved long series of plant improvements over and above the
addition of two machines at Chillicothe, two others at Kingsport, the first of
which required $850,000, as well as additional machines at Sylva and Lynch-
burg. On October 26, 1933, for instance, the board approved the following
items:

A moisture control system for better regulation of drying.
A ball-bearing clipper for safer, more continuous and less manual handling of
wood.
Gravity filters to remove excess iron from water and thus to ensure more uniform
color with less consumption of time, less lost times and fewer rejections.
A water recovery system.
A double shake arrangement for No. 10 machine for quality improvement.
An automatic shaker for No. 3 rotary incinerator to permit the use of cheaper
grades of coal.
A new layout of circulating pumps to provide an increased supply of cooling
water and greater soda recovery.
A portable elevator on a lifting machine to pile paper higher and increase storage.
At Lynchburg, a second suction press-roll to increase production.
At Sylva, a three-arm lever mechanism on a turbine to decrease costs and increase
production.
At Nashville, a suction roll and alterations on the wet end of the board machine.

The total bill for these improvements was $194,255.30, excluding repairs
which amounted to an additional $43,199.18, totals that were typical of
quarterly expenditures throughout the period for continuing improvements
and maintenance. Major improvements came much higher. The first of
Kingsport's two additional paper machines came to $850,000 even though
it was a used machine.

George and Elsie Mead at their Cape Cod summer home, "Little House,"
At Great Island, Hyannis.

A Balanced Operation

Expansion was not undertaken for its own sake. George Mead was seeking what he described repeatedly throughout the thirties as a balanced operation, and he even decided, in one case in 1936, to forego an opportunity for a huge volume of sales so as not to upset the balance. This case involved the new magazine, *Life,* whose initial print order called for enough paper for 400,000 copies, but whose first-copy circulation actually amounted to 800,000, straining Mead capacity to the utmost, and, incidentally, saddling its publisher, Time, Inc., with heavy initial losses resulting from setting advertising rates based on the original circulation estimate. The Mead Corporation added another paper machine at Kingsport to the one it had already built for *Life* paper, but, as noted earlier, George Mead declined to become an exclusive supplier—even though he had been supplying *Time* and *Fortune* since their respective beginnings in 1923 and 1930—on the grounds that single sources of supply could work potential hardship both on the customer and the supplier.

The balance that George Mead was seeking required an extension of the Mead paperboard line, limited at the beginning of the thirties largely to nine-point corrugated board, and to a diversification in white paper that led within ten years to Mead's producing the widest variety of paper products in the world: almost everything in fact except towels, tissues and wrapping paper.

The first formal step in this direction was taken in the New York office in the presence of Sydney Ferguson in 1931. The president of Dill & Collins, Inc., highly regarded producers of merchant paper with a solid group of jobber outlets, and owners of properties that included the first paper mill established in America (in Philadelphia by William Rittenhouse in 1690), called to say, "George, we're in receivership. We need your help." George Mead answered at once, "Turn the balance sheet over to Sydney, and we'll talk terms at the mill."

Terms were immediately proposed, although they were not immediately acceptable to the bankers involved. The receivership was, like so many of that period, a highly involved and confused affair because of the variety of creditors with divergent interests. When terms were accepted in 1932, the price to the Mead Corporation was considerably lower than the original offer.

George Mead's apparently lightning-like decision to diversify had actually been made at least a decade before. In 1921, when Sydney Ferguson, had just begun taking on Crowell responsibilities, he suggested that there were dangers in being limited to one principle customer. George Mead agreed so readily that Sydney Ferguson surmised that the idea was in no sense novel to him. During the late twenties and very early thirties, Chillicothe kept turning out trial quantities of merchant grades of paper—e.g., business papers, envelope papers, writing papers—but the sales company found jobbers unwilling to buy. When Dill & Collins called for help, George Mead had been looking a long time for an opportunity to build a jobber system, and now the opportunity came to buy outright one of the best in the country, together with mill properties that were themselves valuable, although run down. The cash cost of the acquisition, moreover, was not high. During the first year cash advances required for working capital amounted to only $100,000, and the transfer of ownership was later effected by a transfer of 4,473 shares of Mead common stock.

In 1934, after two years' discussion with another group of receivers, the Geo. W. Wheelwright Company was acquired on comparable terms. Here, too, an original offer was turned down and the purchase eventually made at a lower price; and here, too, there was an excellent distribution system for merchant grades of paper—in particular fine bristol and index boards, mill blanks and box boards—together with valuable property, including the original Wheelwright mill, founded in 1796 at Leominster, Massachusetts.

George Mead had no idea of going piecemeal into the jobber business. He refused to go in until there was certainty that the paper machines could be run full long enough to make future profits propheciable. He had sacrificed the jobber business when the Company was small because he knew that constant changes of paper grades were uneconomical, and had based his strategy of growth on the one thing that would permit the machines to run full—magazine paper. Now that he had the Dill & Collins and Wheelwright distribution systems, the Chillicothe mill began to add still other grades of merchant paper, which had the promise of more profit per ton, and to market these grades under the Mead name. The Dill & Collins and Wheelwright names were maintained for more than a decade. These plants functioned as separate subsidiaries of the Company, until the Mead name was applied to all lines of Mead-produced paper.

The alteration in Chillicothe production occasioned not a little surprise among some executives and even some controversy centered around the introduction of Mead Moistrite Bond, a high-quality, moisture-proof business paper. In the course of stilling the controversy, George Mead discussed his strategy:

> This Moistrite Bond is an outstanding sheet. So far we have lost money on every pound of it we have turned out, and will probably continue to lose money on it until we can get enough money to run it on one machine all the time. The only way you can do that is by selling hundreds of small printers little jags of it—in other words make little orders for little customers. You have got to make it in big volumes and distribute in small lots, and to that end we are building a couple of warehouses . . . We have had plans for those warehouses for ten years, and each year we would set them aside again. We did not feel that the time had come when we actually needed them. There were good chances to sell that product far and wide, but we were not sure of the product. This year we made up our minds that we were sure we knew what we were doing, and when we started out to make a product we would make it like we said we would make it. Now we believe we are entitled to build these warehouses and we built a big lot of them—roll warehouse and warehouse for the stocking of these papers. . . .
>
> If we can get out in front as the best paper manufacturing organization in the United States we will have a machine running Moistrite Bond 12 months a year and having difficulty keeping up with the business. Now we are not making anything like the money we would like to make out of it, but we have one machine running on it and five years ago we did not make a pound of Moistrite Bond. It is not a profitable grade of paper, but you can imagine if we could run say No. 11 machine on Moistrite Bond at top speed 322 days a year, then that would be a very profitable business for us—we could run it right straight through, and a little company cannot do it; they have to make half a dozen grades on their machine. . . .
>
> We can't choose to make nothing but magazine paper in this mill. Twenty years ago this decision was in order and we decided to specialize in this mill in nothing but magazine and gradually let all other business go, because we could make magazine paper best and possibly cheaper here. However, we couldn't do this for two reasons. A lot of other people who were envious of our position began competing with us and, if we had left ourselves in that position, we might have reached the point where we had nothing left to do, for there would be no money left in magazine paper. For the last 15 or 18 years, as I have told you before, this Company has been trying to diversify its products, to get into various fields of paper, but we are interested in manufacturing only as many different grades of paper as we can possibly find to manufacture profitably.

Brown Paper Crisis

In the brown paper area of the Mead operation, the search for balance and growth as a means of combatting the depression quickly became critical. The paperboard business of the country was so new that it had never been shaken down by economic fluctuations; it included numerous marginal plants; and it quickly gave signs of participating in the feast-and-famine character of the paper industry in general. Indeed, brown paper was struck by severe famine even earlier than white paper, its production breaking at the same time as industrial production in general and recovering with it; while white paper, with volume tied to advertising contracts, fell off and picked up a year or so later. By 1932, the brown paper business was down to 50 per cent of capacity, and every mill in the country was in the red.

The Mead attack on the brown paper crisis was based on the general strategy of expanding production to economic levels at existing plants, but it was carried out by two particular tactics: participation in an industry-wide program for buying up distressed properties and concentrating their production in modern high-yield, low-cost plants, and searching through the southern states for the right location for a Kraft mill to produce linerboard and thus to enable Mead to sell both of the components used in containers instead of only one. In the course of this search, moreover, the company stumbled, as it were, upon an excellent site for a bleached-sulphate pulp mill and immediately took advantage of the discovery to add further balance to its operations by increasing its self-sufficiency in a basic raw material for white paper.

The industry-wide program came to be known as the Becker plan. It provided for the payment into a trust fund of a dollar per ton of brown paper production by established and efficient companies, and for the purchase of distressed paperboard properties by the individual companies from their contributions to the fund. The consequent concentration of production in low-cost mills effected savings of up to five dollars a ton, rescued both efficient and marginal mills, and actually made possible price benefits to the consumer. There were over a hundred companies in the brown paper business, not one of which had as much as 10 per cent of production. The Department of Justice examined the plan twice, the Federal Trade Commission once, and both gave it a clean bill of health.

This was a plan whose cooperative aspects had strong appeal to George Mead's cooperative convictions. Indeed, he tried in vain for years to persuade the white paper industry to adopt a comparable one. Meanwhile, the Mead Corporation became active, both before and after the Becker plan formally went into effect, in seeking out and buying up distressed properties. Acquired in 1933 were mills at Rockport, Indiana, Menasha, Wisconsin, and Nashville, Tennessee, at prices respectively of $157,000, $135,000 and $300,000. In 1935 the Company bought a board mill property at Newark, New Jersey, for $105,069 and in 1939 one at Cedarville, Ohio, for

$150,000. Of these acquisitions, the Nashville property alone was in good operating order; it was rebuilt and refitted at a cost greater than its purchase price and made into an integral part of Mead's nine-point corrugating operation. The purchase of the other four plants brought almost at once new production to other Mead paperboard plants, making possible a markedly better operating ratio. But the mills themselves could only be dismantled for disposal of equipment and real estate, although two were operated intermittently for a brief time.

In the search for a location for a linerboard mill, Mead cruisers and engineers studied stands of wood all over the South for years and eventually came up with 200,000 acres of timberland at Brunswick, Georgia. Negotiations for this property had just been launched by Alan Goldsmith when George Mead learned that the Scott Paper Company was anxious to build a pulp mill to produce bleached sulphate pulp. At this same time, C. R. Van de Carr was serving on the Scott board of directors and thus was in a good position to act as an intermediary between Scott and Mead. Scott realized that if it was to build a Georgia plant for just its own use, it wouldn't be large enough to be efficient and thus a joint effort with Mead seemed logical. In addition, Scott could benefit from the survey work already completed by Mead. At the same time, Mr. Van de Carr and Al. H. Mahrt reported that Alfred I. du Pont, who owned 750,000 acres of timberland in northern Florida, was considering the building of a Kraft liner mill at Port St. Joe. Thereupon George Mead, working inseparably with his colleagues as usual, conceived of a large, bold plan: to enter into a cooperative relationship with Scott and build a pulp mill big enough to supply both Mead and Scott and lessen the dependence of both companies on imports of Scandinavian pulp for their white paper mills, and at the same time to enter into a similar relationship with Alfred du Pont so that Mead could move substantially into the Kraft linerboard business. The plan went through. Agreements were reached with Scott and, Alfred du Pont having died, with his estate, the Almours Security Company. Two huge plants were erected and Brunswick was in production at a rate of 150-tons-per-day by the spring of 1937 and St. Joe by the spring of 1938 with 300 tons a day.

During the discussions which led to the joint development of the Brunswick mill, George Mead and Thomas B. McCabe Sr. of Scott became close friends. Recalling those discussions, Mr. McCabe says:

> When the agreement was consummated, George Mead and I had an understanding with the respective organizations of Scott and Mead that the partnership was

to be considered a very important relationship and that neither George Mead nor I would tolerate any grave differences of opinion between our respective organizations. We agreed that if any disagreements should arise, they would be brought to the attention of George Mead and myself and our decision would be final, and we would not tolerate any undue bickerings as this was to be a partnership in spirit as well as form. During Mr. Mead's lifetime, no serious disagreement arose. We often discussed policies and programs relating to the Brunswick Pulp & Paper Co. and these discussions were amicable and resulted in a mutually satisfactory agreement. We became intimate friends and both of us held the other in high esteem, and the friendship became one of the richest things in our lives. When I called to see Mr. Mead shortly before he died, we had a delightful time reminiscing about our partnership and told each other nothing in our business experience would have been more satisfactory.

Mr. McCabe's admiration for George Mead and his organization was evidenced by the fact that even though Scott financed the major share of the Brunswick development, it didn't attempt to take more than a 50 percent share in the operation. Commenting later on George Mead's approach to such developments, Mr. McCabe recalled, "He was a very bold operator and I had to admire his imagination and great courage." The relationship between the heads of Scott and Mead continued to flower over the years and at one point George Mead and Tom McCabe were taking a walk along the golf course at Pebble Beach, California when Mr. Mead suddenly said, "Tom, we ought to consider putting our two organizations together." Both of them went over the possibility very carefully before finally deciding it would probably end up being too much of a conglomerate to suit either's tastes.

George Mead held back from the planning of the details of construction of the plants in Brunswick and St. Joe to the extent that he did not study the blueprints. His technical grasp of papermaking was so great, however, that in the course of his first trip through the Brunswick mill—a pioneer development in producing bleached sulphate from Southern pine—he so promptly understood the technical details of making bleached sulphate pulp—an operation he had never seen—that he was at once in conversation with the manager about matters ranging from the layout of pipes and the location of auxiliary engines to possible solutions of future technological problems.

Both mills grew rapidly. The initial Mead and Scott investments of $1,000,000 each were increased by $3,500,000 each, and production rose during the first three years to 300 tons a day, each company taking half. Relationships between the two companies, equally represented on the board with an impartial referee serving as a tie-breaking member, began cordially and remained so over the years to come. At Port St. Joe, Herbert E. Kidd was installed as manager, and the plant promptly began turning out its scheduled daily production of 400 tons of pulp and 300 tons of liner of unexcelled quality. St. Joe was generally held to be the finest linerboard mill in the country, and by 1940 it was clearing no less than a million dollars before taxes.

A Goal Reached . . . and Delayed

At this point many of the long-range plans George Mead had been revolving in his mind since 1910 had been fulfilled on a scale that surprised him no less than it did his colleagues. He was persuaded, moreover, that the Mead Company had achieved at last a balanced operation. In May of 1939, he reported this belief to the men at Chillicothe:

So far as I know, and I have been the one responsible for this expansion more than anyone perhaps, The Mead Corporation has now reached the point where it is a balanced unit. This doesn't mean that we will not add to our capacity in any way; but the big job is behind us. You in this room know that we have our steam plants, our plants to make soda pulp and raw materials fairly worked out. . . . During the last year we have completed and placed in fine operation, due to Mr. Van de Carr and his group, the sulphate pulp mill at Brunswick, Georgia. We have made Brunswick a real producer of very high-grade pulp so that we are not entirely dependent upon foreign sources. . . .

We think we are now protected from a sulphate pulp standpoint; we know we are protected on our soda pulp; we know we have balance in operation in our nine-point mills. As you know, we went into the development at Port St. Joe, which I am happy to report is running very well due to the very hard work of the organization under Mr. Van de Carr's leadership and Herb Kidd's immediate direction, and that operation is going very smoothly. Both of these operations are now in what we call the profitable period of their development. I told you last year the reason for going into the St. Joe development was because we had a large investment in our nine-point mills and our customers began using liner so we felt it necessary to produce liner in order to meet competition. . . .

Now we have this balanced operation throughout the Corporation and we are prepared for the first time to give our every hour and minute to the economic and intensive management of these plants. We are turning out better and better products at a cheaper and cheaper cost, and it is the first time in 35 years we have been in this position.

Unhappily, however, the relationship at St. Joe with the Almours Security Company, which had no experience in the paper business, was not proving cordial. Difficulties became acute, and differences arose even about the car-

rying out of contractual relationships. No other of George Mead's cooperative relationships had ever gone sour, nor were any to go sour in the future,
but he had no desire to continue a discordant relationship, however profitable. He offered to buy or sell; the sell offer was immediately accepted; and
the Mead Corporation severed its St. Joe connection, taking only a 6 per
cent interest on its $2,150,000 investment. The company instantly launched
plans for another linerboard mill, but the plans were only in the preliminary
blueprint stage when World War II intervened, and George Mead and the
Company had to wait six years to achieve the balance he wanted.

CHAPTER 10

A Republican Helps The New Deal

IN 1933, George Mead added a new balance to his own life by beginning his 20-year career not so much for as with the federal government. This was work for which he was not paid—he declined anything more than the token dollar a year—and work which he did not seek. The work simply happened. He made himself available, and his availability led to his deep involvement in matters affecting the industry of the country from the beginnings of the National Recovery Administration to the end of the Korean War. George Mead's contribution was incalculable since he encouraged the great shift of opinion among business leaders throughout the country from simple profit-seeking to broad social and economic concern. Its incalculability resulted from George Mead's reticence in describing what he did, apart from the posts he held and the general convictions to which he subscribed.

The depression undoubtedly increased his own sense of social responsibility, but it did not create it. During World War I, for instance, he had agreed to take the presidency of the Spanish River company only because its principal executives were being called to war posts in England. He had served also as a dollar-a-year man for the Wright brothers aircraft operation in Dayton. Social responsibility, moreover, had become inherent in his sense of responsibility to his Company and his industry through his pioneer work in mutual relations with employees and through his practice of cooperation both within the Company and within the paper industry. His scale of responsibilities put country above industry and industry above company. As he saw it, the Company, which he indeed cherished, could not flourish unless the industry of which it was a part was flourishing, while the health of that industry, like any other, was indistinguishable from the health of the country. Moreover, he had that clarity of mind and conversation that kept him, even in discussion of complicated issues, from further complication by verbal gymnastics. He often said, in effect, that what was good for the country was good for the industry and thus for the Company, but it would never have occurred to him to turn this proposition around.

His political background was Republican and remained so throughout his life, but in affairs political he distrusted rigid adherence to the book as much as he did in matters of daily business. While no Bull-mooser, he preferred Theodore Roosevelt to William Howard Taft in 1912, but voted instead for Wilson because he was strongly against Presidential third terms. In 1920 he supported his close friend, Governor James M. Cox, against Warren Harding, also a friend and a customer of the Mead Company, having heard personally from Harding that he felt himself unequal to the Presidency and hoped to avoid being nominated for it. He was disturbed by Coolidge's passivity as a President, and when he eventually met Coolidge's opponent, John W. Davis—under the interesting circumstances of a debate in 1934 on the NRA, in which Davis was on the other side—George Mead reported that he was convinced that Davis would have made an excellent President. He admitted regret that he did not vote for Franklin D. Roosevelt in 1932, but later on declared with much force that he was unalterably opposed to a third-term in 1940.

Moreover, he did not feel uneasy about absences from the Company. His Canadian experience had taught him that he could delegate responsibility among his colleagues by not being on hand to assume it himself. He never alluded to this lesson in words, nor did he even present it as an argument for his involvement in Washington. Indeed, he regularly and frankly asked his board of directors whether he was spending too much time away from work, often adding humorously that he would consider giving up Washington if some of the directors would go there. (Clarence Francis actually did.) But he was in the process of transferring responsibility to fourth-generation management and of helping bring up a fifth generation at a critical time when a word from him carried unusual weight.

He was first called to Washington in 1933 when he was appointed one of the original members of the Business Advisory Committee of the Department of Commerce, a group of business leaders who acted as President Roosevelt's counselors on business and economic problems. Half of the men, including George Mead, were selected from a group that had been meeting informally in New York for discussions once a month ever since the severity of the depression became evident in 1931. George Mead additionally found himself involved in working on the NRA code for the paper industry, and then in 1934 he was appointed first as member and then as chairman of the

NRA's Industrial Advisory Board. By the time this work was phasing out, he was named chairman of the Business Advisory Council itself, and served as chief link between the President of the country and the country's industrialists. During the years between 1934 and 1937, in fact, he managed to carry a full-time job in Washington and a full-time job in the Mead Corporation—accomplished while working half of a 16-hour day for each—and thereafter had a comparative respite for four years, when he acted simply as a member of the Business Advisory Council and as appointee only to a committee preparing a special report on the NRA. In 1941, with the war at hand, he was made a member of the National Defense Board and his time was again fully engaged.

A Counselor of Leaders

During the intense 1934-1937 period, he had regular, often weekly, conferences with President Roosevelt, sometimes alone, sometimes together with Secretary Roper. The purposes of these conferences was to keep the President informed of the ideas and proposals of the business community, but George Mead never revealed a word of what went on in them. He was constantly in touch with other industrialists and with government officials in the NRA and other recovery programs, and frequently in conversation with labor leaders George Meany, John L. Lewis, Philip Murray and Sidney Hillman. He revealed nothing about these discussions either. From the first he saw no newsmen, held no press conferences, and reported little more to his friends than he did to his men in Chillicothe during his regular talks, confining himself to a brief statement of what he was doing and a longer expression of his views on the course of national affairs.

From these remarks, from his comments on a few additional matters he happened to mention to friends and from the recollection of Washington associates, there emerges a picture of a man whose influence was as great as it was inconspicuous. In Washington, he was entirely the same man he was in Dayton or Chillicothe: warm, courteous, concerned, and entirely lacking in a compulsion to express himself. He never claimed to be anything other than what he was—an industrialist, not an economist, nor political scientist nor financial expert—and for 20 years he remained strictly an industry spokesman, but much more an industrialist speaking for the country than a countryman speaking for industry. He made it his business to know as precisely as possible what was going on, and to that end consumed with typical

George and Elsie Mead at the Meadowbrook International Polo Game
in the mid-thirties.

rapidity a great volume of records and reports. Given a task to do, he accepted without hesitation and immediately went to work informing himself about it in a matter quite at variance with that of typical Washington advice-givers. He never betrayed confidences, never claimed credit, never asked favors. (Once when a wildcat strike developed at the Lynchburg plant, labor leaders informed him that they would settle it for him, and he replied, "No thank you; we'll handle it our own way.")

He quickly displayed a talent for negotiation in the government that was quite the equal of the talent for merchandising for which he was so widely admired in the industry. Actually, the two talents were the same, both based on exact knowledge of the facts an unfailing interest in other persons, and a remarkably low-pressure sort of persuasiveness that led others to reach George Mead's conclusions in the process of making those conclusions their own. It was not that he worked out compromises. He studied both sides, recognized the merits of each, and instead of taking a position in the middle, took one off to one side as it were. From this point of vantage, he encouraged discussion. He would congratulate both sides on their sincerity and their presentation of views, but he would wait until asked for an expression of his own position, and then only just before or after the discussion was adjourned.

His interest in people was patent. His open door policy, utilized so well in the Mead plants, extended to his Washington work. In Washington as elsewhere he looked for the best in everyone he met and usually found it. Indeed his remarks about the labor leaders, industrialists and political figures with whom he worked were entirely and sincerely full of praise. One of the few critical remarks he ever dropped among close friends was that in political maneuvering Franklin Roosevelt had "a heart of stone." He understood thoroughly, however, the confinements and the necessities of politics, genuinely liked the President, admired his way of doing things—possibly because the President liked to use conversation as a way of getting things done—warmed to his confidence in the future of the country and deeply respected his sense of responsibility.

It is known that George Mead was active in support of the NRA. While he felt it tried to do too much too quickly, he recognized that speed was essential to the renewal of business confidence. Also, he felt that many of the program's cooperative measures were ones that had been slowly and properly evolving in the course of daily business. He was no friend of price-fixing; he believed that this practice, legal in some respects in Canada, weakened businessmen's ability to merchandise; but he was convinced that the country needed temporarily even such a measure as that. He was also active in the discussions that led to the Wages and Hours Act, eventually passed by Congress in 1938; he supported the Administration bill strongly and sat in on the congressional hearings at the President's request. And more and more he was active in discussions with the President and with labor and industrial leaders about the causes and possible cures of the wave of strikes that was moving across the already demoralized country in the mid-thirties. It is to be remembered that George Mead first went to work as a roll tender, that the actualities of blue-collar labor remained in his mind all his life, and that he interposed between himself and his men none of the distance felt by some managers who rise from the ranks. Moreover, he was now persuaded that, in addition to the causes to which he had earlier attributed the depression, a serious gap between productive power and consuming capacity was responsible for the human misery and economic severity of the Great Depression.

Abuse and Honor

His principal achievement during these years, however, was his participation in the substantial change of atmosphere among the business leaders of the country. It was not that sudden alteration which, during the first hundred days of the Roosevelt Administration, led many industrialists to hail the arrival of salvation, but the much slower change that took place in attitudes toward cooperation with labor and toward cooperation with the government itself. Many industrialists came to Washington believing that George Mead—supporter of the NRA, the Wages and Hours Act and, of all things, the Wagner Labor Act—was a muddle-headed theorist and ended by moving towards his own position. He even encouraged such men to come to Washington. For some years, his standard answer to vituperation against the Administration was a recruiting message to come to work in the capital and do something about the Administration. In fact, he recruited scores of critics and supporters, as well as men like himself, into the Business Advisory Council and other government posts; and the Council itself retained him for many years as chairman of its membership committee. When he sought to recruit his friend R. R. Deupree of Proctor & Gamble, Deupree replied, "I'll agree to come to three meetings as long as I don't have to talk and can resign at the end of three months." George Mead promptly replied,

"Yes, that's a fair proposition." A concerned man, Deupree stayed for years, eventually joined George Mead on the War Labor Board, and thereafter served a term as Business Advisory Council chairman.

In the mid-thirties, however, many men were not Deuprees, including many members of the Business Advisory Council itself. By this time, hating the President and denouncing him as a traitor to his class had followed the early welcoming of him as a messiah. He and all his acts were verbally dispatched to perdition, and it was thought that Alfred M. Landon would easily win the presidential election of 1936. Tumult broke out in the Business Advisory Council; resignations were threatened; and upon George Mead fell the role of chief supporter for the Administration. He talked very quietly, reasonably, factually, but the burden of his message lay in one sentence which he kept repeating: "We will all resign or we will all stay." A secret vote was taken at the end of a morning's discussion and tabulated during lunch time. The "stays" won by two votes out of 40 cast. Very shortly thereafter, the Business Advisory Council elected George Mead to be its next chairman.

CHAPTER 11

War and Reconversion

WHEN GEORGE MEAD was called back to Washington in 1941, it was to engage in a task initially frustrating and controversial, and soon critical and demanding but no less controversial. The year before the United States entered World War II, sentiment concerning the conflict in Europe and Asia had by no means crystallized; strikes were so frequent and so general that the Roosevelt program of aid to England and preparedness at home was endangered. The National Defense Mediation Board was created to deal with the labor problems, and George Mead was promptly named by President Roosevelt as an industry representative. The work was not a tax on his time. The Board had no real effective power, met for only several days of discussion each month, and informed itself about the gravity of a situation it could not change. Anti-isolationist in conviction and a strong supporter of aid to Britain, George Mead believed strongly even before Pearl Harbor that the war would be won and that the errors of World War I could be avoided if Americans rose to the tasks before them. As a consequence, work on the board in the pre-war atmosphere was somewhat frustrating.

"I have been asked a good many times," he reported at the time to the Foreman's Club at Chillicothe, "why it is that the Administration or Congress or those in authority do not pass proper laws and stop this labor trouble that we are all finding ourselves in, and I have sat for hours listening to various and sundry [thoughts] as to what kind of laws might be put on the statute books to prevent the strikes and labor upheavals we are seeing every day of our lives, and which—with a million men under arms who are offering to go to war if necessary to fight for our country . . . just seems ridiculous and deplorable." But, he said, no laws can be made to stop labor trouble without the support of the American people. In other words, citizens are responsible for the state of the Union.

With the attack on Pearl Harbor and the instant crystallization of conviction throughout the country, the support of the people for all aspects of the war effort became obvious. In January, 1942, President Roosevelt transformed the Defense Mediation Board into the War Labor Board by executive authority and gave it powers to mediate disputes and to formulate labor policies, responsibilities confirmed in October of that year by Congress, at which time the board took on the added duty of holding down wages and salaries in somewhat the same way as the Office of Price Administration was holding down prices. The board had to delineate such policies as nationwide maintenance of union membership, which upset many businessmen, and the "Little Steel Formula," strongly opposed by labor. It had to deal with the rambunctious John L. Lewis and the recalcitrant Sewell Avery, and with practically every labor problem in the country. Originally the board was supposed to settle any wage dispute that affected production for the war effort, but a hotel strike in San Francisco assumed such a character that the board had to take it up, and thereby, in George Mead's words, "We *opened the door* to almost every labor controversy in America, and therefore under the law we were compelled to take any labor dispute on our Board for final determination that had any indirect influence on the war...."*

Total Immersion

Shortly after his appointment to the board, George Mead had taken up residence in Washington, rented a small house in Georgetown, and spent the next two years in patient, painstaking and precise labor on a task that was as thankless as it was important. He did not grumble. "The work is very absorbing," he reported, "the hearings last all day and in the evening the different groups have to get together to discuss the procedure to be followed the next day. Frequently I have found I work every day and every night to midnight for a week at a time, and when your mind is completely absorbed in that way it is just impossible for you to stop and take in the arguments that should properly be given to this particular business in which we are all interested." In 1942, he insisted on his resignation from the presidency of the Mead Corporation, remained Chairman of the Board, but insisted that he be relieved of any decisions for the time he was ab-

*See Appendix IV for George Mead's wartime views in general and for comments on the War Labor Board at the time of the Sewell Avery fracas.

George Mead and Marianna in front of their Georgetown residence—
the Mead's home-away-from-home during his service to the war-time government.

sorbed in Washington, designating Sydney Ferguson and C. R. Van de Carr
to take full responsibility and active management.

The work of the War Labor Board, despite the controversies that
attended many of the cases it handled, was marked with success in avoiding
production dislocations and in preventing the type of inflation that occurred
in World War I, largely because it was composed of citizens of the stature
of George Mead. Moreover, in disputatious Washington it was remarkably
free from dissention. But it was as lacking in glamor as it was demanding of
laborious attention. George Mead had no complaint, and he remained on
the board much longer than most of its original members.

Wider in scope and probably more challenging intellectually was his entirely informal and unofficial role in the continuing series of private discussions that during the war generally preceded official decisions. He already had a decade of Washington experience; his talents in informal discussion were highly developed; and he knew well many industrialists, labor leaders and officials elected and appointed, in high posts, middle posts, or in no posts at all, many of whom came to see him or asked him to come to see them. He would not talk about these discussions, of course, nor would he allow anyone else to talk about them, but it is known that he regularly frequented the famous park bench of Bernard M. Baruch, and that he frequently spent a daily half hour with James F. Byrnes, whom he had known well since early days in Aiken, South Carolina. (Unaware of the nature of these meetings, labor union members of the War Labor Board protested them to Byrnes under the mistaken belief that labor matters were being discussed behind their backs.)

Baruch was, of course, the architect of much of the machinery with which Washington sought to win the home-front battle for production and economic stability. After October 2, 1942, James Byrnes was, in effect, acting president of the country for domestic affairs, with responsibilities not only for the wartime agencies but also for Congressional and Supreme Court contacts. George Mead did ask James Byrnes if he could be relieved of his War Labor post, but not until he had spent two and a half years in it as well as the additional year on the Defense Mediation Board that preceded it. And then he did not ask for anything else. Indeed, by Washington standards, his behavior was highly unconventional, since a man's effectiveness there is typically measured in terms of the authority and prestige his position entails and the publicity he receives. George Mead was not, however, inclined to follow any book, whether it dealt with the standard operating practices of business or those of politics. It is indicative of the man and of the vitality of his inner convictions that he was valuable in Washington precisely because he followed his own rules. His counsel was sought not only because of his knowledge, his experience and his mental capability, but also because he was inconspicuous, because he took no credit and sought no favor. Indeed it was for such reasons that Baruch and Byrnes alike considered his contribution immeasurably great.

For his own part, George Mead considered these two men principally responsible for the country's achievement on the home front and for the success with which it shifted from war to peace without the economic disloca-

President Truman with the War Mobilization Board.
George Mead is at left in the back row.

tion and depression that followed World War I. On this subject, he was willing even to surrender part of the silence with which he surrounded his
Washington activities. In January, 1942, a time of one of the recurrent crises
of the War Production Board, whose activities were frequently a source of
wranglings and maneuverings, President Roosevelt was beset by divergent
counsels about continuing Donald Nelson as head of the board or appointing one of a number of other men who were being urged upon him. (Coin-
cidentally, Donald Nelson had been recruited into Washington service as a

consequence of an appeal made by George Mead to a specially called meeting of Council members when he was chairman of the Business Advisory Council. George Mead urged them to recruit more qualified industrialists to come to Washington for continuing work with the government, and not simply for hit-and-run advice-giving. General Robert E. Wood of Sears Roebuck responded by promising to send his most able vice-president, who was, of course, Donald Nelson.)

The President sent for Baruch, who counseled the retention of Nelson, but urged the appointment of Byrnes and an advisory committee to a new Office of War Mobilization and Reconversion, the legislation for which Baruch had been planning. "My experience in Washington and with the country's economy," George Mead said many years later, "developed a belief in my mind that Mr. Baruch's advice was greatly helpful to war production. The legislation he proposed was largely responsible for the successful conversion to a new economy, a contribution for which Mr. Baruch has never received proper credit."

President Roosevelt was reluctant to ask Byrnes to sacrifice his job on the Supreme Court, to which he had been appointed only a year before, but Byrnes volunteered his readiness. George Mead reported:

The President said he would appoint him with the understanding that he would be reappointed to the court after the war was over, and that he would also leave a memorandum to that effect for whomever would succeed him as President. This Mr. Byrnes refused to accept, saying he would risk his chances in the future, as his first consideration was winning the war. The consequence was improved direction of the war effort, which was so complex no one man could cover it properly, and the avoidance of reconversion problems. I feel that in the foregoing development, Governor Byrnes performed a remarkable job that has never been fully appreciated in the country.

New Responsibilities

As for his own role in these matters, George Mead said nothing beyond a few off-the-cuff and off-the-record remarks at Chillicothe:

Now, on account of my closeness to Mr. Byrnes, last fall he called me up one day confidentially when I was in the West on a trip, and said that he would allow me to retire from the War Labor Board at the end of the year if I would accept another appointment. After a good deal of argument over the telephone, I told him that I would do so. I tried to talk him out of it; I thought there were other men in America that should be chosen in my place; and I told him that I would try to get one of them. But he said "No," the decision had been made, and that I was to become a member of the Board that was set up in the Act of Congress passed last fall determining the Director of Reconversion.

That Act made one man not only War Mobilization Director, but the Director of Reconversion, so that office was combined. That seemed to be necessary because of the transition from war to peace through the Japanese phase being contemplated. It is quite a long one and obviously you can't have one man prosecuting the war while another is setting up the peacetime economy, so that Mr. Baruch, who formulated the Act, along with his assistant, Mr. Hassett, and the Congress in passing the Act, agreed . . . that the job should be given to one man. But it was seemingly such a colossal undertaking and such a great responsibility to be in the hands of one individual, since it covers all the other war agencies in Washington and peacetime agencies that are still to be set up, that it was determined by the Congress that a board of 12 men, 12 persons, should be appointed by the President and confirmed by the Senate, and that is called the Advisory Board to the Office of War Mobilization and Reconversion, and is the Board that Mr. Byrnes and the President asked that I serve on. The public is represented on that Board by three persons, one of whom is the Chairman of the Board; the law reads that three persons shall be familiar with labor, shall be experienced in labor matters, three experienced in management matters, and three experienced in farm or agricultural matters. . . .

That Board sits every other week starting Monday morning for two days and sometimes three, and so far practically every member has attended every meeting. There is no chance of substitution because we were confirmed by the Senate, which means that the individual name has to appear or else the place is empty, there is no chance of substitute votes. You can perhaps visualize the activities of the Board since I have told you some of what the Director has to cover and the Director sits with us during the two-day discussions and we try to give the best we can of our judgment and experience to him in helping him make the decisions which he has to make to carry on his work for the next week or ten days. We are also subject to call at any time.

After accepting that responsibility, Mr. Davis, who has been chairman of the War Labor Board ever since the war started, and with whom I have had a very close association—Mr. Davis when he was made director of Economic Stabilization had a vacancy caused by the resignation of Mr. Ralph Flanders of New England in his Board, and asked me to take that job because it comes the day after these other meetings and didn't seem to require very much more time, and I was persuaded to accept that responsibility also.

However, I can assure you that this is the limit. I have gone to the end of the road and it means that I am in Washington four days every other week and the rest of the time I am happy to tell you I am coming back to Ohio to live and I am going to get to the paper business. My wife and I have given up our house in Washington the first of the year with the idea of getting back where we belong. . . .

George Mead and Mrs. Mead got back even sooner than planned. In May they were again resident in Dayton, and while George Mead's two Washington jobs continued into 1946, he managed them by spending four days in Washington every two weeks. Then in October, very shortly after these responsibilities ended, President Truman, who had been in attendance at a number of White House meetings of the War Mobilization and Reconversion Board, telephoned to ask George Mead to take the chairmanship of the Price Decontrol Board. He declined the chairmanship on the grounds that an industrialist should not preside over a group concerned largely with agricultural commodities; he accepted membership. This task lasted only three months, required but one day a week, and is memorable not only for the speed but also for the secrecy with which it worked.* This task done, George Mead was before long called to take on others, and it was not until 1952 that he was free of Washington responsibilities, but compared to the four intense years of the war his time had become relatively free.

A Tragedy

What, it may be asked, induced George Mead to take leave of home and work and take on the burdens of those four years? Obviously, he was not out to make a name and impress others; he did not traffic in bright new schemes for winning the war; he did not presume on his acquaintance with President Roosevelt or, for that matter, with any other man. In short, he acted successfully in Washington the way he was more and more seeking to act in Dayton: as a consultant ready to do a job well and without fuss. His social life was quiet. Mrs. Mead would always join George for the social functions in Washington. One time, she arrived at the airport late, changed into her formal clothes in an airport washroom, and met George at the White House. Those they entertained at dinners were Washington colleagues only. There were short weekend vacations from time to time at the Cape and at Aiken. And that was all.

There was also a great grief, the loss of his oldest son, George Houk Mead, Jr., a 1941 Yale graduate who had immediately entered the Marines and who was killed on Guadalcanal at the head of his platoon on August 19, 1942. A young man of great promise both at Yale and at Mead mills during summer work, young George had developed an early and intense interest in papermaking, and undoubtedly he had not only parental affection but also some measure of parental hope that he would someday represent the Mead family interest in the company.

---

*Any premature disclosures would, of course, have afforded enormous opportunities for commodity speculation. The two other members of the board, bankers, were entirely alert to the need to keep the public uninformed, but some apprehension was felt concerning the numerous staff, under heavy pressure from outsiders. On one occasion the pressure was unusually great—wheat was about to be decontrolled—and George Mead hit upon the tactic of refusing to agree with the rest of the Board until two minutes before the scheduled press-release time.

Before the war—George Mead and his son, George Jr.
quail hunting at Aiken in 1938.

If it be thought that the dedication and austerity of George Mead's Washington life was a reaction to this loss, such speculation cannot be supported. The Mead scale of living was as simple in the months before the death of young George as it was afterwards. The George Mead style of human warmth, reflective conversation and precise study of facts had been long established and remained unchanged; long established and unchanged were his attitudes to such things as money-getting and prestige-seeking. He had come to Washington to serve and, it being required of him and Mrs. Mead to suffer, they suffered, as they told one another, together with other American families. Literally and immediately they went on with their work: Mrs. Mead served as a nurses' aide and took care of Navy wives right after their babies were born; George Mead continued at the War Labor Board. He visibly aged and he abruptly gave up singing, which theretofore had given him pleasure. But his way of life and his way of work were not altered.

His absence from the Company was in no sense the consequence of any decline of interest in it. The occasion for intense public service coincided with a time when he was seeking gradually to spread responsibility further among the fourth generation of Mead managers, and ever since he had gone to Canada in 1911, he had been using his absence as well as his presence to train his men. Moreover, he was less absent from the Company than his physical separation from Dayton suggested. He missed no board meetings, paid regular if infrequent visits to Chillicothe and other plants, kept up with reports, and saw a great deal of his colleagues. Many were on leave to the government: for example, H. E. Whitaker and D. F. Morris, heads-to-be of the fifth generation of managers, were dollar-a-year troubleshooters for the War Production Board, Whitaker serving also on the interallied Combined Production and Resources Board. And even more Mead men were making the hurried and harried trip to Washington, typical of the times, in an effort to straighten out wartime rulings so the mills could get on with their job.

Mead men visiting in Washington, however, and Mead men working in Washington had to maintain a dichotomy in their inter-relationships; neither group of men could discuss what the other was doing there. George Mead himself, who scrupulously avoided all possible conflicts of interest, had the additional task of presiding over the principal industry trade group, the American Paper and Pulp Association—a task he took on because the Association was moving more actively toward the type of cooperation he favored—without being able to discuss with his peers any of the current affairs about which he was fully informed and they were most anxious for information.

In World War II as in World War I, government regulatory bodies started off with the mistaken premise that paper was not essential. This time the decision resulted in part from a War Production Board ruling that none of its industry divisions could be headed by anyone from the industry concerned. A lumberman, as a matter of fact, decreed the non-essentiality of paper, and by the time the mistake was rectified almost half the war was over, and the entire industry was having trouble in securing enough maintenance equipment to keep its mills running full. Once the mills were thoroughly upset, it took months—in many cases more than a year—to get them back in order. Meanwhile, shortages in such areas as wood and steel were increasing calls upon containerboard of all sorts, and all sorts of new uses were being discovered overnight: from weatherproof containers to laminated bomb rings. So many were the uses and so many were the war materials dispatched in containers, that once non-essential paperboard had to be allocated before the end of the war. Mead actually had to make nine-point corrugated board out of waste paper pulp in its Chillicothe plant to meet pressing customer needs. At the same time, Chillicothe and the other white-paper plants had to deal with shortages in everything from chlorine to pulp, and, together with the rest of the industry, had to decrease both the brightness of printing papers and their basic weight.

Under these particular circumstances, combined with the general price and profit controls of wartime, the Mead Corporation stood still despite its furious production pace. Total assets in 1945 were only $2.1 million higher than their 1941 figure of $37 million, and net plant actually declined almost $3 million. Dollar sales increased slowly from $32.5 million to $40 million. but excess profit taxes siphoned off earnings to such an extent that the $2.1 million profit figure of 1941 was cut in half.

Postwar Plans Get Priority

The possibilities of present growth being eliminated, the Company's managerial energies were channeled into planning for the future, an activity into which George Mead could and did enter without impropriety. A formal postwar plan was approved by the board of directors as early as the summer of 1943 with a tentative budget of from $2.5 million to $5 million for improvements to existing mills alone, a sum that increased to nearly $7.5 million by the time the plan went into effect. Even before 1943, however, Mead moved to strengthen its postwar position. Plans were perfected for the linerboard mill to be built immediately after the war to fill the gap left by the loss of the St. Joe mill in the company's operations.

Two paper mills in Michigan that had formerly made newsprint and that had long been under Mead management were brought into the Company's structure—the Escanaba Paper Company and the nearby Manistique Pulp and Paper Company, in both of which the Mead Investment Company had maintained an interest after George Mead's withdrawal from his Canadian enterprises. Escanaba had already been transformed into a groundwood specialties mill whose principal product was hanging paper (trade name for wallpaper); it was secured for an exchange of 7,481 shares of Mead preferred stock and 68,000 shares of common. Manistique, a mill making the same type of paper but with only half the capacity, was purchased for $850,000 with the thought that it could be transformed into an efficient producer of coated paper. Before long changes in public taste forced changes in these plans. The market for hanging paper dwindled, that for coated paper swelled. Escanaba, with two 166-inch Fourdriniers and a capacity of 150 tons a day, was turned into a specialized coated paper mill, and Manistique was sold in 1951 to the owners of *The Trenton Times* at a significant profit.

Finally, in 1945, the Company elected to make the best of a confused situation in the independent LaBoiteaux Company, resulting from the death of the company's president, and took into a new subsidiary, Mead Board Sales, Inc., the functions of its former independent sales outlet for paperboard. The transaction gained Robert J. Blum, future vice-president of Mead itself, and three other experienced paperboard sales managers, together with a 40 per cent interest in a small paper-converting operation owned by the group, and not purchased in part so that the men might not suffer conflict of interest.

Stepping Out of Management

The principal step for the future, however, was the move that George Mead made early in 1942 in resigning as President of the Mead Corporation and in expressing his intention of concentrating for the future on policy and planning. George Mead spoke of this as involving nominal changes:

I say nominal changes because, as all of you know, Mr. Ferguson, Mr. Van de Carr and myself have operated as an executive committee for the last ten years, and as I have told you several times, no decision has been made in the corporation of any importance regarding any of its affairs without the unanimous agreement of this committee of three. I repeat that the reason for establishing this committee some ten years ago, was because I felt that any concern that depended upon any one man's judgment was not properly directed—three heads are better than one—and by establishing a rule of obtaining the unanimous agreement of three men we were safeguarding the stockholders and all people associated with us; therefore, all activities have been along very definite lines that we were unanimous in our opinion.

When I undertook the management of this company a good many years ago I was quite a young man . . . and I had observed, particularly in my own home town of Dayton, that companies which were directed by older men found themselves in difficulties, because men advanced in years become more set in their ways and are likely to become autocratic in their thinking. Particularly one company that I knew well in Dayton that was headed by a very fine man got into serious difficulties because this man felt he was wiser than his own directors, and in a number of decisions over-ruled them and insisted on policies that lead ultimately to great financial difficulty, and finally a rather disastrous conclusion for that organization. I gradually made up my mind that when I had the full responsi-

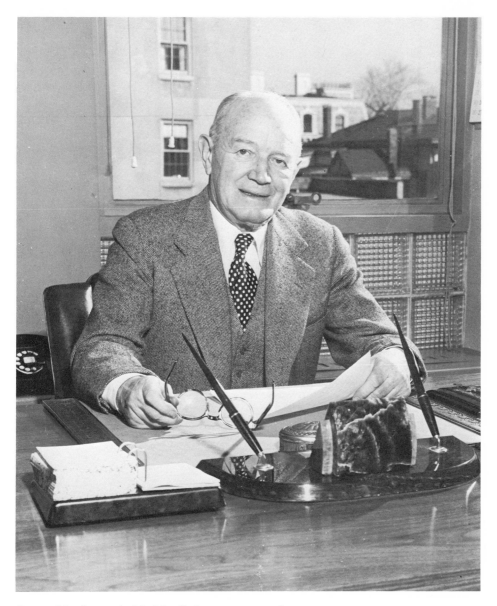

George Mead at work: Mr. Mead's dynamic personality "left lasting and graphic impressions upon his business and government colleagues, friends and family."

bility of this Corporation I would establish certain rules for retirement as time went on and see that they were lived up to.

When I became president 30 years ago I established these rules and told the Directors that under no circumstances did I want them to be broken in my behalf if I reached the ages stated in the general formula set up. I said that I probably would be just as stubborn and headstrong as any old codger I knew and therefore they would have to take me out and shoot me or kick me out if I did not behave properly. . . .

On November 5th of this year I will be 65 years old—I might have waited until the next Annual Meeting to make this change but . . . I decided yesterday that this was the proper date. The Board of Directors has requested me to continue as an active executive of the Company and I propose to do so as long as they desire; however the active direction is placed in the hands of Mr. Sydney Ferguson. In a company, as in an army, it is necessary in my judgment to have someone who is always available, who can make an immediate decision if it is necessary; if it is not necessary we have a committee meeting. . . .

We go on the theory that when a man makes a decision he does it with all the conscience that is possible, and with the best judgment that he knows, and if he is wrong we are all wrong with him—that goes right down through this Corporation, from top to bottom, for all the time I have had anything to do with the management of the Company. If it is not necessary to make a quick decision immediately, and if advice can be had from associates that is a pretty smart thing to do. . . .

We have an executive committee which has been enlarged from three of us to ten, and that executive committee meets monthly. The chairman of this committee is the Chairman of the Board, when present, otherwise Mr. Ferguson or Mr. Van de Carr will act in my absence. You can see I think from the details, and I have gone into great detail with you all, that there is very little change in our organization as it has been functioning for the last ten years, except for the direct management of the Company. I will only give advice and assistance to Mr. Van de Carr and Mr. Ferguson when they ask for it. I may make a suggestion now and then. The letter being sent out to the stockholders says that the general policy of the Company and its future development should remain in the hands of the Chairman of the Board—that gives me some leeway, also, because I have had a good deal of fun in the last 30 years in the development of this Company.

Thus was effected the transition to the fourth generation of Mead management.

CHAPTER 12

Senior Statesman

O NE DAY IN 1947, George Mead revealed many years later, he was sitting at his Dayton desk, perusing reports on the Company's postwar plan and devising the steps he would take to effect his retirement from the chairmanship in anticipation of his 70th birthday on November 5.

At this point, President Truman called by telephone, said immediately, "I want you to work on another committee."

"All right," said George Mead.

He knew already that the President was referring to the Commission on the Executive Branch of the Government, recently approved together with a plan to man it with a bi-partisan group of citizens and government officials, to be selected by the President himself, the President of the Senate, and the Speaker of the House. George Mead, the President said, was to be his Republican civilian appointee, James Forrestal his government appointee.

"I want you to know," he continued, "that Joe Martin has just appointed Mr. Hoover as his civilian nominee," and added that he thought the appointment was excellent and wished he had thought of it himself.

George Mead said he felt very strongly that if Hoover accepted, he should be made chairman of the Committee.

President Truman immediately approved and said that he would be present at the first meeting of the Committee and receive Mr. Hoover as chairman.

To George Mead, the point of this account of the birth of the Hoover Commission—and the reason why he related it—was the broad-mindedness of President Truman, not an indication of any personal stature he himself might have had. This, of course, he did have, and he was by now a senior statesman of the country as well as of his own industry.

The job on the Hoover Commission was a mammoth one, requiring the members to spend three days in Washington every other week with frequent meetings in between during a period of 12 months, with an additional six months of almost constant conferences in Washington. Mr. Hoover appointed a series of three-man committees, each of which was to study four branches of the government and draft reports for their reorganization. George Mead was assigned to the Bureau of the Budget and the Departments of the Post Office, Commerce, and War, for the last of which he found that he had the responsibility of writing the final report, one of his co-members having been taken to the hospital and the other called away by the exigencies of government.

From his work with this committee, he emerged in 1949 with an obviously thorough knowledge of organization systems and their applicability to the largest institution in the country. This knowledge was, just as obviously, kept alive if not increased by his work in subsequent government posts, which continued until the end of the Korean war. From 1948 to 1951, he was a member of the Public Advisory Board of the Economic Cooperation Administration (the Marshall Plan), from 1950 to 1951, a member of the Committee on Mobilization Policy of the National Security Resources Board, and the following year a member of the Advisory Board of the Mutual Security Agency as well as a member of a comparable board on Mobilization Policy of the Office of Defense Mobilization.

Style for Mead Management

Meanwhile, the Mead Corporation was growing larger and more complex—sales during the last year of George Mead's government service were almost twice what they had been the year after the war—but he at no time made any effort to apply to the Company any of the organizational procedures he had studied and observed in his Washington posts, unlike many business leaders who were persuaded that the organizational logic of government structures had wide applicability. "The Government is so massive," George Mead once said, "and its operation is so difficult that it is impossible to compare it with a private corporation." Preferring a style of getting work done to a system for getting it done, he was wary of formalisms, logical or otherwise. There was not even an organizational chart of the Mead Corporation until Ford T. Shepherd, a Washington friend hired at the end of World War II as assistant to the president, drew up a rough chart so that he personally could tell who was who.

Certainly it was difficult to compare the Government with George Mead's

The Hoover Commission was a monumental task.
Two who gave their time for this work were
Herbert Hoover and George Mead.

private organization as he organized it or, more precisely, as he let it organize itself. The only alteration in its basic functioning that took place during the postwar years was George Mead's own almost imperceptible withdrawal from direction of Company affairs. In 1947, he shifted as planned to the post of honorary chairman, Sydney Ferguson succeeding him as active chairman, and C. R. Van de Carr, Jr., taking the presidency. Yet the affairs of the Company were handled in almost the same way after that change as before it. The same men, including George Mead, still talked with the same men with similar results. The new honorary chairman still visited plants, gave talks to Chillicothe foremen and addressed in the same manner as before the new Manager's Meetings, devised to bring the now-scattered executives together more frequently. While still chairman, he had successfully removed himself from problems of current operations, even though he kept himself as fully informed as ever about them. Now, very slowly, he became less emphatic in discussions about current financing and future plans—not from any decrease of physical and mental vigor, which he still possessed in as formidable measure as ever, but from a wisdom that informed him that men learn to do things by doing them and not by being directed how to do them.

This wisdom would have been foolishness, of course, had he not assembled an unusual group of able executives with minds and views and characters of their own, together with an appreciation of the Mead way of business. Shortly before the newest of his right-hand men, Ford Shepherd, arrived in Dayton, George Mead extolled to him the excellence of the Mead group. Shepherd commented that there had to be a heel in any organization. But some years later, when George Mead asked him whether he had found a heel yet, he had to admit he hadn't.

In two areas of the Company, George Mead did see the need for prearrangement. One was the area of precise accounting, and he was pleased when experience in postwar planning led to the formal practice of projecting sales, costs and earnings into the future. (He himself had been doing this informally all along.) Moreover, he maintained his conviction that the Company needed lasting participation by the Mead family in its affairs, to the extent that when his two sons, H. Talbott Mead and Nelson Strobridge Mead, returned from service in World War II to go to work for the Company, he saw to it in 1946 that the older, H. T., was named a director although he was not yet out of his twenties, and that he began work as a white collar employee so that he might, if qualified, move quickly into an executive post.

In this action, there appears to have been no nepotistic desire to advance his own and to hand down authority from father to son, but rather a will to insure the active representation of the family interest. Nelson S. Mead, the younger son, was started off in a blue-collar job; both sons were allowed to find their own way and make their own progress; and they were handled differently from other employees only in being kept more sharply under the scrutiny of the man who was, whatever his title, still the head of the busi-

Celebrating George Mead's 50 anniversary with the company are:
back row (l. to r.) N. S. Talbott Jr., A. W. Jones, Murray Smith,
Al. H. Mahrt, Harold Talbott, Sidney Ferguson, Rufus Worrell,
Charles Deeds, Clarence Frances, Gates Lloyd;
front row (seated) H. T. Mead, Charles Van de Carr,
Governor James M. Cox, George Mead, Matt Smith, Edward T. Gardner, Speed Warren;
front row (on floor) Nelson Talbott and Nelson Mead.

ness. H. T. Mead revealed an aptitude for finance and eventually became, nine years after he was put on the board, a vice-president. Nelson, with marked talents in merchandising, rose to the head position in pulp sales before he was named a director in 1959.

The Fifth Generation

Meanwhile, in all his conversations with his colleagues, George Mead kept referring to the future in terms of new generation of managers. He was determined that he would, so far as he could, try to preserve his company's personality. He was persuaded that the personality of some corporations had been destroyed as they grew in size and were managed by people who did not see the lasting value of such an intangible. In talking with such members of the fourth-generation Mead management as Sydney Ferguson and Alan Goldsmith, he left no doubt that he wanted to be and would be active in evaluating members of the fifth generation and in choosing their leaders.

By the beginning of the fifties, there was urgency involved in this choice. In 1952, President Van de Carr reached the age for mandatory retirement from the presidency; his retirement was followed by those of J. O. Mason and J. H. Cunningham, now comptroller. In the late-fifties, Vice-President Alan G. Goldsmith and A. H. Mahrt retired; by the early-sixties, R. H. Savage, who had been in charge of research, and George Robinson, treasurer had left the company. And Sydney Ferguson, perhaps the most indispensable to George Mead of his associates, could not remain as chairman of the board after reaching retirement age in 1957. Already retired were Speed Warren—after 33 years of service—and Rufus I. Worrel and T. W. Fernald.

In 1952, upon C. R. Van de Carr's retirement to a consultant post, the Board of Directors named H. E. Whitaker and D. F. Morris president and first vice-president, respectively, but there was no question that these were the men whom George Mead had personally chosen to head the new fifth generation management. Both men had wide experience in technical and operations direction throughout the Company; Howard Whitaker had been Operations vice-president since 1946, and Donald Morris had additional experience in research and sales service. Both men had given themselves to government and community service. It is undoubtedly a fact, however, that they were chosen not because of the jobs they held, but rather for the manner in which they held them: in short, for the type of men they were. They

C. F. Kettering and George Mead at the opening of Mead
research labs in Chillicothe about 1948.
Also a Dayton resident, Kettering was one of
George Mead's closest friends.
An independent inventor and manufacturer (he was responsible for
such developments as the electric self-starter in automobiles
as well as quick-drying lacquer for auto bodies, the two-cycle diesel,
the storage battery and freon gas for refrigerators),
Kettering served as head of research for General Motors for 27 years and
was a director of the Mead Corporation for 32 years.

were clearly Mead men who had an instinctive grasp of the Mead way of business.

Named at the same time as new vice-presidents were George H. Pringle (white paper operations), Leonard R. Growdon (paperboard operations), and Ford T. Shepherd (public relations), while W. Walker Lewis, Jr., was appointed secretary, since age was forcing George Mead's long-time legal advisor Murray Smith into retirement. Of this group, Howard Whitaker himself had strongly urged the appointment of George Pringle, a mechanical engineer with brilliant technical achievements and a flair for personnel problems which had led him on his own initiative to develop full-scale training and recruiting programs after World War II, when Mead suddenly saw wisdom in hiring twice as many college graduates as the Company immediately needed. His subsequent success in directing white paper operations increased not only his stature but that of Howard Whitaker, responsible for his appointment, and George Mead made it known to his oldest colleagues that he was very much pleased.

Throughout his long business career, the extent and nature of George Mead's involvement with the company was determined by his conception of what his role should be, not by his response to external demands on his time. The period between 1911 and 1928 when he was most active in running the Company was also the time of his most time-consuming outside activity, the Canadian venture. His taking on a more active role during the depression did not result from his having more time available but from the critical impact of the depression itself. His unusual facility for holding in his mind at the same time many different considerations and for shifting his attention readily and easily from one to the other freed him to a considerable extent from the ordinary confinements of time. At any moment he could have intervened actively in matters in which he had chosen not to be active. He retired altogether from government activity in 1952, but there was no subsequent change whatsoever in his relationship to his Company: he simply kept up his slow extension of responsibility to others by progressively assuming less responsibility himself.

Had he wished, he could probably have run the Company by single-handed dictation until the day illness disabled him. In such case, of course, the Company would probably have become his tombstone rather than his lasting monument, and it is hardly to be wondered that he wished to avoid the sort of dictation that would lead to such a consequence. The remarkable fact is that he really carried out his wish, and moreover carried it out in such a way as to make his withdrawal from active direction almost unnoticeable.

During the ten years following the war, there were other outside interests. For instance he helped form, along with his oldest daughter, Louise, the Dayton Council on World Affairs and served as its first chairman. George Mead's principal task with the Council was to serve as its "Father Confessor." He knew how to organize, and the Council members recognized and respected this. If he were detained, they would wait the meeting for him—an example of the high esteem in which he was held. He often secured the service of an international figure, such as James Byrnes, to speak at Council meetings. He became a member of the National Citizens Committee for Public Schools; he conferred frequently with other papermakers about industry problems; and he gave counsel to whoever sought it: Washington friends, young people, his own associates, his customers.

(Old customer Time, Inc. turned to him and Sydney Ferguson for advice when that company began buying up newsprint plants all over North America immediately after World War II to ensure supplies for its big postwar circulation growth.) But these were the sort of things he had been doing all his life. The privacy with which he had pursued his work in Washington proved to be a help to him: he was well known to the few, known not at all to the many; and his correspondence never became unduly burdensome.

Cooperative Effort

As World War II drew to a close, the scope of the Mead postwar plan increased: in 1946 it was estimated that $23 million would be spent by 1949 in improvements and expansion of existing plant alone. In addition, there were separate plans in the Company's brown paper area for the new kraft linerboard plant to fill the hole created by the separation from the St. Joe operation, and for the conversion of the chestnut-chip corrugated mills to the processing by semi-chemical means of other woods, a change involving heavy research effort and substantial capital investment. In the white paper area, aside from the purchase and subsequent disposal of two plants needed to help meet heavy postwar demand,* major plans were

*The Buena Vista, Virginia, and Bristol, Virginia, plants of the Columbian Paper Company, purchased in January, 1946, for 26,000 shares of common stock and 7,000 shares of preferred, were disposed of in 1950 and 1954.

centered around sales, warehousing, and research to take care of ever increasing production.

Blueprints for the new linerboard mill were prepared long before the war ended, and the order for the paper machine itself was placed long before it was needed to avoid the delays that were likely to be present—and indeed were present—after the war. George Mead determined again upon a cooperative venture, and several container manufacturers were anxious to participate, among them the Inland Container Corporation, headed by H. C. Krannert, long Mead's biggest customer for nine-point corrugated board. Mead began negotiating with Inland, this time on the basis of holding 60 per cent instead of 50 per cent of the stock, perhaps as a consequence of the St. Joe experience. A tidewater location was rejected—so many seaboard mills had been built that available timberland had been greatly reduced—and decision was made for the inland location of Macon, Georgia. Accordingly, the Macon Kraft Company was incorporated early in 1946, and construction began on a 650 ton-per-day mill whose cost was to be $17,500,000—an example of the consequences of inflation since the days St. Joe had been built. The mill almost got into production in April of 1948, after the construction delays that were inevitable during the immediate postwar period, but an evaporator boiler—delivered defective from its manufacturer—blew up and spewed pollution into the air above Macon and into the water of the Ocmulgee River. Every precaution had been taken and all known anti-pollution devices had been installed: George Mead had been an early pioneer in the design of recovery systems, and the Company had long engaged in special anti-pollution research. For weeks, however, the plant was subjected to investigation and litigation, in the middle of which another explosion took place, this time in the stack, and the mill was down six weeks while it was being rebuilt.

By July 1, the mill was in production under the management of Herbert Kidd, who had been Mead's manager at St. Joe, and it immediately began to turn out paper and profit in substantial quantities. One day in 1950, when running on heavy grade linerboard, it set a record of 835 tons, more than any one paper machine had ever produced. Its success, together with the increase of the Company's brown paper business, prompted Mead and Inland to agree on another mill in Rome, Georgia, 170 miles from Macon. Decision for this mill was made in 1951; although its scheduled capacity was 10 per cent lower than Macon's, its cost, by process of inflation, reached

The principals in the Rome Kraft Company meet to inspect
construction of the mill in Rome, Georgia in 1952.
They are (seated l. to r.) George Mead, Al. H. Mahrt and H. C. Krannert.
Standing are Herbert A. Kidd and C. L. Ohl.

$29 million. By the end of 1954, however, it was already producing an average of 435 tons of linerboard a day.

The relationship between George Mead and Herman Krannert of Inland Container was typically a case of mutual respect. After initial negotiations, both agreed on a 50-50 ownership of the Georgia kraft operations and a continuation of the Mead-fostered policy of unanimous board decisions. Mr.

Krannert explains, "We just kept discussing things until a single decision had complete support." (The Rome decision provoked the only known instance in the history of the Mead Board of Directors of an absence of that unanimity which George Mead insisted was essential to any decision. E. T. Gardner, close friend since childhood, owner of a paper converting plant of his own, and a Mead director since 1930, found himself opposed to the Rome venture, finally decided not to stand in its way out of deference to George Mead.)

No entire new white paper plants were built during the postwar period, but construction in the mills at Chillicothe, Kingsport, Escanaba and Leominster added up to considerably more productive capacity than a new plant could have provided. The diversification program attempted in the twenties and launched during the thirties was now in full swing, and Mead's products were so varied that the Company had adopted the slogan "Papermakers to America." Now in the fifties, the Company had cemented so well its relationships to jobbers and merchants that it dropped the Dill & Collins and Wheelwright trade names and sold all paper under the name of Mead itself.

The formula for the success of this operation involved George Mead's familiar factors of high-quality production and long paper machine runs. Quality sold the paper; long runs made the production of various grades economical. It was a new instance of running the machines full, even if the paper so produced could not be sold immediately, and of storing it wherever space was available until it found purchasers. This procedure now required more storage space, and the Company invested $2,200,000 in warehouses in the early 1950's and turned the Dill & Collins mill in Philadelphia, which was becoming too expensive to operate, into a vast paper depot.

The new multiplicity of products underlined the need for more and more research, both in new processes to make paper more economically, and in new products to strengthen Mead diversification. In 1947, Russel H. Savage became Research vice-president and under his direction was developed a New Products Division in the same year. It was designed to see new ideas through pilot-plant production. In 1948 a corporate technical research staff was formed to take laboratory discoveries into the mills themselves (one such discovery increased the capacity of Kingsport's digesters by about one-third). In the following years, an increasing population of resident scientists was hired. In the early 1950's Director Harold E. Talbott pro-

George and Elsie Mead (second and third from left)
meet with traveling companions T. J. Hilliard,
Alfred W. Jones and Katharine T. Jones (Katharine Jones was Elsie Mead's sister;
T. J. Hilliard and Alfred Jones, brothers-in-law).

posed an idea that was already in George Mead's mind: a new $3 million research building with the finest specialized equipment, including small experimental versions of all types of papermaking equipment, and when it was opened in 1953, it had a staff of 40 graduate chemists, physicists and engineers.

When the abilities of the new top team of Howard Whitaker and Donald Morris became available, the operations and the structure of the Mead Corporation had as last achieved the balance that George Mead was seeking in the days before the war, and had achieved it on a scale that would have seemed impossible during the depression-ridden thirties. The scale of the Mead operation is suggested in the table of year-end figures in the appendices.

Important Decisions Are Reached

So far, the growth of the Company had proceeded almost precisely along the lines that George Mead had been planning, and that he had been hoping his colleagues would carry out successfully. Indeed the realization of his hope was greater than the hope itself. In the 1950's however, three nettlesome issues arose that were to lead the Company in directions he had not planned.

The first of these was a comparatively minor issue and one resolved readily by George Mead himself. It concerned the Company's sales organization, the Mead Sales Company, owned in large part by the salesmen who composed it, and kept legally and organizationally separate to help stimulate esprit. In 1951 a strike or stockholder's derivative suit was brought against the Company charging that the arrangements between the sales company and the Mead Corporation were improper. The suit was defended with entire success, and in 1955 the courts found unreservedly for Mead. But George Mead could not bear the existence of anything that had even the appearance of impropriety and, albeit unwillingly, decided that the Company should take up its long standing option to purchase the sales company. Thus was created Mead Papers, Inc., kept distinct so far as possible, yet an integral part of the Company, and Mead Pulp Sales, an equally distinct and equally integrated entity formed to handle the Company's increasing sales of pulp.

Issue two concerned a new approach to financing the Company's growth, and here George Mead, although he indicated initial lack of enthusiasm, declined for the first time to enter into a decision that involved long-term

George Mead: "Affection was welcome; awe was not."

planning. Financial experts among the new generation of management proposed that growth thereafter should be effected almost entirely by ex-
changes of stock and, to that end, special efforts should be made to acquaint
investors and brokerages with the Mead Corporation and with its securities
so that the price of its stock would rise and more capital would become
available for expansion. To George Mead, providing full information was a
basic responsibility of any business, but publicizing one's own stock to the
financial community had aspects of bad taste and was almost comparable to
publicizing one's own self. More important, the proposal ran counter to his
own low-pressure type of merchandising, whose precepts he had followed
throughout his life, and whose merits he had sought to instill in the Company. Finally, he was persuaded that stock prices behave as they behave,
not as people want them to, and that the financial community would sooner
or later spot successful companies without any assistance. Yet, having these
objections, and having the much deeper concern that the Company hold to
its established style of business, he declined to enter into the decision-
making process, possibly considering—here only conjecture is possible—that
it was a greater evil for him to stand in the way of younger men whose
independence he was encouraging than it was to suffer a comparatively
slight change in the Company's personality. There was publicity, and Mead
stock did rise, as did numerous other securities in the then-rising market.
Whether it rose because of the publicity is not known: stock prices it is
known, after all, behave only as they behave.

The third issue was a very large one, and it involved the direction in
which the Company should expand in the future. During the early thirties,
paperboard manufacturers began weighing the merits of acquiring companies that converted their products into cartons, containers and packag-
ings of various sorts, and several alert young Mead executives proposed that
Mead enter the container business by buying up established manufacturers
and so anticipate the moves of competing paperboard manufacturers. This
proposal was received with attention but without initial enthusiasm by the
now-established fifth generation managers, and it was discussed and
debated over a period of two years.

Here George Mead displayed his talents for seeing both sides of a question, advancing arguments now for one side, now for the other. In this case,
however, he did not define his own position, nor did Chairman Sydney
Ferguson, so that surmise alone, based on George Mead's past actions and
convictions, can give a clue to this thinking.

Decision to go into the box business could mean, of course, competition with some old customers and the absorption of others. To move into a new area of enterprise for no purpose other than expansion probably held little appeal to George Mead. Expansionist though he was in temperament, he had always liked to move into areas opened by a breakthrough in research or technology, as for instance the chestnut chip paperboard area, or into other areas where the balance of Company operations could be improved, as for instance merchant paper and pulp. His great dream still was to rationalize papermaking to the degree that the machines ran full day after day, each on its own grade of paper. He remarked in 1954, "Of course the war interfered with a lot of things that might have developed in the last 20 years. Whether it was worthwhile is for someone else to determine in the future. I won't be here long enough to find these things out." It may be assumed, however, that George Mead would have preferred to see his new generation of managers working out facets of his big idea rather than to see them going into an already established field. New products, new processes, new systems of organization—these were to him basic challenges for growth. Finally, entrance into the container business would mean entrance into the Mead Corporation of many executives who had not been exposed to the Mead way of doing business, and who might as a consequence alter that great intangible—the Company's personality.

Here it is to be remembered that George Mead was not in any sense a conservative businessman yearning for bygone days. He was a distinct unconventionalist in business, and he was hoping for a humane and purposeful future—one that did not follow the book—for the Company he had created. His mind and his memory were as keen as ever, as his court testimony in 1954 gave witness. The proposal to move into the container business had about it much of the book as it was currently being followed by U. S. business in general.

While the Company talked, however, the competition was actually moving into the container field so strongly that a danger arose that the Company would lose much of its market for brown paper as well. Decision had to be made, and it was decided to enter the container field. President Howard Whitaker reported the conclusion of the matter: "All the facts were collected, analyzed and discussed at length. Mr. Mead examined the data, asked probing questions, argued the merits of both sides of the question. I am not certain today which decision he preferred absolutely. The fact is that he forced us to make the decision ourselves."

CHAPTER 13

Corporation Dynamics

DECISION REACHED to go into the box business, George Mead was not discomfited by it; nor was he upset by the earlier decision to publicize Mead stock. Fully aware as he was of the deep impact that these steps could have on the Company, he was even more urgently aware that the new fifth generation of Mead leaders must take the steps themselves. As soon as they did, he gave enthusiastic approval and support. He was gratified, first of all, by the way the steps had been taken. Mead's entry in a new field proceeded in no accidental manner. It had been prepared by thorough and exceptionally detailed study of all conceivably pertinent facts and statistics. The Company moved into the new field in a way that suggested no interest either in parading on it or dumping spare production on it, but an interest rather in tending and cultivating it with as much care and thoroughness as the established areas of the business. Moreover, it was entirely clear to George Mead that the Company had made its move from business necessity—Mead was actually the last kraft manufacturer to start buying box companies—and not from any delusions about size or growth for their own sakes. He was now reassured that the Company was not going to suffer any marked alteration in its personality, and his confidence in his new fifth generation team of Whitaker, Morris and Pringle was, to his mind, reconfirmed.

His personal problem was to keep himself on the sidelines. George Mead was a man of extremely vigorous and decisive temperament. The restraint which he had been placing progressively upon his own decisiveness resulted from no passivity of temperament, but from a conscious recognition that the long-term health of the Company would benefit from a corresponding activity of temperament on the part of the new management group.

On one occasion—indeed, in the very middle of the argument about the box business—he even let his own temperament outrun his conscious caution and once more made one of his lightning decisions. At that time, the argument focused on whether or not Mead should buy the Jackson Box Company, a substantial organization with several plants controlled by a prominent Cincinnati family, which for reasons of age and taxes wanted to sell. While Mead debated its decision, the West Virginia Pulp and Paper Company made an offer to the family, and Jackson President William J. Cassady, Jr., immediately informed Mead executives Al. H. Mahrt and Robert J. Blum, who in turn promptly took him to George Mead's office. Cassady, a talented executive and an excellent organizer, by this time was well known to George Mead, and it is not unlikely that his personal abilities as well as his company's assets influenced the following brief transaction:

"Can you buy a controlling interest?" George Mead asked the Mead men in his office.

"Yes."

"Very well. Buy a minority interest as an insurance policy." This was done immediately and for a full year before Mead finally decided to buy the Jackson Box Company in 1955, Mead owned 49 per cent of it.

As his age increased—in 1955, he was 77—and the years remaining to him decreased, George Mead's interest in the Company grew even more intense. He kept himself as meticulously informed as ever about all of its activities, even those with which he refused to have anything at all to do, and only a belief in extreme self-control kept him from interfering in matters where he was convinced he should not. When he was asked to be present at various inspections and negotiations concerning box company properties, he avoided altogether the role of negotiator and acted as if he was a part of the stage scenery. As such scenery, he was of course enormously effective, not only because he was on view as the industry's senior statesman, but also because his interest in people was as active as ever. This interest he saw no reason to alter. He genuinely wanted to know everything about the prospective seller; he was keenly aware of the emotions involved in selling one's own business (he himself hated to part with anything he had worked to build up and was actually downcast when the Manistique mill had to be sold) and readily put himself in the seller's place. Not only during negotiations but after them, he was looked upon with affectionate awe by the men who were selling out to his Company.

Affection was welcome; awe was not. It was even widespread among the younger men in his own Company, and it represented an additional tax on his self-control. When he came into a room, everyone promptly stood up, and he would say, with slightly more emphasis than was his wont, "Sit down, gentlemen, sit down!" To a man who was seeking to defer to younger men and to give them their heads, such deference was frustrating.

New Managers Continue Expansion

He therefore held back his views, not himself, for he conceived his interest in the new generation of men in the Company to be beneficial—and only in the case of the return to the Mead Corporation in 1955 of the Chillicothe Paper Company, founded with his help three decades before and now a going concern with sales of $3 million a year, did he play a role of prominence. For the rest, he kept practically all of his views on new projects and acquisitions to himself, leaving negotiations entirely to the direction of Howard Whitaker and Donald Morris, together with Al. H. Mahrt, a still-active member of the fourth generation, and to James McSwiney, H. T. Mead and William Cassady, who in 1957 became a Mead vice-president. Chairman Sydney Ferguson, whose mind worked in a manner at once comparable and complementary to that of his friend now of so many years standing, joined George Mead on the sidelines to exchange remarks and give encouragement while the younger men got on with the game.

As time progressed, the following facts became evident:

In the new men that were coming into the organization as a consequence of the acquisitions, Mead was gaining talent rather than suffering a dilution of its personality. There was, for instance, new Vice-President William Cassady. There was Robert J. Blum, a skilled and imaginative merchandiser already head of Mead Board Sales; in 1958, the Excello Company, which he and his associates had owned, became an integral part of Mead, and he himself became even more active than before as a Company vice-president particularly in the development of new container products. There was also Arthur J. Harris, a dynamic and experienced executive, who came into the organization in 1958 at the time of the acquisition of his Atlanta Paper Company, which served as the base for Mead's substantial entry into the field of packaging (folding cartons largely for consumer uses as contrasted to corrugated boxes for industrial shipping).

The new box and packaging activities were being handled as integral parts of the Mead operation and not as sidelines. From the beginning, quality was made a first principle. Financial controls, operating standards and merchandising systems were given as thorough attention as they had always been given in the established areas of paper and pulp. New research and development programs were created, and with the opening of a New Products Division in 1960, provision was made for the systematic application of new ideas, of which there were literally thousands, to the entire container and packaging fields.

The Mead impetus to growth in its long established white paper operations was in no way arrested by the expansion into boxes and packaging. Research, development, improvement and expansion programs were pressed as vigorously as ever. An entire foreign operation was set up. Moreover, with the purchase in 1957 of the Hurlbut Paper Company of South Lee, Massachusetts, and in 1958 of the Wrenn Paper Company of Middletown, Ohio, the Company moved strongly into the field of technical and industrial papers, including such advanced items as flameproof and reinforced papers, ceramic fiber papers and glass filter papers.

It became the obvious, although not announced, goal of the Company to concern itself both in basic research and in future expansion with any product that could be made of fibers—cellulose or others or even of such things as foams—if the product could issue from papermaking technology, or if it could be used for printing, writing or packaging. In sum, the Company had established guidelines for the future that would stimulate its growth along the lines in which it was experienced and expert and not in directions foreign to it, and certainly not in the direction of any amorphous and conglomerate series of unrelated operations.

Involved in the expansion which George Mead studied from the sidelines between 1955 and 1963 were the companies shown in the appendices. The year-end results of the intensive activity of acquiring them, together with the results of equally intense activity in other parts of the Company are shown on tables also in the appendices. The Company, which from its beginnings had been doubling the scale of its activities roughly every six years, except during World War II and the first years of the depression, now almost tripled its scale over a comparable period of time. When in 1957, the Crowell company ceased publication of the magazines that had once taken Mead's entire production of paper, the tonnage loss was only 11 per cent of white paper production alone, and it was made up in less than two years. At the end of 1962, the Mead Corporation was fifth in size among all paper companies—121st among all the industrial companies in the country—and at the time George Mead still liked to think that it was still not the *biggest* but the *best* in the business.

Although he kept himself on the sidelines, probably no one in the industry and certainly no one in the Mead management imagined that the Company's recent spurt of growth was attributable to any cause other than George Mead. Over many years he had established the dynamics of his Corporation through experiment with its own workings and—even more daringly—through experiment with the workings of the U. S. economy. As a rule, long-term decisions of large corporations do not show up in year-end figures until ten or twenty years later. Mead's year-end figures of 1962, with sales rapidly approaching a half billion dollars, were directly traceable to decisions made as early as the depression and the mid-twenties. Indirectly they were traceable to everything that had occurred since the day George Mead took over the small family company and an ancient boiler burst the first night.

A Means to an End

The tremendous expansion of the Corporation during the period between 1955 and 1962—in size, in product diversity and in geographical dispersement—brought with it a need for a degree of formality and rationalization in its system of organization that had previously been foreign to it. Required now were definitions of authority and responsibility, together with designations of channels of communication, systems, procedures and, of course, a constantly changing organization chart. Even the services of management consultants were required; and George Mead, with his profound distrust of the book, was not inclined to be cordial to those who made their business writing it. He believed that their experience lay in what was common among well-run companies, not in what was unique, and above all he wanted the Mead Corporation to be a unique institution. But he recognized fully that organization, whether systematic or voluntaristic, was the only means whereby a large institution endures. His deepest interest in his older years, together with his most constant attention, was centered on this topic, all aspects of which he discussed with Sydney Ferguson, Howard Whitaker and Donald Morris. He was ready to evaluate openmindedly the procedures of companies quite foreign in their style of business to that of his own, but here again he kept his own conclusions to himself and, while entering freely into discussion, abstained entirely from decisions.

It would have been easy enough for him to make them himself. He was, after all, the man who Herbert Hoover had selected to deal with the organi-

In the wood yard at the Rome Kraft mill:
(l. to r.) Clarence Frances, Charles Cheston and George Mead.

zational problems of such critical and vast entities as the Bureau of the
Budget, and the Departments of the Post Office, Commerce and the Army.
Moreover, he had worked out in his own Company his unique principles of
flexible and voluntaristic organization which, had he chosen, he could have
codified into a guide for the Company's future. He did not choose to do so.
He did not choose to write down or even to talk out the principles that had
guided him; he chose to act upon them, even if acting upon them meant
inaction on something so close to him as the organizational structure of his
Company.

One thing he reserved to himself: a deep and unceasing personal interest in all his colleagues and particularly in those of the sixth generation. He wanted to know the strengths, abilities, the personalities of the men who composed it. He could control his urges to make decisions. He could not have controlled, even had he wanted to, the sustaining force of his life, interest in other persons. He did not expect to be alive when the sixth generation assumed office, but he was certainly going to get to know its men as well as he could in the time left to him.

Realizing that there was not much time left, he began removing himself from the board committees of which he was still a member. In 1956, when he felt H. T. Mead was capable of representing the family financial interest, he resigned from the finance committee; in the same year he gave up his chairmanship of the executive committee, four years later giving up his membership on it and retaining of all his innumerable functions only the title of Honorary Chairman of the Board. Actually, these steps were important only because they made evident his will to give way to his younger men. In 1957, the time for his retirement was at hand, and George Mead found it easier to imagine the Company without himself than without the man who had come to him so long ago as his auditor and assistant, and who had become his intimate friend, his close associate and his confidant. He wanted him to remain to watch the shop, and Sydney Ferguson himself had to refuse, although he agreed to remain for a time as director. In 1957, therefore, the move from fourth to fifth generation management was complete: Howard Whitaker became Chairman of the Board, Donald Morris president, and George Pringle executive vice-president. The duties of expanding the Company and of providing it with an organizational structure now devolved entirely upon them, with primary responsibility going to Whitaker for long-term planning and to Morris for current operations.

The organization structure built by these men and the colleagues of their generation and the next was remarkable not so much for the way that it looked on paper as for the style in which it functioned. It provided for a divisional separation whereby different areas of the business were organized as separate profit centers, but it had such distinct and added merits as formally bringing together men who had been working together informally. In describing the plan in its 1961 form, Howard Whitaker concluded with the observation that "the organization plan itself is, of course, merely a means to an end. Charts and position descriptions alone cannot manage the business and we should take care not to place too much emphasis on the

George Mead inspires another generation of Meads
—his grandchildren.

plan rather than on getting the job done. Strong individuals working together as a team are the key elements in all organization effectiveness. The
plan of organization described here does not indicate required lines of contact or communication. Common sense and good judgment should determine the channels of contact conducive to the most expeditious handling
of the work."

Later he alluded more informally to the thinking behind the plan:

We now have 42 plants in the United States and we have extended our operations in five separate ventures overseas. We are particularly concerned with keeping in touch with the world markets. Our sales offices and warehouses are considerably more numerous than our plants, and our 1,000-odd list of products
receives regular additions from research and development. . . . One particular task
of my generation of Mead management, therefore, has been to build a system of
organization that will not hinder the voluntary and personal aspects of the individuals which have made Mead an effective and humane enterprise. This task
has proved less difficult than it might have been, basically because we began

with Mr. Mead's principles and policies and built an organization structure around these. Had we proceeded otherwise, starting with an organization system that looked ideal on paper and applying it rigidly to our Company, we could have destroyed the great intangible asset of our Company: its humanity.

Time Runs Out

During this time, when George Mead was in his seventies, he maintained a vigorous personal schedule. He had always enjoyed the outdoor life and did so now. Canoe trips on Canadian vacations, long walks and a program of exercises kept his body in tune with his spirited business life. However, in spite of all this, time began to press upon George Mead. In November of 1958, he suffered the first of a series of strokes, each one of which was so severe that it was believed impossible for him to survive. That twice he did survive, and survived not to invalidism but to a return to active work despite limited use of the right side of his body, is an indication both of his extraordinary vitality and extraordinary self-control. He showed astonishingly few indications of the symptoms that universally follow crippling cerebral accidents in the form of querulousness and depression, and that often prostrate men as active and vigorous as George Mead. George Mead had himself so remarkably under control that he seldom gave any indication of any sense of depression he felt—and then not about matters close at hand like his family or his business, but about some manner depressing in its own nature, such as current international politics. He regained poise, punctiliousness in person, agility in mind, and, notably, warmth of personality to such a marked degree that it was impossible to entertain the idea while talking to him that he was indeed sick, actually mortally sick. The very few lapses from his normal courteousness of speech and his more recent withdrawal from decision making were so minor as to be entertaining; they seemed to his associates to indicate his vitality, and stories about them were circulated affectionately around the Company.

And in no way but one did he alter his new relationship to the Company. As always he read reports thoroughly, asked questions, sought details about anything and anybody, and remembered events both past and present with a precision remarkable not only for a man of more than 80 years but also for a man of any years, let alone one incapacitated by a stroke. He discussed the organization of the Company with precisely the same degrees of interest and detachment with which he had been discussing them before his illness. The only change in his activity was increased discussion with his

A family reunion at Little Woods in 1961:
(standing l. to r.) Nelson S. Mead, John M. Walker Jr., John M. Walker Sr.,
Daniel E. Mead, George H. Mead III, H. T. Mead Sr., H. T. Mead Jr., Whittaker Mead;
(seated l. to r.) Nelson Mead Jr., Ruth C. Mead (in front),
Ruth C. Mead, Louise M. Walker, Randolf Walker, Katherine T. Mead,
George H. Mead, Elsie Mead, Mimi Mead, Dudley H. Mead,
Mary W. Mead, Marianna M. O'Brien;
(in front) Elsie O'Brien, Dorothy O'Brien, Louise O'Brien.
Missing from the picture are Frank O'Brien, Jr.,
George M. Walker and Elsie M. Walker.

younger executives. He knew clearly now that he had very little time. He did not want to instruct his young men, inform them, or exhort them. He gave them no lectures about the history of the Company, no disquisitions about its future. He simply wanted to talk freely and openly with them. He wanted to know the coming sixth generation as well as he had known the fifth and the fourth.

After he was struck by another and equally severe stroke, he drew once again on his vitality, and before long he had rehabilitated himself so well that he picked up his conversations where he had left them. Inherent in his will to live was his deepest conviction that the meaning of life and the purpose of men, both in their inward lives and in their work in the outside world, lie in the profound relationships of one human person to another. This was the witness of his life; it was his testimony to his Company and, more broadly, to his industry and to the country he had sought to serve.

He was seized by yet another stroke, and died in the early hours of the new year 1963.

The Humane Corporation

THE CREATION of George Mead was the Mead style of doing business, and the success of that creation rests where he left it, upon the Company itself or, more precisely, upon the capacity of other companies and other institutions to develop humane and voluntaristic styles of their own.

For persons who follow the book—that is, for conventionalists—the applicability of humane and voluntary principles to the affairs of a sizeable corporation is likely to seem dubious. George Mead, for all the neatness of his dress and the courteousness of his speech, was strongly unconventional in his subordination of material values to human values, and persons who dislike such subordination are likely to shrug off his life's work or to try to explain it away. It is common enough to make speeches about human values in business, but it is uncommon to try to build a corporation about these values and then to make no speeches. It can be argued that George Mead, after making a marked personal success financially, simply lost interest in the ordinary affairs of life and devoted himself to an ideal of public service and an idealistic view of business. This argument, however, is negated by the entire course of his career. It can also be argued that he worked out for a small company a style of business that was simply overwhelmed by the size to which it eventually grew. The full and experimental proof or disproof of this argument rests with the future of the Company and with the future of U. S. business as well. But it should be noted that George Mead staked the whole of his life on the proposition that persons were persons in small institutions or large, and that, if left to their own devices, they were capable of developing an organization that embodied their values. This capability was not a matter of theory to him; it was a matter of experience.

It is perhaps regrettable that he did not choose to theorize, that he did not express his experience in terms of logical concepts and formal statements, that he did not, so to speak, write a rule book of his own. But this was his talent. Not only did he hold his deepest convictions entirely to himself, but also, when he sought to record abstractions of lesser import, he did not possess facility in discussing them. He attempted to deal with important generalities in the prefaces to Mead annual reports about the state of the world or of the economy—subjects on which he was widely and intimately informed—but they had none of the life or force they had when he spoke informally of his experience of them. Moreover, his modesty was so genuine and so pervasive that he said little about the experiences that touched him most. He chose to act rather than talk about acting. Indeed, he could hardly do otherwise. A permissive way of running a business ceases to be permissive as soon as it is formally described as such, just as the permissive upbringing of children becomes calculated direction when they are lectured on how permissively they are being brought up. George Mead sought for the only type of growth possible as regards profound inward values—a growth that is natural, organic, voluntary. Talking about such growth impedes it. He was an example not a text book.

Hence arose the difficulty of some persons, even some who knew him well, in understanding fully what he was about. For example, some persons felt that he was not delegating authority because he was not delegating it formally, thus overlooking the fact that formal delegation is much the same thing as formal dictation. Others felt that he delegated authority in some spheres of his business life much more than in others, thus overlooking the fact that with him delegation increased progressively as his Company grew larger and that its degree depended not on where he was but on what the time was in the Company's expanding history. The true George Mead is discernible only if his life is seen whole and not as a series of parts.

Seen thus, his life illustrates a series of convictions about the nature of economic activity, both as regards its tactics and as regards its motivation. In the area of tactics, George Mead made for himself a variety of pioneer discoveries that are now generally accepted and somewhat widely applied:

That attention to the equation of production, price, profit and pay creates opportunities for dynamic growth.

That this dynamic relationship works no less in bad times than in good, and that the best time to expand is when times are bad.

That employees are productive when they are treated like human beings.

That large organizations can be handled more easily if they are broken down into small units.

That group meetings are most successful if it is pre-agreed that they must work toward unanimous conclusions.

George Mead: He accomplished so very much in quiet ways.
(Grandson is George Mead Walker.)

That products sell because they are worth buying, not simply because they are worth selling.

That the well being of a company depends more on the general health of the country than on any health measures of its own, and that its social responsibility takes precedence over its economic responsibility.

These tactical propositions have by now become part of the language of business if not always part of the practice of it. The still unconventional aspect of George Mead's convictions have to do with business motivations. These can be summed up in a statement whose reality is considerably more complex than its expression:

The values in business life as in the rest of life are person-to-person relationships; institutions are to be adapted to persons, not persons to institutions.

This conclusion, obviously, is not one to be spread by exhortation. Rarely do people listen to edifying remarks in the evening and wake up in the morning with a resolve to act like a human being; rarely is dissension within a corporation removed by ordering its executives to be humane. Humane convictions spread largely by osmosis. The one concrete step that George Mead took in his own Company was to hire men who seemed capable of being humane if they were left free to be so.

Hence the looseness of the Mead organizational structure, kept as informal and as flexible as possible so that persons could have the chance to be persons within it. The degree of informality and flexibility varied, to be sure, according to the situation and the size of the Company at any given time, but the important fact was not the precise degree of freedom but the general atmosphere of it, an intangible, to be sure, but one independent of size or situation. George Mead was not alone in seeking motivation for business activity in this sort of atmosphere, now increasingly prevalent in a number of other large corporations. He was unique in the whole-heartedness with which he made it a part of everyday life.

Business motivation of this order is entirely different from that postulated by the classical economic theorists of the 17th and 18th centuries, but just as different are the tactics of modern business from the small commercial transactions of those times. The characteristics of personal competitiveness and aggrandizement that seemed to be economic virtues long ago when it could be said that "man's self-interest is God's providence," are hardly applicable to the complexities of life that have been multiplying relentlessly ever since the industrial revolution.

George Mead's answer to these complexities is that cooperation is more vital to business life than aggrandizement, whether a man tries to make himself greater by seeking position or chasing wealth, that there remains one unchanging verity in times even of the greatest confusion of spirit, the relationship of one human being with another. The alternative to this truth is that there is no truth, that a man's self is by itself and not in relationship to any other self, that there is no purpose in life and no satisfaction other than the narcissistic adoration of self by self.

George Mead was an original and no man's copy. His impact on business even today remains distinct. Speaking shortly after George Mead's death in 1963, Board Chairman Howard E. Whitaker said:

> To his Company and to associates his strength was, and still is, a rock amidst the swirling scenes of social, economic and political events, and yet he never possessed rock-like immobility . . . I am convinced that it never occurred to Mr. Mead to doubt that person-to-person relationships constitute the chief purpose of life on this earth. Mr. Mead and the Company witnessed devastating and demoralizing wars and depressions. Both in their respective ways suffered public and private alarms and discouragements. In a world that appears to be only too often out of joint, the reality of personal relationships is perhaps the one fact that cannot be shaken, the one fact that can confidently be clasped, the one fact that remains pertinent in private, business and public life. . . .
>
> It is this asset, created for us by Mr. Mead, that we wish at all costs to preserve and perpetuate. It has given meaning to ourselves, to our families, to our communities, to our work. It has required hard labor; it has posed many difficult decisions. But it has created an atmosphere of warmth and humaneness, free—in the words of Mr. Mead—of jealousies and conceits. It has buoyed us up. It has given direction and purpose to our lives.

George Mead found purpose in his life. He gave purpose to the lives of others.

APPENDICES

APPENDIX I
CHRONOLOGY

APPENDIX II
HISTORICAL STATISTICS

APPENDIX III
1905 REPORT

APPENDIX IV
REMARKS AND SPEECHES

Chronology

GEO. H. MEAD	THE MEAD CORPORATION

THE MEAD CORPORATION

1846. Ellis, Chaflin & Company, the first direct forerunner of The Mead Corporation, was established in Dayton, Ohio, Colonel Daniel E. Mead participating as one of the partners.

1856. Ellis, Chaflin & Company was succeeded by Weston and Mead.

1861. Weston and Mead was succeeded by Mead and Weston.

1866. Mead and Weston became Mead and Nixon.

1873. April 1. The firm was changed into a joint stock company, The Mead & Nixon Paper Company, with a capitalization of $250,000.

GEO. H. MEAD

1877. November 5. George Houk Mead was born in Dayton, son of Marianna Houk and Harry Eldridge Mead, grandson of Ellen Demarest and Daniel E. Mead and of Eliza Thruston and George Washington Houk.

1881. July 13. Colonel Daniel E. Mead acquired full ownership of the company, excluding inventory and receivables, recapitalized the company at $150,000, and adopted the name of The Mead Paper Company.

1890, December 6. The Mead Paper company purchased the Chillicothe Pulp & Paper Mills of Ingham Mills and Company. Founded in 1847 by Em Trekin, Green & Company. The company was already making paper for the Crowell Publishing Company.

1891. Daniel E. Mead, grandfather of Geo. H. Mead, died.

1897. Geo. H. Mead was graduated from Hobart College with degree of Bachelor of Laws.

1897. Marianna Houk Mead, mother of George H. Mead, died.

GEO. H. MEAD

1897. Began playing golf and helped found Dayton's first country club.

1897. Geo. H. Mead was employed as roll boy and tour worker by The Mead Paper Company until 1898.

1898. Studied chemical engineering at Massachusetts Institute of Technology. Graduated in 1900 with degree of Bachelor of Science.

1900. Employed as research chemist by Cellulose Products Company of Boston, Massachusetts, until 1902.

1902. Served as Pulp Mill Superintendent at the Mead Paper Company's Chillicothe Works, until 1903.

1903. General Manager and Treasurer, General Artificial Silk Company of Philadelphia, Pennsylvania, until 1905.

1905. Geo. H. Mead reorganized the Mead Paper Company as the Mead Pulp & Paper Company and became its Vice President and General Manager.

1905. Resided in Chillicothe from the end of 1905 until 1907, at which time took up residence in Dayton.

1910. Elected president of the Mead Pulp & Paper Company.

1911. Organized with Colonel H. E. Talbott the Lake Superior Paper Company and served as its Vice President until 1913, when it was consolidated with the Spanish River Pulp & Paper Mills, Ltd. Began selling Canadian newsprint under the name Geo. H. Mead.

1913. Began playing polo. Some years later founded Miami Valley Hunt & Polo Club; thereafter served four years as Treasurer of the U.S. Polo Association and as member of the committee to select the U.S. International Polo Team.

THE MEAD CORPORATION

1904. The operation of the Mead Paper Company was placed in the hands of Trustees nominated by banks in Dayton, Chillicothe, and Cincinnati.

1905. On September 14 the Mead Paper Company was reorganized as the Mead Pulp & Paper Company, an Ohio corporation, with an initial capitalization of $300,000.

1906. The machinery in the Dayton paper mill was moved to Chillicothe and the Dayton real estate sold the subsequent year. The principal offices of the company remained in Dayton.

1909. The capitalization of the Mead Pulp & Paper Company was increased to $800,000.

GEO. H. MEAD

1914. Elected Vice President of the Spanish River Pulp & Paper Mills, Ltd., and President the following year.

1914. Geo H. Mead and Elsie Louise Talbott were married on November 22.

1915. Louise Mead was born September 6.

1916. Mr. Mead's newsprint selling organization became the Geo. H. Mead Company.

1916. Colonel Harry E. Mead, Mr. Mead's father, died in Dayton.

1917. George Houk Mead, Jr., was born August 3, 1917.

191?. Mr. Mead founded the Mead Investment Company.

1918. Harry Talbott Mead was born October 16, 1918.

1919. Mr. Mead was relieved, at his request, of the position of General Manager of the Mead Pulp & Paper Company.

1919. After World War I, Mr. Mead developed four new Canadian newsprint mills: The Fort William Paper Company, The Manitoka Paper Company, St. Anne Paper Company, and The Murray Bay Paper Company. Became President of a U.S. newsprint mill: Escanaba Paper Company.

THE MEAD CORPORATION

1915. Capitalization was increased to $1,500,000.

1916. The Board of Directors authorized company purchase of a portion of the shares of the Kingsport Pulp Corporation, a soda-pulp company in whose origins Mr. Mead was instrumental.

1916. The company purchased the entire capital stock of the Peerless Paper Company of Dayton.

1916. The Board of Directors approved Mr. Mead's plan for employee stock purchases.

1917. The company entered into its first substantial contract with the Crowell Publishing Company.

1918. The Management Engineering and Development Company was organized in Dayton as a separate company to supervise the engineering of the Mead plants and to sell its services to other paper companies.

1918. Control of the Peerless Paper Company was sold to S. L. Roger, former Treasurer of the Mead Pulp & Paper Company, at his request.

1919. Capitalization was increased to $6,300,000.

1920. The Mead Fibre Company, incorporated as a separate organization, purchased the Kingsport Pulp Corporation. (In 1926, the company became a subsidiary of the Mead Pulp & Paper Company and in 1931 dissolved into part of the Mead Corporation.)

GEO. H. MEAD

1921. Nelson Strobridge Mead was born October 28.

1922. Mr. and Mrs. Mead completed the building of "The Little Woods," their home in Dayton.

1923. Purchased winter home in Aiken, South Carolina.

1924. Katherine Mead born October 12.

1928. Upon the merger of the Spanish River Pulp & Paper Mills, Ltd., and the other of Mr. Mead's newsprint companies in Canada with the Abitibi Power & Paper Company, he became Chairman of the new Abitibi board, in which position he served until 1930.

Became active in the Dayton Community Chest, which he served in various positions until 1949.

THE MEAD CORPORATION

1921. The Mead Sales Company was founded as a separate corporation to sell the white paper produced by the Mead Pulp & Paper Company mills together with the white paper of other mills in the United States and Canada.

1922. Research into the use of spent chestnut chips (a waste product resulting from the extraction of tannin) in paper manufacture was transferred from Dayton to the Forest Products Laboratory in Madison, Wisconsin.

1924. The company acquired all the stock of the Peerless Paper Company, the latter organization having fallen into difficulties and its president having become ill.

Mead became the first paper company to overcome the two-sidedness of coated paper.

1925. Equity base of company changed from 30,000 $100-par shares to 100,000 no-par shares.

First production began of paperboard pulp from the chestnut chips used in the extraction of tannin; the first use of the semi-chemical method of pulp manufacture.

1927. The Mead Paperboard Corporation was founded as a holding company for a group of southern companies which had been engaged in the extraction of tannin from chestnut chips but which, after Mead research, and under Mead direction, were branching into the manufacture of paperboard from the spent chips. The southern companies included The Sylvia Paperboard Company, The Harriman Company, The Southern Extract Company, the Chillicothe Company.

1928. Raffield, a calcium carbonate and calcium waste product, was developed for use as a filler in white paper manufacture to produce a brighter and more opaque sheet and thus an improved printing surface.

1929. The Mead Straw Pulp Company was organized as a subsidiary of the Mead Pulp &

GEO. H. MEAD

1930. Marianna Mead was born March 28.

Geo. H. Mead was elected President of the newly formed Mead Corporation.

The Mead family began to spend summers on Cape Cod.

1933. Became a member of the Business Advisory Council at the time of its formation, remaining active until 1944.

1934. Appointed Chairman, Industrial Advisory Board of the National Reconstruction Administration; served in this capacity until 1944.

1936. Became Chairman of the Business Advisory Council and served until 1937.

THE MEAD CORPORATION

Paper Company to convert straw into paperboard, but the process did not prove economical and the subsidiary was dissolved in 1930.

1930. The Mead Corporation was formed to include the activities of the Mead Pulp & Paper Company, the Mead Paperboard Corporation, and the Management Engineering & Development Company, although the legal existence of these organizations and/or some of their parts did not terminate for some years.

The Corporation sold $9,500,000 of First Mortgage Gold Bonds, Series A, through the National City Company.

1932. The Corporation acquired Dill & Collins, Inc., a manufacturer of book papers with an established system of distribution through paper merchants. (Dill & Collins' history began in 1690 when the first paper mill was put in operation in the United States.)

1933. The principal offices of the Corporation were moved to Chillicothe.

A chestnut pulp and paperboard mill at Nashville, Tennessee, was acquired under a purchase contract.

1934. The Corporation purchased the assets of the Geo. W. Wheelwright Paper Company of Leominster, Massachusetts, a manufacturer of fine bristol and under boards, mill blanks, and box boards.

Mead began participation in the Becker Plan, a concerted industry operation to buy up distressed paperboard manufacturers.

1935. The common and preferred stock of the Mead Corporation was listed on the New York Stock Exchange.

Mead and Kimberly-Clark entered into a pooling agreement to facilitate research in coating methods. (The agreement continued until 1953, when it was renewed with modifications.)

1936. The Mead Corporation, in a 50-50 arrangement with Almours Securities, Inc., organized the St. Joe Paper Company to erect and operate a paperboard mill at Port St. Joe, Florida. (The Corporation sold its share of the assets in 1940.)

GEO. H. MEAD

THE MEAD CORPORATION

The Mead Corporation, in a 50-50 arrangement with the Scott Paper Company, organized the Brunswick Pulp & Paper Company to erect and operate a pulp mill at Brunswick, Georgia.

1937. Named Chairman of the Board of the Mead Corporation; renamed as President.

1937. The Corporation sold 50,000 shares of Cumulative Preferred Stock, Series B, through Lehman Brothers for $4,800,000.

1938. Coating of white paper on-the-machine was perfected sufficiently for first exclusive commercial use.

1940. Became member of the Committee for Economic Development, served until 1949.

1940. The Corporation sold $6,000,000 of First Mortgage Bonds through Lehman Brothers, et al.

1941. Appointed member, National Defense Mediation Board.

1942. Took up residence in Washington, D. C.

1942. Sydney Ferguson became President of the Corporation.

Mr. Mead became a member of the Board of Trustees of Dayton's Miami Valley Hospital.

The Escanaba Paper Company of Escanaba, Michigan, was acquired.

Resigned as President of the Mead Corporation, continuing as Chairman of the Board.

George Houk Mead, Jr., Lt. USMC, was killed on Guadalcanal, August 19.

Mr. Mead was appointed member of the National War Labor Board, on which he served until 1944, acting in 1943 and 1944 as Chairman of the Industry Group.

Elected President of the American Pulp & Paper Association; served until 1943.

1943. The Manistique Pulp & Paper Company of Manistique, Michigan, a ground wood manufacturer, was acquired. (This acquisition did not prove profitable, and its physical assets were sold in 1951 and in the first months of 1952.)

1944. Appointed as Industry Member of the Advisory Board, War Mobilization and Reconversion, a post held until 1946.

1944. The principal offices of the Corporation were moved back to Dayton.

Appointed Member of the Economic Stabilization Board, a post held until 1946.

1946. Appointed member of Federal Price Recontrol Board; served until 1947. Returned to residence in Dayton.

1946. The Corporation sold $24,000,000 of First Mortgage Bonds, Cumulative Preferred Shares, and Cumulative Second Preferred Shares through Drexel & Company, et al.

GEO. H. MEAD

THE MEAD CORPORATION

The Columbian Paper Company, with a pulp mill at Bristol, Virginia, and a paper mill at Buena Vista, Virginia, was acquired. These operations were discontinued in 1951, and part of the equipment and inventory was moved to the Wheelwright plant.

Mead Board Sales, Inc., was incorporated as a separate organization to sell paperboard.

The Corporation, in a 60-40 arrangement with the Inland Container Company, organized the Macon Kraft Company to construct and operate a paperboard mill at Macon, Georgia.

1947. Became Chairman of the Dayton Council of World Affairs, of which he was one of the founders.

Appointed Member of the Commission on the Organization of the Executive Branch of the Government (the first Hoover Commission); served until 1949.

1948. Resigned as Chairman of the Board of the Mead Corporation; named Honorary Chairman.

1948. Sydney Ferguson elected Chairman of the Board; Charles R. Van de Carr, Jr. elected President.

Appointed Member of the Public Advisory Board of the Economic Cooperation Administration (the agency that administered the Marshall Plan); served until 1951.

Served as Member of the National Citizens Committee for the Public Schools until 1954.

Scored hole-in-one from fifth tee of Moraine Country Club, Dayton.

1950. Appointed Member of the Committee on Mobilization Policy of the National Security Resources Board; served until 1951.

Awarded TAPPI Medal for technical advances to the pulp and paper industry. (TAPPI = Technical Association of the Pulp and Paper Industry.)

1951. Appointed Member of the Advisory Board, Mutual Security Agency, a post held until 1952.

1951. The Corporation, in a 60-40 arrangement with the Inland Container Company, organized the Rome Kraft Company to construct and operate a paperboard mill at Rome, Georgia.

Appointed Member of the National Advisory Board on Mobilization Policy of the Office of Defense Mobilization; served until 1952.

1952. Howard E. Whitaker elected President of the Corporation.

GEO. H. MEAD

THE MEAD CORPORATION

1954. The Corporation sold $7,500,000 of Cumulative Second Preferred Shares through Drexel & Company, et al.

Mead Pulp Sales, Inc., was founded as a subsidiary of the Mead Sales Company to handle pulp sales to and from the Corporation.

1955. The Macon Kraft Company was reorganized into the Georgia Kraft Company, and the capitalization both of this company and of the Rome Kraft Company was readjusted to provide equal shares to the Corporation and to the Inland Container Corporation.

The Corporation purchased a controlling interest in the Jackson Box Company of Cincinnati, Ohio, a manufacturer of shipping containers with interests in plants in three other locations. (This company became a wholly owned subsidiary in 1956.)

The Corporation acquired the Chillicothe Paper Company by means of exchanged shares. (The latter company had been formed in 1919 by former Mead employees with the assistance of Geo. H. Mead.)

A wholly owned subsidiary, Mead Papers, Inc. was formed to acquire the assets of the Mead Sales Company, whose chief business had been the sale of the Corporation's white paper.

The Corporation announced the installation of a neutral-sulphite-semi-chemical recovery plant at Lynchburg, Virginia.

1957. Howard E. Whitaker named Chairman of the Board; Donald F. Morris named President.

The Corporation acquired the assets of the Atlanta Paper Company, a manufacturer specializing in bottle containers, together with its recently acquired subsidiary, Palm Container Corporation of Miami, Florida.

The Crowell-Collier Publishing Company suspended magazine publication.

The Corporation acquired the Hurlbut Paper Company of South Lee, Massachusetts, a company specializing in special industrial technical papers.

The Corporation acquired the Cleveland Paper Company, a wholesale distributor.

GEO. H. MEAD

THE MEAD CORPORATION

The Corporation acquired Mead Board Sales, Inc.

The Corporation acquired the Excello Paper Products Company of Cincinnati, Ohio, a container board manufacturer.

Mead Containers, Inc., was formed to unify box manufacturing and marketing operations.

The Corporation acquired the Shelby Paper Company of Memphis, Tennessee, a container manufacturer.

Sales offices were established in Dusseldorf, Germany, and in London, United Kingdom.

1958. The Corporation sold $25,000,000 of debentures through Drexel & Company and Harriman Ripley & Company.

The Corporation acquired Bermingham & Prosser Company, a wholesale white paper house with headquarters in Chicago, Illinois and branches in four other cities.

The Corporation acquired the Ottawa Paper Company with container plants in Toledo, Ohio and Flint, Michigan.

Acquired also: the Miller Container Corporation of Louisville, Kentucky, the Grand Rapids Container Company, and the Wrenn Paper Company of Middletown, Ohio, a manufacturer of technical and industrial papers.

1959. The Corporation acquired the assets of the A & P Corrugated Box Company of Gardner, Massachusetts, together with two of its affiliates, the Associated Folding Box Company of Lawrence, Massachusetts and the Industrial Container Corporation of Maryland.

Further acquisitions: Gibralter Corrugated Paper Company, Inc. of North Bergen, New Jersey; and 354,356 square feet of building space for container manufacture expansion at Louisville, Kentucky.

Mead Containers, Inc. became the Mead Containers Division of the Mead Corporation.

During 1959, the Corporation acquired two paperboard mills and seven paperboard converting plants.

1960. Plans developed for doubling the output of Brunswick Pulp & Paper Company's output.

GEO. H. MEAD

THE MEAD CORPORATION

The Corporation acquired the Gilbert Paper Company of Menasha, Wisconsin, a white paper manufacturer.

1961. The Corporation acquired several new subsidiaries: the Chatfield & Woods Company, a distributing organization with outlets in eleven cities; the Dixon Paper Company, a white paper and industrial paper manufacturer with nine branches; the Waterloo Corrugated Box Company with plants at Waterloo and Fort Dodge, Iowa.

Agreement reached with Nippon Pulp Industry Company, Inc. for use of machine coating processes in Japan.

Mead, Société Anonyme, Switzerland, established. Subsequent participation with Mead-Branson, N. V., of the Netherlands; Papeteries de Tisselt, S.A., Belgium; and Hurlbut-Scheuflen G.M.B.H.

New Mead Research Center in Chillicothe inaugurated.

1963. Geo. H. Mead died in the early hours of the New Year.

Historical Statistics

Accounting is an ever-changing art that is always seeking to become more scientific; it is a convention that is forever trying to achieve greater actuality. The paradox results from the fact that business life is always more complex than numbers indicate while it is understandable basically in terms of them. Procedures change with the years so that accounting can become more utilitarian.

In the survey of Mead statistics, tables of which occupy most of this appendix, the statistical procedures are based as far as possible on those used in the 1962 annual report: e.g., depreciation is always subtracted from plant, except in 1905, when it was incalculable, and in 1907, when the plant had been so refurbished that the auditor concluded it was not subject to depreciation at all. Sometimes, present day procedures are not applicable: it is impossible to give even a sketch of Mead's comparative statistics without using the catch-all of "Other Deductions," up until 1957 when the company abandoned it, only to resurrect it in 1961 to take care of "Extraordinary Charges." Generally speaking, changes in capitalization, gains or losses from specific transactions, even outstanding events are not noted, not even changes in accounting, which as the tables show become more complex and complete. To take advantage of these changes, figures since 1951 are based on the accounting for two adjoining years and thus make use of figures that have had the benefit of an additional year's thought. Read in conjunction with the text and with the chronological appendix, the tables should be largely self-explanatory.

Tables covering 58 years, however, are not likely to provide the sharp sense of contrast between the Mead Pulp and Paper Company of 1905 and the Mead Corporation of 1962. An introductory page of contrasting figures therefore precedes the tables. In addition there are tables that illustrate the tremendous growth of the corporation between 1955 and 1962 and a list of the corporation's acquisitions to broaden, diversify and enlarge its already extensive operations.

THE MEAD PULP & PAPER COMPANY Balance Sheet November 1, 1905	THE MEAD CORPORATION Comparative Balance Sheet December 31, 1962

ASSETS

Plant & Equipment..........	$320,089[1]	$158,327,431[2]
Inventory..................	46,071	49,342,531
Bills & Accounts Receivable...	72,358	43,605,980
Cash......................	258	13,509,373[3]
Prepaid Expenses...........	100	2,176,068
Investments, Other Assets.....	nil	48,270,424
	$438,909	$315,231,807

LIABILITIES

Capital Invested.............	$250,000	$115,583,779
Bills & Accounts Payable.....	155,906	44,638,351[4]
Surplus and Reserve.........	33,033[5]	83,009,677
Long-Term Liabilities........	nil	72,000,000
	$438,909	$315,231,807

TONNAGE

1905......................	6,340	1962.................	1,180,412[6]

SALES

1905......................	$460,520	1962...................	$435,116,370

EARNINGS

1905......................	(deficit)	1962...................	$ 14,048,824

EMPLOYEES

1905......................	75	1962.................	17,383

STOCKHOLDERS

1952......................	7	1962.................	10,345

---

[1]"Of course, it would have been much better if we had started with a vacant lot and built a new mill . . . ." Geo. H. Mead, January 10, 1926.

[2]The value of plant and equipment is given after provision of $125,350,182 in accumulated depreciation.

[3]Cash includes $3,487,126 in marketable securities.

[4]Of accounts payable, $7,118,849 is not a current liability. It represents largely income tax adjustments.

[5]The 1905 figures were highly fictitious. Capital had been dissipated; many bills and accounts payable were dubious; and surplus and reserve served largely to achieve a paper balance with assets.

[6]The 1962 tonnage does not include 440,000 tons of paperboard converted into cartons, boxes, and other articles.

Year	Current Assets	Investments, Other Assets	Gross Plant	Less Accumulated Depreciation	Net Plant
1905	$ 118,720	$ 100	$ 320,089	N.A.	$ 320,089
1906					
1907					
1908					
1909	141,623	3,813	414,415		414,415
1910	266,193	3,259	680,993	16,177	664,815
1911	244,053	10,327	739,443	25,053	714,390
1912	314,245	14,014	759,020	60,967	698,053
1913	341,168	33,341	779,650	60,997	718,653
1914	345,682	37,895	821,475	60,997	760,478
1915	321,682	45,405	875,237	80,977	794,240
1916	631,511	147,890	1,362,534	125,844	1,236,690
1917	765,235	530,347	1,355,277	183,293	1,171,994
1918	924,105	283,169	1,403,830	259,880	1,143,950
1919	796,165	278,096	1,456,742	337,335	1,119,407
1920	1,657,850	354,860	4,339,532	421,581	3,917,951
1921	1,363,270	293,272	4,832,922	632,013	4,200,909
1922	1,770,420	261,973	4,899,538	849,201	4,050,337
1923	1,316,661	341,260	4,928,499	1,066,155	3,862,344
1924	1,708,874	438,911	6,257,589	1,054,863	4,752,726
1925	2,045,330	1,467,741	6,999,856	1,764,807	5,234,779
1926	2,256,296	2,535,208	8,362,851	2,063,500	6,299,351
1927	2,432,121	902,256	12,475,587	2,590,956	9,884,991
1928	3,360,496	2,389,578	13,824,026	2,896,600	10,956,024
1929	3,291,500	797,792	18,254,324	3,380,614	14,873,710
1930	5,591,759	2,014,713	27,575,810	4,452,759	23,123,051
1931	5,140,210	2,411,589	27,990,720	5,425,587	22,565,132
1932	4,218,374	1,276,728	28,267,795	6,389,760	21,878,036
1933	4,379,748	2,491,997	28,592,923	7,230,367	21,362,547
1934	5,063,143	2,654,514	28,935,229	8,525,531	20,406,698
1935	5,232,539	2,613,777	29,793,412	9,737,620	20,055,793
1936	6,799,094	2,288,356	31,790,618	11,125,763	20,644,855
1937	8,304,045	3,497,217	34,842,593	12,262,217	22,580,376
1938	7,560,579	4,188,649	35,961,174	13,417,362	22,543,812
1939	8,059,400	4,595,212	36,582,060	14,697,591	21,884,469
1940	10,209,758	3,605,141	37,076,685	15,255,003	21,821,682
1941	11,628,621	3,188,041	39,913,077	16,205,483	22,707,634
1942	13,126,551	3,341,699	41,647,913	19,717,444	21,930,469
1943	13,197,510	3,579,269	42,401,226	21,462,873	21,012,348
1944	13,762,511	3,868,127	42,754,843	22,997,802	19,756,414
1945	14,351,218	5,342,508	44,190,169	24,268,486	19,921,683
1946	18,327,372	9,444,780	50,585,330	26,641,639	23,943,691
1947	20,791,595	9,649,592	56,398,857	27,978,089	28,420,768
1948	24,388,649	8,627,773	61,931,280	29,541,267	32,390,013
1949	23,780,058	9,296,771	64,206,629	30,566,581	33,640,079
1950	24,622,509	12,304,412	66,192,079	22,456,623	33,735,456
1951	28,540,592	11,510,869	71,535,923	32,079,977	39,455,946
1952	31 031,463	13,689,481	74,658,694	33,400,245	41,258,449
1953	28,827,656	13,709,631	80,736,565	35,142,028	45,594,537
1954	37,590,043	20,109,012	91,457,242	39,239,460	52,217,782
1955	39,947,068	23,067,978	99,555,690	42,117,838	57,437,852
1956	47,867,852	20,776,347	123,369,819	47,895,303	75,474,516
1957	56,258,752	14,434,337	148,985,796	55,481,635	93,504,161
1958	74,045,651	24,100,793	185,562,527	68,336,595	117,225,932
1959	87,474,730	21,014,792	228,007,567	88,931,750	141,075,817
1960	95,305,567	18,818,514	246,302,304	100,155,230	146,147,074
1961	108,242,975	46,120,028	266,365,815	113,165,847	153,200,028
1962	108,683,952	48,270,424	283,677,613	125,350,128	158,327,431

Year	Net Assets	Current Liabilities	Other Liabilities	Long-term Debt	Share-holders' Equity
1905	$ 438,909	$ 155,906			$ 283,003
1906					
1907					
1908					
1909	559,851	144,338	$ 2,115		413,398
1910	934,267	258,925			675,432
1911	968,770	124,047			845,723
1912	1,026,315	173,652			852,663
1913	1,093,162	225,824			867,338
1914	1,143,859	280,669	112		928,990
1915	1,161,327	132,230			1,029,097
1916	2,016,091	276,781			1,739,310
1917	2,458,566	684,872			1,803,694
1918	2,351,243	574,246			1,776,995
1919	2,202,788	366,619			1,836,169
1920	5,930,660	888,661		$ 1,100,000	3,942,000
1921	5,857,451	669,576	27,501	1,200,000	4,060,374
1922	6,082,730	1,011,290	40,000	970,000	4,071,434
1923	5,520,924	534,445	75,348	840,000	4,071,131
1924	6,901,071	828,065	57,497	1,205,000	4,810,508
1925	8,747,120	820,614	53,709	2,922,500	4,920,292
1926	11,090,854	1,076,215	80,362	2,922,500	7,011,777
1927	13,219,009	1,041,512	49,362	3,331,000	8,797,135
1928	16,706,097	1,320,936	45,646	2,991,500	12,348,117
1929	18,961,000	3,784,953	58,526	2,362,500	12,755,023
1930	30,819,521	835,218	1,808,501	9,500,000	18,675,803
1931	30,118,931	633,190	1,651,959	9,344,000	18,487,782
1932	28,373,138	423,193	1,327,092	9,017,000	17,605,853
1933	28,234,292	736,357	1,415,987	8,582,945	17,499,003
1934	28,394,565	998,504	1,497,286	7,974,323	17,654,471
1935	27,902,110	953,376	990,962	7,495,242	18,123,004
1936	29,752,305	2,473,527	1,359,281	7,240,151	18,643,254
1937	34,111,638	2,569,159	1,184,515	6,657,169	23,712,795
1938	34,294,040	2,019,694	1,137,484	7,885,232	23,250,630
1939	34,505,080	2,235,110	1,206,124	7,536,000	23,527,845
1940	35,636,581	2,277,401	1,273,676	7,750,000	24,335,485
1941	37,571,296	3,560,348	844,868	7,650,000	24,466,080
1942	38,398,712	4,581,195	1,059,103	6,790,000	25,968,420
1943	37,798,183	4,340,974	822,615	6,580,000	26,045,578
1944	37,387,046	4,167,528	918,479	6,000,000	26,292,039
1945	39,615,409	4,129,208	954,727	8,000,000	26,531,473
1946	51,715,941	5,643,385	1,178,260	12,000,000	32,894,296
1947	58,861,946	7,932,229	1,203,440	12,000,000	37,725,878
1948	65,574,965	9,153,647	1,219,387	14,518,400	40,683,522
1949	66,872,159	7,165,347	722,213	16,167,800	42,806,778
1950	70,804,197	7,009,074	693,756	16,257,200	46,754,397
1951	79,507,407	9,568,350	680,076	18,120,000	51,138,981
1952	85,979,393	10,998,780	853,850	19,250,000	54,875,000
1953	88,131,824	6,989,825	1,168,227	22,070,000	57,903,772
1954	109,916,837	10,218,074	1,600,636	21,630,000	76,468,127
1955	118,452,898	11,855,321	2,399,703	21,180,000	82,987,874
1956	144,118,715	17,017,544	3,448,285	24,745,000	98,907,886
1957	164,197,250	18,072,111	3,727,868	29,070,000	113,327,271
1958	215,372,376	28,268,462	4,408,431	45,000,000	137,695,483
1959	249,565,339	36,405,044	4,715,156	47,000,000	161,445,139
1960	257,586,258	36,646,856	4,448,428	47,000,000	170,490,974
1961	307,563,031	39,539,408	2,867,657	72,000,000	193,155,966
1962	315,231,807	37,512,502	7,118,849	72,000,000	198,593,456

Year	Net Sales	Total Income	Selling, Administrative, Other	Interest and Debt Expense	Depreciation and Depletion
1905	$?460,520				
1906	?410,585				
1907	?518,912				
1908	?489,967				
1909	?485,444				$ 16,178
1910	830,179				21,178
1911	1,039,620				
1912	1,147,573			$ 5,474	66,359
1913	1,093,762		$ 37,045	7,543	
1914	1,178,951				
1915	1,268,350				20,000
1916	2,300,820				47,483
1917	3,745,585				59,826
1918	2,812,591				76,818
1919	2,574,885				79,840
1920	3,869,303				85,435
1921	3,271,034				232,301
1922	3,829,247				222,164
1923	4,800,004				226,954
1924	5,756,560				248,065
1925	6,709,638				292,626
1926	6,854,618				330,575
1927	9,793,463				455,916
1928	9,862,719				499,186
1929	12,889,396				
1930	16,707,101	$ 20,020,401	909,419		
1931	12,821,679				
1932	9,295,510	9,458,093	730,101		
1933	10,497,824	10,708,317	823,665		
1934	12,277,923	12,578,579	913,332		
1935	14,130,119	14,443,713	1,018,461		
1936	19,413,529	19,688,947	1,357,793	449,952	1,446,884
1937	25,743,711	26,048,856	1,701,871	445,167	1,417,406
1938	19,664,856	19,892,980	1,456,514	447,111	1,586,450
1939	21,986,587	22,270,170	1,490,212	486,498	1,707,720
1940	24,506,440	24,809,638	1,691,437	404,462	1,661,032
1941	32,452,149	38,835,694	2,071,783	386,703	1,640,174
1942	33,858,432	34,148,962	2,097,634	656,371	1,799,527
1943	36,878,042	37,251,439	2,180,219	270,827	1,829,491
1944	39,919,882	40,230,049	2,312,524	263,962	1,692,308
1945	40,857,380	41,341,116	2,364,420	443,349	1,862,127
1946	53,429,125	53,787,871	2,922,036	547,167	1,730,301
1947	72,273,305	72,901,600	4,000,583	373,038	1,862,252
1948	84,837,549	85,196,015	4,396,065	429,788	2,357,876
1949	76,648,806	77,107,891	4,338,503	505,012	2,208,126
1950	93,452,506	93,854,566	5,124,666	513,674	2,234,233
1951	112,030,825	112,543,539	6,193,186	596,271	2,382,548
1952	100,304,905	110,910,318	6,091,968	678,434	2,593,824
1953	111,365,154	112,269,946	7,252,372	813,205	2,911,177
1954	121,182,360	122,333,507	7,287,138	852,227	7,417,599
1955	150,525,636	152,246,525	8,574,710	835,251	3,815,982
1956	192,548,200	194,588,793	12,756,215	1,114,778	4,387,971
1957	208,123,788	210,264,654	16,423,917	1,048,144	6,170,640
1958	256,244,183	258,631,873	22,932,224	1,739,349	8,775,589
1959	331,814,735	333,901,704	31,854,888	2,000,255	11,293,621
1960	359,869,465	362,729,072	36,563,852	2,108,781	12,717,359
1961	405,504,091	408,595,219	42,848,829	3,150,666	13,627,202
1962	435,116,370	437,792,340	45,706,839	3,231,032	13,270,921

Year	Other Deductions	Taxes on Income	Net Earnings	Retained Earnings: End-of-Year Shareholders' Equity
1905				
1906			$L (3,750)	
1907			24,898	
1908			14,898	
1909			20,914	
1910	$ 27,698 ?		30,640	
1911	35,944 ?		31,766	
1912			67,770	
1913	12,479		44,232	
1914			43,739	
1915			79,235	
1916			365,678	
1917	P 29,466		112,851	
1918	P 30,508	$ 7,425	42,387	
1919	P 30,508	6,076	141,484	
1920			277,750	
1921			226,862	
1922			202,351	
1923			480,400	
1924			331,584	
1925			369,288	
1926			401,575	
1927			767,899	
1928			828,780	
1929	1,939,290		1,151,210	
1930	868,905	161,505	1,215,984	
1931			439,837	
1932	1,515,457	L (1,493)	L (713,279)	
1933	1,870,766	L (29,182)	L (384,620)	
1934	2,346,115	85,692	31,437	
1935	2,197,586	107,319	501,607	
1936	428,570	225,643	955,020	$ 382,465
1937	540,037	437,024	1,841,111	893,893
1938	540,398	63,790	L (105,802)	193,615
1939	288,550	170,550	744,028	470,830
1940	200,770	1,590,615	1,426,881	1,400,889
1941	633,171	1,650,923	2,109,785	2,595,129
1942	47,721	1,382,273	1,357,470	2,839,176
1943	732,505	1,097,007	1,078,141	3,039,729
1944	133,251	1,148,659	1,137,831	3,306,780
1945	78,521	1,202,395	1,190,647	3,557,441
1946	267,514	1,959,800	3,449,308	5,503,450
1947	1,221,077	3,698,000	5,685,386	10,364,033
1948	1,285,139	3,058,300	5,013,917	13,467,677
1949	1,656,730	2,264,000	3,416,067	15,831,071
1950	1,508,807	6,006,000	6,377,397	14,892,336
1951	1,934,729	10,230,000	6,109,237	19,410,555
1952	2,108,705	7,000,000	5,093,126	22,731,312
1953	2,014,352	6,975,000	5,424,488	25,284,418
1954	3,491,575	7,417,599	6,961,379	28,862,290
1955	3,354,767	11,600,000	10,643,135	31,375,434
1956	4,193,608	15,628,000	14,186,767	40,505,910
1957		11,900,000	11,930,142	43,648,093
1958		10,950,000	10,690,879	43,979,505
1959		15,665,000	14,002,448	52,113,271
1960		14,930,000	14,552,645	57,938,857
1961	1,764,444	11,000,000	12,025,759	78,525,687
1962		12,850,000	14,042,824	83,009,677

Year	White Paper Tonnage	Paperboard Tonnage	Total Tonnage	Capital Expenditures	Expenditures Inc. Affiliates
1905			6,339		
1906			4,496		
1907			6,838		
1908			6,377		
1909			7,111		
1910			10,675		
1911			13,462		
1912			15,705		
1913			14,768		
1914			14,812	$ 41,475	
1915			14,030	53,762	
1916			19,971	487,298	
1917			19,667	136,713	
1918			18,915	48,573	
1919			18,762	48,553	
1920			21,377	2,841,742	
1921			18,384		
1922					
1923					
1924					
1925			77,000		
1926				1,690,100	
1927			83,705	238,791	
1928					
1929					
1930			238,789		
1931			214,641		
1932			182,972		
1933			213,974		
1934			223,091		
1935			254,963		
1936			331,589		
1937			371,383		
1938			297,456		$ 1,298,803
1939			350,058		
1940			359,948		
1941			440,602		
1942			424,417		
1943			440,142		
1944			453,582		
1945			444,649		
1946			494,251		
1947			522,508	6,339,329	
1948			576,927	6,327,131	
1949	373,244	260,526	510,869	3,458,193	
1950	329,324	324,500	685,492	6,713,885	
1951	344,609	332,150	703,601	8,601,369	7,500,000
1952	274,530	315,038	634,553	9,482,482	16,500,000
1953	296,289	357,912	685,350	7,274,754	13,000,000
1954	292,197	360,616	687,764	7,135,819	12,500,000
1955	369,329	487,993	888,691	9,046,952	10,000,000
1956	412,815	480,179	905,263	16,593,981	19,500,000
1957	366,244	465,471	899,265	19,282,808	21,000,000
1958	371,330	434,080	805,410	17,000,922	19,000,000
1959	420,515	559,960	980,475	20,424,660	25,000,000
1960	452,940	566,911	1,019,851	17,372,724	30,000,000
1961	458,324	640,111	1,098,435	18,914,860	26,000,000
1962	482,891	697,521	1,180,412	17,540,476	31,000,000

Year	Number of Employees	Number of Stockholders	Working Capital Ratio	Net Earnings as a Per Cent of Assets	Net Earnings as a Per Cent of Sales
1905			0.76 to 1		
1906					
1907					4.8%
1908					3.0
1909			0.98 to 1	3.7%	4.3
1910			1.03 to 1	3.3	3.7
1911			1.97 to 1	3.3	3.1
1912			1.81 to 1	6.6	5.9
1913			1.51 to 1	4.0	4.0
1914			1.23 to 1	3.8	3.7
1915			2.43 to 1	6.8	6.2
1916			2.28 to 1	18.1	15.9
1917			1.12 to 1	5.6	3.0
1918			1.61 to 1	1.8	1.5
1919			2.17 to 1	6.4	4.7
1920			1.87 to 1	4.7	7.1
1921			2.04 to 1	3.9	6.9
1922			1.75 to 1	3.3	5.3
1923			2.46 to 1	8.8	10.1
1924			2.06 to 1	4.8	6.9
1925			2.49 to 1	4.2	5.5
1926			2.10 to 1	3.6	5.9
1927			2.34 to 1	5.8	7.8
1928			2.54 to 1	5.0	8.4
1929			0.87 to 1	6.1	8.9
1930	2,298		6.69 to 1	3.9	7.3
1931	1,945		8.12 to 1	1.5	2.4
1932	2,155		9.97 to 1		
1933	2,636		5.95 to 1		
1934	3,259		5.07 to 1	1.1	2.6
1935	3,244		5.49 to 1	1.8	3.5
1936	3,850		2.75 to 1	3.2	4.9
1937	3,750	3,900	3.23 to 1	5.4	7.2
1938			3.74 to 1		
1939	3,877		3.61 to 1	2.2	3.4
1940	4,049		4.48 to 1	4.0	6.5
1941	4,402		3.27 to 1	5.6	6.5
1942			2.87 to 1	3.5	4.0
1943			3.04 to 1	2.9	2.9
1944			3.30 to 1	3.0	2.9
1945			3.48 to 1	3.0	2.9
1946			3.25 to 1	6.7	6.5
1947			2.62 to 1	9.7	7.9
1948	7,500	6,649	2.66 to 1	7.6	5.9
1949		6,526	3.32 to 1	5.1	4.5
1950		5,917	3.51 to 1	9.0	6.8
1951		5,603	2.98 to 1	7.7	5.5
1952		5,792	2.82 to 1	5.9	5.5
1953	7,700	6,019	4.12 to 1	6.2	4.9
1954	6,026	6,185	3.68 to 1	6.3	5.7
1955		6,150	3.37 to 1	9.0	7.1
1956		6,959	2.81 to 1	9.8	7.4
1957		7,303	3.11 to 1	7.3	5.7
1958		7,669	2.62 to 1	5.0	4.2
1959		9,238	2.4 to 1	5.6	4.2
1960		10,197	2.6 to 1	5.6	4.0
1961		10,210	2.74 to 1	3.9	3.0
1962	17,383	10,345	2.9 to 1	4.5	3.2

Year	Net Earnings as a Per Cent of Net Worth	Dividends as a Per Cent of Earnings		Year	Net Earnings as a Per Cent of Net Worth	Dividends as a Per Cent of Earnings
1905				1936	5.1	95.1
1906				1937	7.8	69.8
1907				1938		129.7
1908				1939	3.2	62.2
1909	5.1			1940	5.9	43.0
1910	4.5	98.4		1941	8.6	43.4
1911	3.8	91.4		1942	5.2	73.6
1912	7.9	70.8		1943	4.1	81.3
1913	5.1	?		1944	4.3	76.5
1914	4.7	75.5		1945	4.5	78.9
1915	7.7	63.6		1946	10.5	36.9
1916	21.0	37.6		1947	15.1	28.1
1917	6.3	96.9		1948	12.3	38.1
1918	2.4	166.5		1949	8.0	45.5
1919	7.7	62.6		1950	13.6	38.9
1920	7.0	58.5		1951	11.9	34.0
1921	5.6	108.0		1952	9.3	42.4
1922	5.0	81.7		1953	9.4	39.8
1923	11.8	38.5		1954	9.1	44.4
1924	6.9	71.9		1955	12.8	37.0
1925	7.5	70.3		1956	14.3	35.0
1926	5.7	84.6		1957	10.5	53.1
1927	8.7	65.7		1958	7.8	70.9
1928	6.7	74.4		1959	8.7	62.2
1929	9.0	60.6		1960	8.5	63.0
1930	6.5	55.3		1961	6.2	78.0
1931	2.4	133.3		1962	7.2	68.1
1932						
1933						
1934	1.3					
1935	2.8					

ACQUISITIONS BETWEEN 1955–1963

BOX COMPANIES

The Jackson Box Company, Cincinnati, Ohio, with additional plants in Milwaukee, Wisconsin, York, Pennsylvania and Syracuse, New York; 1956.

The Industrial Container and Paper Corporation, Chicago, Illinois; 1957.

The Excello Paper Products Company, Cincinnati, Ohio; 1957.

The Shelby Paper Company, Memphis, Tennessee; 1957.

The Ottawa River Paper Company with plants in Toledo, Ohio and Flint, Michigan; 1958.

The Miller Corporation, Louisville, Kentucky; 1958.

The Grand Rapids Container Company, Grand Rapids, Michigan; 1958.

The A & P Corrugated Box Company, Lawrence, Massachusetts with two affiliates: The Associated Folding Box Company and The Plymold Corporation, also of Lawrence; 1959.

The Industrial Container Corporation of Maryland, Baltimore, Maryland; 1959.

Gilbralter Corrugated Paper Company, Inc., North Bergen, New Jersey with additional plants at Elizabeth and Jersey City, New Jersey; 1959.

The Waterloo Corrugated Box Company, Waterloo, Iowa with an additional plant at Fort Dodge, Iowa; 1961.

In 1961 the company built a new plant at Louisville, Kentucky.

WHITE PAPER COMPANIES

The Chillicothe Paper Company, Chillicothe, Ohio; 1955.
The Hurlbut Paper Company, South Lee, Massachusetts; 1957.
The Wrenn Paper Company, Middletown, Ohio; 1958.
The Gilbert Paper Company, Menasha, Wisconsin; 1960.

PACKAGING COMPANIES

The Atlanta Paper Company, Atlanta, Georgia, with a subsidiary plant in Miami, Florida;
1957.
(Subsequent plants were established in company properties in Lawrence, Massachusetts;
Los Angeles, California; Charleroi, Pennsylvania; and Oakland, California. An affiliate was
established in Toronto, Canada.)

MERCHANT DISTRIBUTORS

The Cleveland Paper Company, Cleveland, Ohio; 1957.
Birmingham and Prosser, Chicago, Illinois with four branches; 1958.
The Chatfield & Woods Company, with outlets in eleven cities; 1961.
The Dixon Paper Company, with nine branches in the Rocky Mountain area; 1961.

FOREIGN OPERATIONS, DECEMBER 31, 1962

Mead S. A., Zug, Switzerland
Mead-Bramson N.V., Amersfoort, Holland
Hurlbut-Scheufelen G.M.B.H., Frankeneck, West Germany
Mead Pulp and Paper Ltd., London, England
Mead Zellstoff und Papier G.M.B.H., Duesseldorf-Nord and Hamburg-Poppenbuettel, West
Germany
Papeteries de Tisselt S.A., Tisselt, Belgium
Cellox Italiana S.p.A., Milano, Italy

EXPANSION BETWEEN 1955–1962

Year	Gross Plant	Net Plant	Total Assets	Total Income	Net Earnings	White Paper Tonnage	Brown Paper Tonnage
1955	$ 99,555,690	$ 57,437,852	$118,452,898	$152,246,525	$10,643,135	369,329	487,993
1956	123,369,819	75,474,516	144,118,715	194,588,793	14,186,767	412,815	480,179
1957*	148,985,796	93,504,161	164,197,250	210,264,654	11,930,142	366,244	465,471
1958	185,562,527	117,225,932	215,372,376	258,631,873	10,690,879	371,330	434,080
1959	228,007,567	141,075,817	249,565,339	333,901,704	14,002,448	420,515	559,960
1960	246,302,304	146,147,074	257,586,258	362,729,072	14,552,645	452,940	566,911
1961**	266,365,875	153,200,028	307,563,031	408,595,219	12,025,759	458,324	640,111
1962	283,677,613	158,327,431	315,231,807	437,792,340	14,042,824	482,891	697,521***

* In 1957, the Crowell Company abandoned magazine publishing.
** The year 1960–1961 was one of mild business recession.
*** Container and packaging production for this year amounted to an additional 420,000 tons.

1905 Report

G. H. MEAD, *Report on Mead Paper Co.* May 15, 1905
[Private Document Submitted to Bankers and Reorganizers]*

HISTORICAL

The paper mills at present operated by the Mead Paper Co. were established on their present site in Dayton, Ohio, in 1846, by Ells, Chaflin & Co., who were succeeded by Weston & Mead in 1856; then by Mead & Weston in 1861.

On January 1st, 1866, Mr. Thomas Nixon, brother of Martin Nixon, of Philadelphia, purchased Weston's interest and enough of the interest of Col. D. E. Mead to make him an equal partner.

The preserved records date from the formation of the firm of Mead & Nixon, but it is generally conceded that the business was a successful and profitable one for the twenty years preceding their advent.

The Profits of Mead & Nixon were:

1866 for year ending Dec. 31st.		$57,379.55
1867	Do.	38,387.72
1868	Do.	25,337.11
1869	Do.	24,680.38
1870	Do.	48,962.23
1871	Do.	55,525.42
1872	Do. and 3 months to April, '73	62,722.69

On April 1st, 1873, the firm was merged into a Stock Company, The Mead & Nixon Paper Company, capital $250,000.00 without disturbing existing conditions. Profits and Losses as follows:

1874 for year ending April 1st		$53,690.92
1875	Do.	26,218.77
1876	Do.	6,624.04
1877	Do.	15,977.16
1878	Do.	7,230.20
1879	Do. Loss, $12,800.50	
1880	Do.	5,401.46
1881	Do. 11,502.17	

As will be seen from above, the last few years of the business shows a decline in profits due to the changing methods of paper making. Mr. Nixon, the then expert of the Company, still clinging to old ideas, in fact, "not keeping up with the times," consented to a sale of the property, as the mill had to be rebuilt, and he—Nixon—being engaged in other business, had no money to advance his share of the necessary expense.

---

*The first two sections of this report were written by Col. H. E. Mead and were incorporated in their entirety into Mr. Mead's document.

On July 13th, 1881, D. E. Mead purchased the mills and machinery and all corporate property of The Mead & Nixon Paper Company, except bills and accounts receivable, and stock on hand or in process.

The Mead Paper Company was then formed with a capital of $150,000. D. E. Mead, President, C. D. Mead, Secretary.

The last Statement of The Mead & Nixon Paper Co., April 1st, 1881, is as follows:

RESOURCES		LIABILITIES	
Real Estate...............	$152,003.30	Capital Stock............	$250,000.00
Machinery...............	63,828.13	Profit & Loss............	26,551.58
Building Account........	42,386.08	Bills Payable............	67,507.23
Pulp Works.............	24,830.07	Co. owes on Acct.........	19,823.28
New Engine.............	8,861.08		
D. O. Fair Stock.........	500.00		
Thos. Nixon, Per.........	434.91		
D. E. Mead, Per..........	176.59		
Due Company on a/cs ...	23,254.16		
Cash....................	931.43		
Stock on hand...........	33,641.44		
New Boilers.............	115.16		
In Mer. Nat'l. Bank......	1,417.57		
Loss.............	11,502.17		
	$363,882.09		$363,882.09

With these assets The Mead Paper Company began business and began immediately to rebuild the mill. Of course, the first year was unprofitable and the year 1881 was a sort of panic year in the business.

1882 for year ending July 1st.		Loss, $3,862.37		
1883	Do.	Gain,		$21,732.38
1884	Do.	Gain,		30,366.88
1885	Do.	Gain,		33,596.68
1886	Do.	Gain,		19,939.89
1887	Do.	Gain,		13,145.56
1888	Do.	Loss,	238.91	
1889	Do.	Gain,		15,445.49
1890	Do.	Gain,		40,598.27
1891	Do.	Gain,		49,683.08

On December 6th, 1890, the Company purchased the Chillicothe Pulp & Paper Mills of Ingham Mills & Co., which by a peculiar coincidence, had also been established in 1846 and was a large plant which had over-grown itself, become out-classed, and through dissensions among its partners had been allowed to "go to seed" and finally to the hammer. The price paid, about $30,000, was absurd as compared to the value, for it was finely situated near coal mines and in a valley abounding in good pulp wood which could be obtained cheaply.

The Company began immediately to rebuild this important addition to its properties, and had the Paper Mill started in June, 1891, the Pulp Mill in November, 1891.

On July 1st, 1891, the Undivided Profits of the Dayton Mills having become $112,532.02 and the expenditures at Chillicothe being considerably over $100,000, the Board of Directors July 23rd, '91, declared a stock dividend, making the capital stock $250,000.

On November 10th, 1891, D. E. Mead, President of the Company, died, leaving an estate of about half a million dollars in trust to his children. Trustees empowered to endorse for The Mead Paper Co.

The Profits of the Combined Plants in

1892	for the year ending July 1st			$37,711.68
1893	Do.			51,142.37
1894	Do. (The year of the panic)	Loss,	$960.68	
1895	Do.			13,582.43
1896	Do.			18,009.01
1897	Do.			25,557.94

1898   Do.   During this year the north mill at Dayton was remodeled at a cost of about $60,000.

Loss, $2,519.19

1899	Do.		$18,315.53
1900	Do.		33,649.19

The period of demoralization now set in and the losses reached their height.

1901   Loss, $22,586.74
1902   Loss, 13,853.10

(The losses of these two years are not properly figured here, as the interest charges should be deducted from the figures given. The writer has made these corrections on the profit and loss sheet which follows.)

The high water mark was reached Jan. 1st, 1903, with Bills Payable aggregating $200,000 and the Banks began calling loans. The overdraft of the family had then passed $100,000, and at this time the following "Recommendations" were made by the Vice President, which were not put into effect.

RECOMMENDATIONS

I submit that this property—The Mead Paper Co.—can be made a paying investment, and in fact that it now *is* such, but that it is carrying too great an unnecessary expense to prove it. An interest account of near $14,000, officials over $26,000, an overdraft on which the interest is over $6,000, and Expense and Repair Account out of proportion to actual necessities, all unite to drain the paying powers of the business and that it has withstood these attacks for eleven years and is still solvent, proves conclusively that it can be made to pay *largely* by careful and conservative management.

To that end, I recommend—

1st.   That the President and Vice President be required to pay 6% interest on their overdraft; same to be deducted monthly from their salaries.

2nd.   The abolition of the offices of Superintendent and Treasurer and the discontinuance of those officers, whose duties may well be performed by—Superintendent by Vice President, —Treasurer by President.

3rd.   The discontinuance of payment of $100.00 monthly to D. Eldridge Mead and Eleanor B. Mead.

4th.   The employment of a male stenographer at not to exceed $50.00 monthly.

5th.   The immediate prosecution of the work of removal of machinery in South Mill to Chillicothe.

6th.   That monthly meetings of the Board of Directors together with Trustees of D. E. Mead Estate, be jointly held on or about the 10th. of each month and that the books and accounts be audited by such meeting.

7th.   That no further overdrafts be allowed by *any* one.

By the above it is proposed to save the Company—

1st.	6% interest on $80,000	$ 4,800.00
	Salary of Superintendent	3,000.00
	Salary of Treasurer	1,800.00
	Payments to D. E. and E. B. Mead	2,400.00
		$12,000.00
	By the transfer of the South Mill to Chillicothe	6,000.00
	Decrease in expense of running N. Mill separately	2,000.00
		$20,000.00

These last two items are extremely conservative estimates and it is believed will greatly overrun the amount set down. Besides which, the increased efficiency of both plants can not well be estimated, but there is no doubts of the results.

We are now making money as the prices are good and stock prices not exhorbitant. Our showing for month of December may be in some slight degree, attributed to more careful taking of stock Jan. 1st. than usual, but we can safely say we have made $2500 in December. When the new arrangement of machinery is effected, there is little room to doubt our ability to keep the pace, which would be at the rate of $30,000 per year. This with the saving above noted, should give us $50,000 and two years hard work and diligent and intelligent attention to business on the part of the officers should make us whole again and on the road to a prosperous future. These changes should be put in effect at once. Every day's delay means that much loss.

Jan. 15, 1903. H. E. Mead, Vice President.

Losses continued, being in—

1903 . . . . Not Available
1904 . . . . $7,027.91

During the last ten years, probably $200,000 has been spent on the mills for improvements, which amounts have been charged up each year to either Profit & Loss, Expense or Surplus Accounts, thus adding nothing to the Real Estate account, which has in fact been decreased by the transfer of the South Mill in Dayton to Chillicothe. This accounts for the low valuation of plant which is comprised in the account "Real Estate" in the statement taken from the books for July 1st, 1904, which follows. This statement completes the historical part of The Mead Paper Company, as soon afterward the Teutonia National Bank of Dayton precipitated affairs by suit which culminated in a compromise and the present arrangement of Trusteeship.

Statement July 1st, 1904
THE MEAD PAPER CO.

ASSETS		LIABILITIES	
Real Estate	$308,200.00	Capital Stock	$250,000.00
Dempsey Purchase	2,016.95	Surplus	30,726.97
Bills Receivable	2,552.81	D. E. Mead Estate	59,856.04
Improvements	16,061.51	Bills Payable	161,410.00
South Mill moving	248.42	Merchants Nat'l., Dayton	4,972.27
Cash	211.35	Ross Co. Nat'l.	384.49
Dayton Nat'l. Bank	146.86	Rent	81.00
Fourth Nat'l. Bank	9.25	Accounts Payable	26,381.18
Merchants Nat'l. Bank, Cincinnati	226.51		
Teutonia Nat'l. Bank	262.40		
Interstate Stock	590.00		
Interstate Commissions	2,604.85		
Good Accounts	36,541.93		
Doubtful	430.51		
Suspended	8,572.71		
Overdrafts	102,473.08		
Inventory	45,734.90		
Loss to July 1st	7,027.91		
	$533,911.95		$533,911.95

[MR. MEAD CONTINUES:]

This historical sketch of the development of The Mead Paper Company and its progress to the time of the change of management, November 1st, 1904, to the 3 Trustees appointed by the several Banks, was written shortly after this change by the former Vice President of the Company and is included in the present report for two reasons: Firstly, to show that in past years the business has been most successful when operated under proper supervision, the periodic losses having invariably been due to bad practical management, which in the earlier days was promptly changed as soon as proven incapable, always with satisfactory results; and secondly, because the reasons for the final failure of The Mead Paper Co. as such, which brought about the present Trusteeship, can be so clearly seen by an analysis of the "Profit & Loss Account" of the past 13 years, or that period during which the management recently deposed had complete control of the business; that this may be more thoroughly understood, the following *detailed* "Profit & Loss Account," is added:

PROFIT AND LOSS ACCOUNT
1893 to 1905

	Dayton Paper Mills		Chillicothe Paper Mill		Chillicothe Pulp Mill		Totals Profit	Loss
7–1–1893	Profit	$15,799	Profit	$24,205	Profit	$11,137	$51,141	
94	Loss	9,043	Loss	1,609	Profit	9,693		$ 959
95	Loss	4,685	Profit	9,132	Profit	9,135	13,582	
96	Loss	4,833	Profit	12,186	Profit	10,655	18,008	
97	Profit	416	Profit	18,855	Profit	6,285	24,724	
98	Loss	17,965	Profit	11,430	Profit	4,016		2,519
							107,455	3,478
99	Profit	4,416	Profit	12,586	Profit	10,224	27,226	
1900	Profit	1,626	Profit	10,616	Profit	10,111	31,353	
01	Loss	1,973	Loss	4,580	Loss	9,281		15,834
02	Loss	2,363	Profit	8,419	Loss	7,134		1,078
03	Loss	12,460	Profit	7,151	Profit	4,252		1,057
04	Loss	3,902	Profit	10,284	Loss	3,902	2,480	
							61,059	17,969
							17,969	
							*43,090	*Total net profit for 6 years.*
4–1–1905	Loss	4,935	Profit	18,038	Loss	870	12,233	

*NOTE—This profit of $43,090 has been used for interest payments on not only Company loans, but also all private loans. These interest charges have in the past 6 years amounted to $62,629 total, the $19,539 not obtained from profits having been borrowed.

Therefore, from 1901 to 1904 the Company had to not only make good by borrowing, the losses above noted, but also had to borrow over $10,000 per year more for interest payments. [Note by Mr. Mead.]

The control of the Company passed to the management which has continued for the past 13 years, at the death of the former President, Col. D. E. Mead shortly before Jan. 1st, 1892. At this time the business was in most excellent condition, having a good plant in Dayton, including 3 paper machines of medium size, a newly acquired or remodeled plant in Chillicothe, including a complete Pulp Mill, an additional Paper Mill with one medium-sized paper machine.

The following year, ending July 1st, 1893, shows a profit of $51,000, and it should be noted that the Chillicothe plant at this early date showed a big advantage over the Dayton plant. 1894, the panic year, shows a total loss for the three plants, but the Pulp Mill in particular, continued to be a consistent profit maker and the following three years surely should have proved the great value of the Chillicothe situation and its advantages from an economic standpoint over the Dayton location, for while the Dayton Mills were constantly losing money, the Chillicothe Mills were making excellent profits. It is hard to understand how, in face of such figures, $80,000 could be further invested in the Dayton plants in improvements, instead of in the Chillicothe mills, but such was the case and nothing could show more clearly the inefficiency of the management from which the business was suffering.

The moderate success of the concern from 1892 to 1897 was due to the practical man of the Company who, in position of Superintendent, had absolute control of the manufacturing end of the business. He was a hard worker, a great labor driver and economical to an extreme, but very autocratic and bull-headed. Being above all a good paper maker, the product turned out was excellent and practically sold itself and the credit of the Company being of the highest, with large backing from the Estate left by Col. D. E. Mead, the selling and financial departments were quite neglected, and the whole establishment was practically in the Superintendent's hands. The large expenditure in 1897 at Dayton was at his advice and under his direction and was given almost no thought by the President of the Company, and as far as can be learned now, the chief reason for making this improvement in Dayton instead of in Chillicothe, was because the Superintendent did not want to live in Chillicothe, which would have been necessary had the plant there been so increased.

The remodeling of the Dayton plant consisted in the tearing out and discarding of 2 old small machines in the so-called North Mill and putting in its place a new and entirely modern machine of large size and capacity equal to the 2 discarded machines; together with the rebuilding of the whole mill and adding of all the new machinery necessary to the turning out of a high grade paper by the most improved methods.

The results of this big improvement were indeed most disastrous, for during the next two years, which were very good (as shown by the Chillicothe Mills continuing to make excellent profits), the new modern Dayton plant had difficulty in keeping even and as a consequence, the man who had been responsible for the expenditure of $80,000 finally resigned, leaving no one to take his place.

Due to his high handed methods and the fear his subordinates had of him, nobody in the mills could be expected to quickly learn to assume responsibility, and the demoralized condition, particularly in the Chillicothe plant, which had been so consistent a money maker, is shown by the sudden losses of 1901. (It is also an unfortunate fact that the Superintendent, realizing that his resignation was inevitable, did not keep the mills in good repair, but allowed them to run down in a most shameful way.)

The following year, ending 1902, shows the Chillicothe mill again on a profitable basis, as by that time the foreman of the mill became aware of the necessity of the situation and had been given sufficient authority to so operate the mill as to put it back near to its previous condition. In this year a new General Superintendent was also finally obtained, but as he knew nothing of pulp making and very little even about paper making, and mill management, in which he had had a series of failures in various places, he was requested to resign after something over a year's trial and would never have been allowed to stay more than a small fraction of that time had he not been so well recommended by a friend of the President of the Company.

In the spring of 1902 the writer was employed by the Company as manager of the Chillicothe mills and he immediately gave the larger part of his attention to the Pulp Mill which had shown over $9,000 loss in 1901 and showed over $7,000 in the year ending July 1902. The result of careful operation during the following year is shown by the change from the $7,000 loss to the profit of over $4,000, which was all made in 6 months, as, during the latter 6 months of the year, the Pulp Mill ran only part time (for reasons stated later).

During the year July 1901–02 of the writer's management, the paper mill shows no increase in profit over the year before, but during this time the South Mill (so-called) in Dayton was dismantled and the paper machine and all necessary machinery moved to Chillicothe and installed there. Many portions of the Chillicothe Mill were remodeled, all of which was done without a single day's shut down of the regular Chillicothe paper machine and with the plant so torn up and operated under such difficulties, it is surprising that it showed any profit at all.

The moving of the machine was accomplished only after long and continued argument on the part of the writer, but he was so sure of the economies which would result and the value of such a move that he kept on insisting, and the profits of the past two years have more than justified the move and have shown even greater economies than he had expected. Immediately after this moving and rebuilding was completed, the writer resigned, the date being July 1st, 1903.

The following year, ending July 1st, 1904, the Chillicothe Paper Mill progressed fairly satisfactorily under good superintendence of the man who had been foreman for many years, but the Pulp Mill which should have shown much greater profits, than the year before, (having another paper machine in the adjoining mill to supply with pulp which saved much on freight to Dayton), again ran at considerable loss due entirely to the lack of a man who knew anything about the manufacture of pulp.

The Dayton Mill in this year showed considerable improvement due to the removal from there of the General Superintendent before mentioned who had spent a large amount of money in so-called improvements, the most of which were experiments for his own benefit.

The 9 months from July '04 to April '05, will be taken up later in detail as will also the year July '03 to '04, but it is worthy of note here that under the very uncertain and difficult operation of the business during the 4 months preceding the Trusteeship, and the 5 months immediately following, the Chillicothe Paper Mill should show a profit of $18,000, the Pulp Mill a loss of only $870 (it being shut down from September to November on account of fire), while the Dayton Mill lost $4,900 due principally to its running about one-half time from July to November.

This outline of the operation of the Company for the past 13 years shows so clearly how the business has been neglected, that it needs no further comment, and it is the writer's judgment that had it not been for the most extraordinary earning power of the Scioto Pulp & Paper Mills in Chillicothe, the Company would have reached its recent unfortunate climax years ago.

MANUFACTURING

The question of cost of manufacture and the profits which can be made out of the business can only be shown by complete analysis of not only the past profitable periods of the operation of the various plants, but also of the losing periods; and the following reports are therefore purposely filled with figures of detailed *costs* which though tedious and rather difficult to at first grasp, seem to the writer to be well worth study necessary for their understanding, for they show so clearly the causes of loss or gain in the operation of the mills in the past and prove conclusively their ability to make money in the future under proper management.

The process of figuring costs followed with all of the mills is the same, starting with the combined months of "January and February, '05" which are the most recent figures that can be obtained from the present management (and also which months are very good to use as a basis as due to the extreme weather they are usually the most expensive of the year to operate mills in), then taking the year "July 1st, '03–'04" for comparison and from the two showing the causes of loss and gain and the costs under which the mills can be successfully operated.

SCIOTO PULP MILL IN CHILLICOTHE, OHIO

The Pulp Mill statement of March 1st, 1905 shows the following costs for the 2 month period of "Jan. & Feb. '05."

The total pulp made in the two months was 742,766#.

The total number of days the mill was operated was 42½ (out of a possible 50). (Over-supply of pulp being the cause for shutting down.)

Therefore the daily average of the days run was 17,470#.

The five principal items of cost in the manufacture of pulp

The cost of				
Wood =	$5,727.72	= 77.1	Wood	77.1¢. equivalent to $7.71 per cord.
Lime	1,004.44			
Soda Ash	1,673.74 }	= 56.1	Chemicals 56.1¢.	
Bleach	1,496.42			
Labor	2,642.70	= 35.5	Labor	35.5
Fuel	1,552.18	= 20.9	Fuel	20.9
Repairs	142.71	= 1.9		
Expense	1,216.93	= 16.4 }	"O-E"	24.6
Interest & Ins.	466.34	= 6.3		
Total cost		214.2		
Profit	104.63	1.4		

The principal factor in all costs is the output per day, being in the present case (as noted above).

Value of Pulp made—$16,027.81, 215.6. —Being the selling price for pulp for the past two months.

It is apparent from the previous figures, that the five principal items of cost are Wood, Chemicals, Labor, Fuel, and "Other Expenses."

The Wood, which is figured on a basis of $7.71 per cord, the writer does not understand, as the "average per cord" cost should not be over $6.50; therefore, some unusual loss must have come into this item the past two months.

With the previous cost figures as a basis, the causes of loss in the past can best be shown by taking the detailed cost of the year "July 1–03 to July 1–04" for comparison (that being the last complete year before the beginning of the present trouble), which year shows a loss of $6,242.00 (without deducting interest). The costs of the "year 1903–04" on an average output of 16380# per day were:

Wood	61.2¢.	($6.12 per cord)
Chemicals	60.6	
Labor	34.8	
Fuel	27.9	
"O-E"	35.5	Total output for the year was
Tot. cost	220.0	4,732,408#.
Loss	13.0	— Total loss of $6,242.00 for the year.

Selling price, 207.0¢.

A comparison of the above two sets of figures shows that if the "O-E" alone had been reduced during the year of "1903–04" to the figure of the past two months, the loss of the year would have been very nearly eliminated (35.5 − 24.6 = 10.9¢. gain), and that if the selling price of the year had been the same as in the past two months and the "O-E" had been so reduced, a profit of 6.5¢. would have resulted: 215.6 − 207.0 = 8.6¢ − 2.1¢—the difference between loss of 13¢. & gain of 10.9¢. = 6.5—or a profit for the year of $3,121.00.

However, *the greatest cause* of loss in the year "1903–04" as well as at the present time is the low production per day, of pulp, for the 3 items of "Labor," "Fuel" and "O-E" are directly dependent on the production, and it is also a fact that with the mill working up to its capacity, a saving is always effected in "Wood" & "Chemicals," (the only other 2 items of cost), due to the care necessary to the turning out of a greater quantity of pulp.

Comparing the Scioto Pulp Mill with other mills of the country of similar equipment, the production should average 24000# per day at least. The mill is not quite balanced at present, and therefore can not be made to turn out this amount of stock without some additions, but an output of 20,000# should easily be maintained, instead of 17470#, and that this is entirely possible can be shown by past figures, which the writer is doubly sure of, having had charge of the mill at the time (May 1902 Av. for 27 days was 20398#).

The reason for not making this 20000# per day for the past 2 years is that the pulp mill has always been run *only* to supply the paper mills owned by the Company; and that pulp could be manufactured and sold as well as paper, does not seem to have interested the management, although no less than 750 tons of the same kind and quality of pulp are sold by eastern mills in the Miami Valley alone, every month.

(It might be well to mention here, that all the Soda Pulp Mills in the East are and have been for the past year in a well organized association which has very satisfactorily maintained the price at 215.0c. per 100# and as the production and demand are very nearly equal, the association is very sure this price will continue indefinitely, any change being in favor of an increase, especially as there is a demand in Europe for all the soda pulp which can be obtained in this country at the above price.)

The statement of the last 6 months of the year 1902 during which time the pulp mill ran fairly regularly shows the following costs—(The writer has chosen this statement as it is of the only 6 months complete, running full, that he had charge of the mill):

```
Wood................ 48.0c.   ($4.80 per cord).
Chemicals............ 57.1
Labor................ 27.4
Fuel................. 21.5
"O-E"............... 21.5
                    ─────
                    192.0
Profit.............. 11.    —On total output of 2,490,000#—$2739.00
                            (without adding the interest profit.)
```

Selling price, 203.0c.   Daily average = 17,550#.

The following Table gives the Production & Cost of each of the 6 months in detail.

TABLE I

Working days of the month.		Days mill was run.	Average lbs. per day run.	Total lbs. output.	Cost wood per 100#.	Chemicals per 100#.	Labor per 100#.	Fuel per 100#.	Total Mill cost per 100#.
1902.									
July	26	19	15546	295377	45.7	67.8	29.8	24.8	168.1
Aug.	26	23	16550	380656	50.7	57.5	27.2	22.1	157.5
Sept.	25	25	18440	460996	45.9	53.1	24.2	17.8	141.0
Oct.	26	25	18424	478999	50.5	54.4	26.4	20.7	152.0
Nov.	25	25	18044	450949	49.9	53.1	27.0	19.9	149.9
Dec.	24	24	17730	425387	54.4	50.4	26.0	22.5	153.3
Totals.	152	142Av.	17552	2492364	Av48.0	Av57.1	Av27.4	Av21.5	Av154.0

An analysis of the Table shows that the month of July, which was not only a "short" month but also a bad month, due to the low production even on the days run, very materially raises the average cost of the 6 months. However, taking the 6 months, ("Cost A") as a basis for a fair cost of manufacture, the following, "Cost B" results:—

		"A"	"B"
Wood	48.0c.	(4.80 per cord increase to 6.50 per cord)	65.0c. per 100# of pulp made.
Chemicals	57.1	(Price of all chemicals is a little lower now than in '02)	56.5
Labor	27.4	(Wages are same now as in '02)	27.4
Fuel	21.5	(Fuel costs same now as in '02)	21.5
"O-E"	38.0	(Statement of last 2 months shows this to be)	24.6
	192.0	New total cost...........................	195.0c.
		Assuming a selling price of *only*.....................	210.0
		Shows a profit of................................	15.0c.

This profit on an output of *17550#* would make a total of $26.32 per day, for 6 months (of 142 days) of $3737.44, which makes $7474.88 per year. The above cost "B" on an output of 20,000# per day would be reduced as follows:—

COST "C"

Wood	65.0c.	Not affected by increase in output.
Chemicals	56.5	
Labor	24.0	Reduced by increased output to $\frac{17550}{20000}$ of
Fuel	18.8	
"O-E"	21.5	"B" as no more labor, fuel, or "O-E"
Total Cost....	185.8	is required to produce 20000 than 17550#.
Assume	210.0 as selling price (same as above).	
Profit,	24.2c. on 20000# = $48.40 per day or $13745.60 per year	
		(284 days).

NOTE.—The month of "May 1902" which preceded the 6 months of "Table I" not only shows an average output of 20398# per day but also a much lower cost than the above assumed cost "C." Chemicals in "May" cost but 50.7c., Labor 22.8, and Fuel 18.1, and the total cost was 181; however, it is the average month which should be used for a basis of figuring rather than the good one.

That the preceding cost "C" is conservative and that the Pulp Mill can earn under ordinary conditions $13,000 net profit per year is the writer's judgment not only from his personal experience in operating this mill, but also from the figures of the past 6 years (already given in general in the "History"), which show the operation of the plant. (Only the last 6 years are of direct value as the present Dayton Paper Mill was not put into operation until the beginning of the year 1898–99.)

The profits and losses for these years, plus the interest (paid on borrowed money which properly represents profit) ; together with the merchandise sold, are as follows:

Yr. Ending	Profit	Loss	Int.	Total Profit	Net Loss	Total Merchandise sold
July 1–99	$9150		1070	10224		$67910
July 1–00	16767		2344	19111		91891
July 1–01		11716	2435		9281	65427
July 1–02		10285	3151		7134	79193
6 mo. ending Jan. 1–03	2736		1688	4425		50213
July 1–03		1347	1175		173	39608
Yr. ending July 1–04		6242	2340		3902	95946

The above figures may be accounted for as follows: The years '99 and 1900 were profitable and need no comment, except that during the year 1900, the old superintendent, as mentioned in the previous "History," left the Company.

From January 1st., 1901 to July 1st., 1901, the Company having no superintendent or any one in its employ who understood *anything* about pulp making, the mill was operated simply by the workmen without a head. The figures show the disastrous results for the $9281.00 loss above noted occurred practically all in the last 6 months of the year ending July, 1901.

The new superintendent who was employed at this time, although he was supposed to be a general paper maker, had never had charge of, or worked in a pulp mill, and knew nothing of the process of making pulp. This man spent $10,000 (more than the loss) in the year ending July 1, 1902, in repairs, some of which were necessary on account of the run-down condition of the plant, but a great deal of which was used in putting in various pieces of machinery which were not only unnecessary but a part of which has since been discarded for the old which he had torn out.

As previously mentioned, the writer was employed in the spring of this year, 1902, and remained with the Company until July 1st., 1903, as manager of the Scioto Mills. The 6 months following, July 1st., 1902, are shown above as earning a profit of $4425.00, as against a loss of $7134 the previous year. This rate of profit making could have easily been maintained, which would have made a total profit for the year of $8850, but for the shutting down of one of the paper machines (which was moved from Dayton to Chillicothe during January to June, 1903). Of course the excess Pulp *should* have been sold during this period, and the Pulp Mill run on the same or a greater output than in the previous 6 months; but this was not done, and as shown by the "Merchandise" sold, the production was materially cut down, and a natural loss resulted, though of small proportion, ($172.00).

With this above mentioned paper machine added to the Scioto Mill, the pulp Mill should have shown a greater profit in 1903–04 than in the first six months of 1902–03, as the saving in freight alone on pulp was considerable, but again the mill was operated at a loss, due to the lack of a man who knew how to make pulp as well as lack of management all around, and when it is considered that pulp making is essentially a chemical process, it is only natural that the losses from lack of knowledge should reach such figures.

The Pulp Mill is in better condition today than it was in 1903, having recently been improved, after a fire, which fortunately destroyed that part of the mill which needed rebuilding, and the costs of manufacture are almost exactly the same now as then, any change being in favor of the present; the increase in the cost of wood being entirely taken care of by the increase in the selling price of the pulp. Therefore, "Cost C," which shows the manufacturing cost to be approximately 185c. per 100, and a corresponding profit of 25c. based entirely on the present and past operation of the mill, is certainly a most liberal cost upon which to figure future profits, and it should be noted that the many little economies which naturally will result from careful management and improved methods, are in no way figured or included in the estimated profit of .25c. per pound.

SCIOTO PAPER MILL IN CHILLICOTHE, OHIO

The Scioto Paper Mill statement of March 1st., 1905, shows the following costs for the 2 month period of Jan. & Feb., '05:

The total paper made in the 2 months was 1,324,119#.

The number of days the mill was operated was 51.

The daily production of the day's run was 26,000# average per day.

The cost of — Per 100# of paper made.

Wood Pulp	$23780.50	=	179.6c.	Paper stock	202.4
Material	3019.40		22.8		
Labor	4280.02		32.3	Labor	32.2
Repairs	377.51		2.9	Repairs	2.9
Fuel	3266.95		24.6	Expense	45.6
Expense	2776.52		21.0		
Interest	286.53		2.2	Interest	2.2
Profit	3363.89		25.4		285.4
Paper sold	41151.32				25.4
					310.8 Selling price on paper made

NOTE.—These subdivisions are chosen to make comparison with other statements easier. Fuel and Expense are combined because in past years the fuel account has been kept under the "Expense Account."

NOTE #2.—To the above profit there should be added, according to the statement of March 1st., $248.99, being a correction for a loss on a special lot of stock paper.

This would make a total profit for 2 months of $3612.12 or for the year $21677.28 (exclusive of the interest charges.)

Again taking for comparison the costs for the year July '03–July '04, which shows a profit of only $6801.69 (without interest) on an output of 24620# per day.

Wood Pulp cost per 100#	169.3c.	P.S.	193.5
Material	24.2		
Labor	34.2		34.2
Repairs	6.2		6.2
Expense	53.4		53.4
Interest	4.9		4.9
			292.2
Profit ($6801.69)	9.7		9.7
			301.9 Selling price on paper made.

That these costs may better be compared, they are again tabulated as follows:

(Year 03–04)		"Jan. & Feb. '05"	Differences	
Paper Stock	193.5	202.4	8.9	The daily output for the year "July 03–04" being 24620#. The daily output for "Jan. & Feb. 05" being 26000#.
Labor	34.2	32.3	1.9	
Repairs	6.2	2.9	3.3	
Expense	53.4	45.6	7.8	
Interest	4.9	2.2	2.7	
			15.7	
Profits	9.7	25.4	15.7	
Selling Price	301.9	310.8	8.9	

The preceding table shows the increase in cost of "paper stock" to be exactly offset by the increase in selling price, therefore, the difference in the item can be eliminated and the savings which make the increase in profits are all found in the four items of Labor, Repairs, Expense and Interest.

The causes of these savings can best be shown as follows:

Labor at 34.2c. $\times$ 24620# per day = 26000# at 32.2 = Saving of		1.9
Repairs 6.2c. $\times$ 24620# per day = 26000# at 5.8 = Saving of	.4	
Economy of management effected in Repairs, a further saving of	2.9	3.3
Expense at 53.4 $\times$ 24620# per day = 26000# at 50.6 = Saving of	2.8	
Salaries included in expense for "03–04" were 7.8c.;		
in "05" were 2.8c. = Saving of	5.0	7.8
Interest at 4.9 $\times$ 24620# per day = 26000# at 4.6 = Saving of	.3	
Other difference in interest charges = Saving of	2.4	2.7
Total saving of		15.7
Add to this the real profit of "03–04" of 9.7 giving a total of		9.7
and the result is the same as the profit of "Jan. & Feb. 05."		25.4

The above shows that simply by an increase in output of 1380# per day a saving of 5.4c. per 100 pound has been effected, that by reduction in the salary account, a savings of 5c. per 100 pound has been effected, that by reduction in repairs, a saving of 2.9c. has been effected, and in interest 2.4.

The above comparisons clearly show that the only causes for the mill not making over $20,000 profit during the year 1903–04 were extravagance in management (large expense) and lack of pressure on the practical operation of the mill, resulting in not getting out of the plant the production of which it was capable.

That the past two months have not only been not particularly good ones but below the average, is shown by a comparison with the statement of March 1st, 1905, which gives the total profit for the 8 months of the current fiscal year. This statement shows the profits to be so far $14,450.52, and the interest charges to be $1,902.33 or a total net profit of $16,353.85 for the past 8 months, which is at the rate of $24,530.00 per year (quite as high a rate as for the past 2 months).

When the chaotic condition of the company is considered, and also the fact that only recently have reductions been made in expenses, it seems extraordinary that this mill can show such a good record; for from July 1st to Nov. 1st., the management remained the same as in past years, and since the Company has been in the hands of the present Trustees, very little time or thought indeed has been given to the practical end of the business.

It is the opinion of the writer that this mill has proven completely by this 8 months record (the conditions in the paper trade being perfectly normal) its ability to make under ordinary conditions at least $25,000 with every possibility of a much greater profit. It has been a consistent money maker for the past ten years, having in that time run but one year at a loss (1901 the year the whole plant was operated without a superintendent or practical man of any sort, and everything lost money); and in this ten years with but one paper machine, and an output of approximately only 13,000# per day it has *averaged* a profit of over $10,000 per year (including the 1901 loss).

DAYTON PAPER MILL IN DAYTON, OHIO

The Dayton Paper Mill statement of March 1st, 1905, shows the following costs for the 2 months period of "Jan. & Feb. 05."

The total paper made in 2 months was 893,147#.

The number of days the mill was operated was 50.

The daily production of the day's run was 17,860# average per day.

		Per 100# of			
The cost of		paper made			

The cost of			Per 100# of paper made		
Wood Pulp	=	$15,074.97 =	168.8	⎱—Paper stock..........194.1c.	
Material	=	2,255.97	25.3	⎰	
Labor	=	3,991.05	44.7	—Labor..........	44.7
Repairs	=	249.21	2.8	—Repairs.........	2.8
Fuel	=	1,539.12	17.2	—Expense........	53.4
Expense	=	3,233.59	36.2		
Interest	=	264.34	3.0	—Interest.........	3.0
Drayage	=	62.55	.7	—Drayage........	.7
Profit		468.06	5.3	—Profit...........	5.3
Paper sold		27,300.03	304.0	—Selling price.........	304.0

The statement for the year "July 1–03 to July 1–04" shows the following costs with an average daily output of 20982# (for 254½ days = total of 5,339,919#).

Wood Pulp per 100# paper made...............	162.3⎱ P.S.		188.8
Material per 100# paper made...................	26.5⎰		45.1
Labor...................................	45.1		45.1
Repairs...................................	2.7		2.7
Expense...................................	64.9		64.9
Interest...................................	6.8		6.8
Drayage...................................	1.2		1.2
Loss ($7,586.76)...............14.2		14.2	
Paper sold...................................	295.4	14	295.4

The statements for the year "July 03–04" shows that this mill averaged throughout the year 20982# per day output. It is therefore entirely fair to assume that it can again be made to run at such an average output or at least 20,000# per day, and upon a 20,000# a day output we will base our further costs.

The reasons for so low a daily output as 17,860#, which has been the average for the past two months, are the paper machine having been down so much in the preceding 6 months (on account of the Interstate Paper Co. connection) which not only effect somewhat the smoothness of the machine's running, but also demoralized the labor in the mill; and the class of paper which has been made on the machine. Both of these troubles would have been avoided had the Company not become connected with the Interstate Paper Company.

For comparison the costs of the past 2 months on a 17860# basis and deduced to a 20000# basis, and also the costs of "July 03–04" are tabulated below.

	Jan. & Feb. 05 on 17860#	Jan. & Feb. 05 on 20000#	July 03–04 on 20980#		Diff. & Bet. II & III
Paper Stock...	194.1	194.1	188.8	5.3	
Labor........	44.7	39.9	45.1		— 5.2
Repairs......	2.8	2.4	2.7		— .3
Expense......	53.4	47.7	64.9		— 17.2
Interest......	3.	2.7	6.8		— 4.1
Drayage......	.7	.6	1.2		— .6
					27.4 Total
					14.2 Loss
Selling price..	304.0	304.0	295.4	8.6	
				Profit	3.3 plus 13.2 = 16.5c.
					Total profit
Profit........	5.3c.	16.6c.	14.2		
		Loss			

Represents a profit on the paper made of $9,960.00

Represents a profit of $9,900.

The preceding table shows that if the past two months had been on a 20000# per day basis, the profits would have been at the rate of $9,960.00 per year; and that if the same economies had been in effect in "July 03–04" as in the past 2 months, the profits would have been approximately the same as the 2 month's rate, being according to the above figures $9,900.00 for the year.

It should be noted that both of the above profits are figured *without* adding the interest charges; and with the interest added the rate of profit making for the past 2 months would be $11,580.00 per year.

The statement of Jan. 1st, 1905 of the Dayton Mill, shows a loss for the 6 months since July 1st, 1904 of $7,094.97, or over $1,000 per month; however, the total sales for this same 6 months amounted to only $48,677.00 or $8,113 per month, while the sales for the past 2 months have averaged $13,650 per month. The very low average sales for the 6 months period are accounted for by the fact of the mill being shut down for such a great portion of that time for the lack of orders. The number of days run out of a possible 150 was 89 and the average number of pounds made per day was 18890. Such loss as a result of such mill operation is only natural.

The machinery in the Dayton Mill is all comparatively new, since the mill was entirely rebuilt is 1898 and a new and modern paper machine installed, and as the plant is in entirely good condition today, it should make a profit of $10,000 per year if properly managed.

This mill with its comparatively new and entirely modern machinery, particularly the paper machine itself (which was built to turn out a daily production of not less than 22,000# per day), should properly show a greater profit per pound of paper made than the Chillicothe paper mill and this unquestionably would be the result were it so located that labor, fuel, etc., could be obtained at the same figure as in Chillicothe. In its present position the mill should show a cost and profit as figured, and $10,000 a year total for the profit is a reasonable estimate; however, in the writer's judgment in view of the comparative costs of manufacture in Dayton and Chillicothe which show a 100% advantage in profits in favor of Chillicothe, and also the history of the plants of both locations which proves that the mills in Chillicothe have, as a whole, never shown a loss in the 14 years of their existence (except the year they were allowed to run without superintendent or supervision of any sort) it would be a mistake not to move the Dayton plant to Chillicothe at the earliest opportunity.

So placed, this Dayton Mill machinery would show a profit of not less than $20,000 per year and that more surely than $10,000 in its present position for the advantages of a concentrated plant are innumerable.

The foregoing pages of costs and profits may be summarized as follows:

CHILLICOTHE PLANT

	Daily Product	Days run	Prod. per Year	Total Value	Profits
Pulp Mill......	20000#	300	6,000,000#	$126,000	$13,000
Paper Mill.....	26000#	305	7,800,000#	245,830	25,000
				$371,830	$38,000

DAYTON PLANT

	Daily Product	Days run	Prod. per Year	Total Value	Profits
Paper Mill.....	20000#	300	6,000,000	183,000	10,000
				$554,830	$48,000

It should be noted that the total net profit is not even 10% of the total value of the manufactured product (which represents total business done), and certainly 10% is a conservative manufacturing profit in any business.

A consolidation of the plants in Chillicothe would, in the writer's judgment, result in the following increases:

	Daily Product	Days run	Prod. per Year	Total Value	Profits
Pulp Mill......	20000#	300	6,000,000#	$126,000	$13,000
Combined Paper Mills.........	50000#	300	15,000,000	465,000	45,000
				$591,000	$58,000

Still figuring a net profit of less than 10% of the total value of the product or business done.

The writer has purposely avoided future possibilities in profits which would result from careful management of the manufacturing end of the business and more energetic and thorough direction of the selling of the product; and has, particularly in the case of the Chillicothe plants, based every figure of cost on the actual operation of the mills under present and past conditions, the only instance of any estimates of profits being higher than have been shown in the past being on the Dayton Mill in its present location.

The Pulp Mill which, in the judgment of several paper mill experts, with whom the writer has consulted, forms the foundation that makes the enterprise particularly valuable, the writer knows thoroughly the condition of and its manufacturing possibilities, and he believes the figures of cost and profit in this department are very conservative. The Chillicothe Paper Mill needs no further comment; it is and has been running for the past 9 months at the same rate of profit making as is used in all present figuring. The intrinsic value of the Dayton Mill is undoubted but it must be understood that while it is at present running at a small profit, it will take careful managing for a few months to bring it to the desired standard, for the margin of profit at best is not nearly so great as in the other mills.

NOTE:—Since the above figures have been compiled, the Statement of April 1st, 1905 has been brought out and shows for the month of "March" costs and profits almost exactly the same as the preceding for "Jan. & Feb. 05."

GENERAL

Quite as important as the past history and the profits that can be made out of the business at the present time, is the question of its value as compared with other plants manufacturing the same product, as well as how it will stand future competition and development.

It has been shown that in the manufacture of pulp the chief items of cost in the order of their importance are: "Wood," "Chemicals," "Labor" and "Fuel," to which is lastly added the "overhead" charges, or so-called "Other Expenses," and these same items of cost in the same order apply to all Soda Pulp Mills in the country.

There are 19 companies in the United States manufacturing Soda Pulp; 4 in New England, 12 in the Eastern States (New York, Pennsylvania, Delaware, Maryland and Virginia), 1 in Montana, 1 in Washington, and 1 in Ohio (The Mead Paper Co.). Therefore, the Pulp Mill in Chillicothe is the only Soda Mill west of the Allegheny Mountains except the two in the far west, which are very small and do a purely local business.

It seems extraordinary that this central section of the country should be so neglected, but while the eastern mills have recognized and quickly taken advantage of the value of this kind of pulp for high grade papers, the western mills seem to still adhere to the older practice, and that the substitutes which they use are inferior is shown by the fact of The Mead Paper Co. having a reputation for making the best sheet of paper of its grade that goes into the Chicago market from the western manufacturers.

Considering the items of cost, the first, "Wood" is lower than in any mill within the writer's knowledge. The group of Pennsylvania, New York, Maryland, and Delaware mills, all pay between $7.00 and $7.50 for their wood which represents an addition to the cost of pulp of from 5 to 10¢ per 100#, and the New England mills costs are quite as high.

The visible wood supply in the vicinity of Chillicothe is adequate for 10 years' production at least, and at the end of that period this plant will be in quite as good a position comparatively, as any of the soda pulp mills now in operation.

"Chemicals" cost exactly the same delivered in Chillicothe as elsewhere and any advantage one mill may have over another is entirely in the care of manipulating them.

The "labor" in Chillicothe is as satisfactory as in any mill in the country and 10% cheaper per man, giving another advantage over competitors; while "Fuel" is likewise cheaper than in any other mill within the writer's knowledge, since natural gas is certainly cheaper than any coal and even coal can be obtained most reasonably in Chillicothe.

Therefore, with almost every factor of cost in favor of this mill, no competitor in the same section of the country, and a ready market for its product at all times in the paper mills of the same company, there isn't any possible reason why this department of the business should not earn more than its share of the necessary profits, for an indefinite future time as well as at present, as it has in the past, when properly operated.

The chief items of cost in the manufacture of paper have been shown to be "Paper Stock," "Labor," "Fuel," and the "overhead" charges or "O-E" (although the "Fuel" item has not been kept separately in the past but has been included in "Expense," it should most assuredly be so considered, as it is by far the largest single items of cost next to Paper Stock and Labor).

"Paper Stock" costs approximately the same in all mills, and therefore excluding the fact of having nearly one-half of it supplied from the Company's own Pulp Mill, this paper mill would be on quite the same footing as its competitors, but the value of having so much of its own supply is indeed considerable, especially in the Chillicothe mill where all freight costs are eliminated as well as expense of handling. Furthermore, it is a fact that a better quality of paper results from the use of pulp which is not dried, which is only possible when it is used directly from a pulp mill or shipped but a short distance.

The items of "Labor" and "Fuel" in the Chillicothe Paper Mill are just as favorable to low cost of manufacture as in the Pulp Mill, and give it a decided advantage over all competitors. The Dayton Mill is not so fortunate for the labor and fuel in the Miami Valley average about the same as in most other industrial sections of the country. While there are many more paper than pulp mills in the United States, manufacturing similar grades of stock, the advantages of Chillicothe as a location for a mill of this character cannot be too strongly emphasized, and with cheap pulp, labor and fuel and the excellent shipping facilities afforded by 3 railroads (the B. & O., N. & W., and C. H. & D.), it is the writer's firm belief that it can compete with any mill in the country in almost any market, not only at the present time, but throughout the future.

The question of the sale of the finished product, requires little comment. The total output of the plants is comparatively small and the trade of the Company is nearly all of long standing and of the highest credit. That this department can be improved there is no question and its proper handling should result in materially increasing the profits of the Company, since for many years the selling of the Mead Paper Company's product has been accomplished with little effort or trouble; and in spite of the recent vicissitudes of the business, its reputation for manufacturing good paper continues.

The value of this business is therefore, quite as great from a general standpoint as from the direct manufacturing point of view, and the writer in a most searching and thorough investigation has failed to find any obstacle whatever to the making of a great success of the enterprise.

That a great deal of money has been made out of the manufacture of book papers in the past, recent and remote, there is no question, and with such market advantages and practically no disadvantages in manufacturing, as compared with its competitors; an established high class trade and good reputation for turning out excellent paper, the writer is convinced not only of the safety of the proposition financially, but also of its being a most profitable business if properly managed, and in this judgment he has been upheld by some very able manufacturers from whom he has asked an opinion.

SUPPLEMENTARY SHEETS SHOWING HOW COSTS WERE FIGURED

ANALYSIS OF JAN. & FEB. 1905, BUSINESS

SCIOTO PULP MILL

Da. Av........................	17470#
Days run.....................	42½
Pulp made...................	742766#

	Jan. 1–05 Statement	Inventory	Balance	Mar. 1–05 Balance	Difference	Cost per 100#
Wood........	$26,137.16	$20,415.00	$5,722.16	$11,449.88	$5,727.72	77.1
Lime.........	1,915.66	230.57	1,685.09	2,689.53	1,004.44	13.5
Fuel.........	3,717.70	....	3,717.70	5,269.88	1,552.18	20.9
Expense.....	4,389.54	434.51	3,955.03	5,171.96	1,216.92	16.4
Labor........	5,195.84	....	5,195.84	7,838.54	2,642.70	35.5
Repairs......	1,082.27	....	1,082.27	1,224.98	142.71	1.9
Bleach.......	3,169.81	131.12	3,038.69	4,535.11	1,496.42	20.1
Soda Ash.....	3,360.88	1,028.00	2,332.88	4,006.62	1,673.74	22.5
Interest......	1,156.99	....	1,156.99	1,340.62	183.63	2.5
Insurance....	....	....	....	282.71	282.71	3.8
				Profit	104.63	1.4
Soda Pulp....	23,651.65	1,631.88	25,283.53	41,311.34	16,027.81	215.6
Loss	2,603.12	....	2,603.12	2,498.49		

Mar. 1–05   Balance

Rearrangement of above cost per 100#

Wood......	$29,856.13	$18,406.25	$11,449.88	Wood 77.1	77.1	77.1	
Lime......	2,895.78	206.25	2,689.53	Lime 13.5			
				Soda			
Fuel.......	5,426.13	156.25	5,269.88	Ash 22.5	36.0		
				Bleach 20.1	20.1	56.1	
Expense....	5,506.21	334.25	5,171.96	Labor 35.5			
Labor......	7,838.54	....	7,838.54	Fuel 20.9		56.4	189.6
Repairs....	1,224.98	....	1,224.98	Rep. 1.9			
Bleach.....	4,577.03	41.92	4,535.11	Expns. 16.4		18.3	
Soda Ash...	4,569.62	563.00	4,006.62	Int. 2.5			
Interest....	1,340.62	....	1,340.62	Insur. 3.8		6.3	24.6 214.2
Insur.......	282.71	....	282.71	Prof. 1.4		1.4	1.4 1.4
Soda Pulp..	40,059.71	1,251.63	41,311.34				215.6
Loss.......	2,498.49	....	2,498.49				

ANALYSIS OF JAN. & FEB. 1905, BUSINESS

SCIOTO PAPER MILL

DA. AV.............	26000#
DAYS RUN........	51
PAPER MADE......	1324119#

	Jan. 1–05 Statement	Inventory	Balance	Mar. 1–05 Balance	Differ- ence	Cost per 100#
Wood Pulp.....	$83,263.86	$15,637.30	$67,626.56	$91,407.06	$23,780.50	179.6
Material........	10,785.70	1,902.77	8,882.93	11,902.33	3,019.40	22.8
Expense........	18,922.02	1,812.02	17,110.00	19,886.52	2,776.52	21.0
Interest........	1,615.80		1,615.80	1,902.33	386.53	2.2
Labor..........	12,364.21		12,364.21	16,644.23	4,280.02	32.3
Fuel...........	1,380.74	215.63	1,165.11	4,432.06	3,266.95	24.6
Repairs........	426.71		426.71	804.22	377.51	2.9
Profit..........	11,086.63		11,086.63	14,450.52	3,363.89	25.4

NOTE:—Actual profit for two months was 248.99 higher than given above due to "Job lot" loss. Therefore, total profit equals $3,612.88 or $21,677.28 per year.

	Jan. 1–05 Statement	Inventory	Balance	Mar. 1–05 Balance	Differ- ence	Cost per 100#
Mdse..........	$113,961.38	$ 6,316.57	$120,277.95	$161,429.27	$41,151.32	310.8

	Mar. 1–05		Balance
Wood Pulp.....	$99,331.86	$ 7,924.80	$91,407.06
Material........	13,213.79	1,311.46	11,902.33
Expense........	22,050.13	2,163.61	19,886.52
Interest........	1,902.33		1,902.33
Labor..........	16,644.23		16,644.23
Fuel...........	4,744.56	312.50	4,432.06
Repairs........	804.22		804.22
Profit..........	14,450.52		14,450.52
Mdse..........	157,015.27	4,414.00	161,429.27

ANALYSIS OF JAN. & FEB. 1905, BUSINESS

DAYTON MILL

Da. Av.	17860#
Days run	50
Paper made	893147#

	Jan. 1–05 Statement	Inventory	Balance	Mar. 1–05 Balance	Diff.	Cost per 100#
Paper Stock	$35,025.79	$7,804.34	$27,221.45	$42,296.42	$15,074.97	168.8
Material...	8,226.93	3,068.34	5,158.59	7,414.56	2,255.97	25.3 (194.1)
Expense...	14,086.35	2,721.02	11,365.33	14,598.92	3,233.59	36.2
Labor.....	8,446.31		8,446.31	12,437.36	3,991.05	44.7
Interest....	1,867.20		1,867.20	2,131.54	264.34	3.0
Fuel......	749.32	191.25	558.07	2,097.19	1,539.12	17.2
Repairs....	968.78		968.78	1,217.99	249.21	2.8
Drayage...	192.14		192.14	254.69	62.55	.7
				Prof.—	468.06	5.3
Mdse......	40,855.37	7,822.08 (Correction)	48,677.45	75,977.48	27,300.03	306.0
Loss......	7,094.97	(125.00)	7,219.97	6,751.91		
					M.M. =	111.9

	March 1–05 Statement	Inventory	Balance
Paper Stock	$46,729.45	$4,433.03	$42,296.42
Material...	9,899.74	2,485.18	7,414.56
Expense...	17,528.90	2,929.98	14,598.92
Labor.....	12,437.36		12,437.36
Interest....	2,131.54		2,131.54
Fuel......	2,224.69	127.50	2,097,19
Repairs....	1,217.99		1,217.99
Drayage...	254.69		254.69
Mdse......	68,935.65	7,041.83 Correction	75,977.48
Loss......	6,441.89	(310.02)	6,751.91

Remarks and Speeches

Mr. Mead spoke regularly and openly to the men with whom he worked. Only one of his speeches extant in the Mead files was prepared ahead of time, and it was one of the very few public addresses directed to persons outside the Mead organization. The others were entirely impromptu and were typically taken down by court stenographers for later circulation throughout the company.

Selections from the Remarks and Speeches of George H. Mead

PRESIDENT'S DINNER, Chillicothe, February 8, 1922

In perhaps fifty years of industrial life in America—perhaps in the entire history of the country—there has never been a year quite so severe in industrial and financial affairs as the past year . . .

At such a time the unfortunate executive of a company is called upon to do many things that do not ordinarily come into the regular routine of his duties . . . I have been compelled to spend many nights and many days travelling in an effort to do my part toward keeping the wheels down at the end of Paint Street turning.

The Mead Pulp and Paper Company made a profit for the year at a time when, to my particular knowledge, no other paper company in the United States has been able to operate without loss . . . Our company was able to accomplish this because of the cooperation of all employees . . .

There is no reason why the Mill Council should not be as much familiar with the policies of the company as the directors are. There is no reason why the Mill Council should not take to the employees these policies and endeavor to have every man working in unison and harmony to the end of accomplishing the policies that are set forth . . . The men who are working at the machines should know exactly what they are working for.

PRESIDENT'S DINNER, Chillicothe, 1923

I am not as interested in production records as I am in quality records. If any man in this room can take back to the mill with him the solemn resolve to try to turn out only A-1 quality, and to teach every man in the mill the same thing, and if the quality is not right to give to the management of the company suggestions and advice that will help to make it right . . . we will have the information that the products of the Mead Pulp and Paper Company cannot be equaled in this country. That is the way to sell paper . . .

The way to sell a product is to make it so good that it advertises itself . . . I am perfectly willing to work as many hours a day as necessary in financing this company and selling its product if you men will assure me that you will make every possible effort to make the production the best that can be produced . . .

We must not only make a better product, but we must develop a new product . . .

Processes that have been in use for the past generation—the methods of manufacture, the way of doing this, that, and the other thing, will soon be forgotten . . . The companies that insist upon following old methods ... will one by one fall by the wayside and lose their identity and finally their lives. The company that can devise new methods, that can forsee the necessity of improved processes for materially decreasing the cost of production and such like will have possibilities such as never before.

You men know me well enough to appreciate that the management of this company does not feel that the proper way to reduce costs of production is by reduction of wages. I am firmly of the opinion, and you men know it, that labor has never been paid an excessive wage and that every man is worthy of his hire. I would rather see advancing wages than declining wages. But unless we have with advancing wages new development and labor-saving devices, the progress of the company will be of short duration, and our end will be one of disaster ...

I believe the most important part of our future development will be in the paper machines. I liken a paper machine at the present time to an automobile of a few years ago ... We are not holding our own with other lines of industry ... we are working almost no changes and we are suffering about as many breaks as we did ten years ago ... The automobile has outclassed us in refinement ...

I feel that throughout the development of this company we have had an understanding spirit that has meant the development of truth for truth's sake. It is only by being real men and dealing honestly and fair in all things that real success is attainable. The dollar success is bound to come as a result of that spirit of cooperation; perhaps not the maximum financial return, but that is not what this company is seeking. It is only seeking a fair return for honest service rendered.*

PRESIDENT'S DINNER, Chillicothe, 1924

The Mead Pulp and Paper Company seldom shuts down. We have a splendid record in that direction ... The only way we can continue that record is by quality of our product. We must, in spite of the increased production, maintain a uniform quality of paper. I am encouraged each year by the improvement made in this regard. If you go over the samples of ten years, seven years, or five years ago, you will see gradual improvement in the quality of our product. We still have a long way to go ... a quality product is the one thing that will insure continued operations ...

I think the next twenty years will show results that are beyond the comprehension of anyone in this room or in the paper industry.

However, we are not after bigness. I am not interested in our company being the biggest unit in the book paper manufacturing industry. I am only interested ... in being the best in our leadership and first in the good we can do to ourselves and our families, and then to our stockholders, then to our very fine customers, and then to the industry and to the world at large.

PRESIDENT'S DINNER, Chillicothe, January 18, 1925

After safety, above all things we must strive for better quality during the year 1925 ...

I hope the time will come when I will act only as an advisor to the organization of the company.

PRESIDENT'S DINNER, Chillicothe, January 10, 1926

It will be difficult to review a period of twenty years without injecting some personality into the discussion. I will take the liberty of so doing, feeling that you men know me well enough to believe that I have no thought that the success of this institution in its past twenty years of growth is due to any one man and perhaps least of all to myself.

The success that the Mead Pulp and Paper Company has enjoyed, and its present position,

---

*Earlier in the evening, another speaker had made a distinction between research for truth that will yield dollars and research for truth for truth's sake.

is due to the splendid record of cooperation that has existed for these twenty years among the men who have worked shoulder to shoulder, from the laborer in the woodyard to the chief executive of the company. No other spirit, gentlemen, will ever bring success to any institution.

We see temporary growths and we see many declines in business. The great majority of failures come from jealousies, from conceit, from characteristics which do not make real men or real development . . .

We are not in this world of business, gentlemen, solely to make money. It should be the object of our work and our daily lives, first, to make our families happy and then to make our fellowmen happy. Fortunately, to accomplish this to the fullest extent, we must be successful from the financial standpoint.

I think the record of accidents in the Mead Pulp and Paper Company plant indicates more clearly than any other how, by giving thought and attention to our fellow workmen, we can reduce suffering and save the greatest of all things—the lives of other men. I am particularly pleased with this endeavor and want to express to the men who have been working on the safety program the delight I feel in the progress made along this line. In the last four years the accidents have been reduced from fifty to seven. That is a greater performance, gentlemen, than paying the dividends which have been paid to our stockholders.

Twenty years ago on the first of November I came to Chillicothe, having previously resided in Philadelphia, and signed a contract with The Ross County Bank of Chillicothe, the Dayton National Bank of Dayton and The Merchants National Bank of Cincinnati to take over the entire business of the then Mead Paper Company. There were associated with me some Chillicothe and Dayton gentlemen who had agreed to put up a modest amount of money to give to the banks a slight margin over the loans that they then held against the company. I have said many times since that if I had had any real experience in the paper business or if I had known one-tenth of what I think I know now I would have taken the next train back to Philadelphia and not signed anything.

You men will later see that the business we took over was almost worthless. The plant in Chillicothe, as well as the plant in Dayton, was in a very dilapidated condition. The boilers were of the old tubular type, of about 125 horsepower each, and leaking so badly that the insurance companies refused to carry insurance on them. There was not a piece of machinery in the mill that was, perhaps, fit to be operated at the time. I am happy to say that there are a great many men in this room who were present when I walked into the mill twenty years ago. I am sure they will feel I am not exaggerating in any of the statements I may make.

The physical part of this institution was in a very dilapidated condition. The financial part of the institution, as you will see from the few figures to be shown, was in a depleted condition. I had worked in this mill two or three years previous as a much despised chemist, a useless chemist who happened along and was given a job to keep the pulp mill from leaking money. I had learned to know intimately a number of the men who worked in the plant. While I figured that the physical and financial ends of the concern were practically useless I felt confident that the personal side of the Mead Paper Company, the men who were working in its plants, were worth any possible effort I might put in the business and that if I could provide a leader for this fine group of individuals the business could not help but succeed no matter what we had to work with . . .

In 1905 the company had $283,000 invested. That is the value that was placed upon the property, pictures of which we saw a few minutes ago. I don't think the property was worth that amount; in fact, I have my doubts if it was worth $3,000. However, as I said a few minutes ago, it was not the physical value that I was interested in but the personal value, the fact that there was here an organization that could do things if it was given a chance.

During the first five years, it was very, very difficult to raise money for the purpose of replacing equipment. We had great difficulty in adding enough equipment to give the organization half a chance and the consequence was that for the years 1905 to 1910 the progress of the company was very slow and its growth not very rapid.

It always takes a few years, gentlemen, for any business to establish credit because bankers and investors are accustomed to failures. It is a matter of statistics that over ninety per cent of the business ventures started in this or any other country fail: in other words, the percentage of success in business is something between seven and ten per cent. Naturally, men of means and those responsible for other people's money must be most cautious and careful. With a young company, and particularly with a young management that is untried and unproved, the bankers must refuse to give assistance until they are convinced by actual operation that the business that is being offered to them for financing is being properly handled and it has a chance of succeeding.

From 1910 to 1915, the development of the company was a little more rapid. I believe most of you men, probably 90 per cent, know of the development that has taken place from 1915 to 1925.

THE MEAD PULP AND PAPER CO.

	Nov. 1, 1905	Nov. 1, 1925
Plant and Equipment........................	$320,089	$ 6,954,238
Inventory.................................	46,071	1,009,953
Bills and Accounts Receivable................	72,358	898,777
Cash.....................................	291	1,171,702
Deferred Charges..........................	100	560,968
	$438,909	$10,595,638
Capital Invested..........................	$250,000	$ 7,043,000
Bills and Accounts Payable..................	155,906	1,061,670
Surplus and Reserve........................	33,003	2,490,968
	$438,909	$10,595,638

This, gentlemen, is what is called the balance sheet of the company. It is reduced to a few figures, and it is my wish that all who are stockholders of the company gradually learn to understand what a balance sheet is. There is no reason why all should not be equally well versed in the analysis of figures, particularly as the great majority of those present* are stockholders in the company, and I propose in the future to have sent to every man who is in our employ and holds stock, the annual statement of the company . . .

Our quick assets are now three to one, which makes a statement any bank in the United States would be delighted to loan money on . . . I was running around with my tongue hanging out borrowing five or ten thousand dollars a few years ago, and now we can sit and think about it . . .

It never occurred to me ten years ago that I should be sitting at a table as chief executive of a company worth ten million dollars. This shows what conscientious honest effort will do and what can be accomplished if you work together and for the purpose of doing something for the benefit of humanity as well as to satisfy your pocketbook.

PRESIDENT'S DINNER, Kingsport, Jan. 17, 1927

We have been having a so-called President's Banquet for many years in Chillicothe and likewise elsewhere in the companies in which I happen to be interested as an executive . . .

Perhaps most important of all, I felt that such an occasion would give me the opportunity of telling the men in the organization the ideals and principles upon which we were building our business and the policies upon which we propose to operate in the future, with the hope of making our undertaking not a moderate or a purely business success, but a real success from the standpoint of the highest ideals that we know in business . . .

The lack of success of the Mead Fibre Company up to the present time has been the fault of the President of the Company . . . I have the responsibility of determining the policies of

---

*Those present were employees of the company.

these companies, and if I cannot determine the policy which makes for success this year or last year or the year before, I think I should be frank enough with myself to acknowledge it . . .

One of the reasons for our lack of success, in spite of the fact that we have been in the worst period of the paper industry, is our failure to manufacture the best product that could be made in the soda pulp industry . . .

There has never been a time since I assumed any authority in the Mead Pulp and Paper Company that my door has not been open to every member of our organization. Any man who is on the payroll knows that he has the privilege of coming to see me to discuss any question that pertains to the operations of our business or any question that pertains to his family affairs.

FOREMEN'S CLUB, Chillicothe, December 3, 1934*

I little thought when I talked with you last year about this time, that before another twelve months passed, I would be a real member of the United States Government. Having been a life-long Republican, the idea of contributing to a Democratic Administration was probably the last thought in my mind. But I told you at our last meeting something about the N.R.A. from the viewpoint of one who had had a part in the making of codes, and how the paper industry in particular, and all other industries in general, had been called to Washington to work upon this part of the New Deal, and to develop a new industrial situation, that to my way of thinking was not particularly new after all. It was the culmination of many years of thinking in business which would permit of association work in industries without fear of infringing upon the anti-trust laws which had been put together over a period of some thirty or more years. I also mentioned to you, if I remember correctly, the fact that I had been working on a Council in Washington called the Business Advisory and Planning Council, which was appointed by Secretary Roper of the Department of Commerce.

Immediately after the present administration was inaugurated into office, there were about fifty men selected by the Secretary of Commerce to serve on what he determined to call his Advisory Council, these men being largely industrial men from different parts of the country, and from different industries. When the N.R.A. was conceived and the Administration set up, General Johnson requested Mr. Roosevelt to appoint three Boards, one representing the consumer, one labor, and one industry to act as Advisory Boards to him, as the chief Administrator of the N.R.A. Mr. Roosevelt asked Mr. Ickes of the Department of the Interior to appoint the Consumers' Board. The Labor Board, he, of course, asked Miss Perkins to appoint, and the Industrial Board he asked Mr. Roper, the Secretary of Commerce to appoint.

Mr. Roper naturally turned to his so-called Advisory Council and selected from that Council seven men to serve as the Industrial Advisory Board to General Johnson. The seven men originally picked were asked to serve for the first few months. The time was not determined at the beginning, and, subsequently, because of the necessity that these men give a great deal of their time, Secretary Roper was asked to relieve the men gradually and appoint others in their places. So he chose to take his entire Advisory Council and divide it up into sections and asked a certain number of men each month to take their places on the Advisory Board of General Johnson to serve for four consecutive months. Under this procedure my turn came on the first of March of the current year. I, therefore, had to arrange my affairs so as to spend a large proportion of my time in Washington from the first of March to the first of July; expecting, of course, that on the first of July I would be relieved of any further responsibility in this matter.

As you may remember from your newspaper reports, and from the general trend of affairs, in May and June, the N.R.A. was in rather a chaotic condition, and we found on the Industrial Advisory Board that the work was so constant and consuming so much time, and in the judgment of the members of the Board had become so important to industry and business through-

---

*Flood waters unfortunately ruined all stenographic records of Mr. Mead's speeches and remarks between 1927 and 1934.

out the country, that the then members of the Board invited the men who had previously served to join them on a three day conference to discuss what was best as to the future procedure, not only of the Board, but of the whole N.R.A. The result of this conference of three days, which was held about the middle of June, was the revision of the Industrial Advisory Board, and the enlargement of that Board to a total of twenty-one members, five of whom should be selected and appointed for a period of twelve months. These men were then to move to Washington and give their entire time to the work. In addition to the five, of course, there were sixteen more, the majority chosen from Mr. Roper's Council, but three of them in particular were from the heads of certain code groups formed during the Spring under General Johnson's direction.

Unfortunately, I had taken a little too active a part in the record of the Board, and as you may usually feel after one of these annual meetings, I talked too much and had gotten myself into a great deal of trouble, to the end that I was asked to continue on the new Board from the first of July to the first of January next. I had, unfortunately for myself, been elected Chairman of the Board on the first of May and also had to continue in this responsibility from the first of July to the end of the current year.

I take the time of you men to give you this brief history of the Industrial Advisory Board because I think it may be of some interest to you to know what the President of the Company has been doing. He certainly hasn't been paying enough attention to the paper business, and you are entitled to know why.

There has been a thought throughout the country that industrial and business men are not giving enough of their time to the affairs at Washington. That is, that the National Recovery Administration, directed by General Johnson, was being entirely too largely influenced by Labor and by Commerce, and the Industrial situation in this country was not being properly represented, either in General Johnson's Councils or in the Councils of the Administration. I can assure you men from my own personal knowledge that the so-called industrial heads of this country have not been neglecting this part of their work. There have been any number of men who have given generously of their time, and their energy and their thinking to the assistance of the entire Administration, and particularly to the direction of the N.R.A. during the past eighteen months; and I think, in turn, both the Administration and the N.R.A. officials have given real and generous consideration to the viewpoints of these men.

In other words, I do not feel that a lot of criticism which has been leveled against the Administration and against the New Deal in general, and against the N.R.A. in particular, is proper criticism. Of course, it is very difficult, gentlemen, to place before this country, with the varied interests represented from coast to coast, the true picture of what goes on in any situation as we know it in Washington.

As I said at the beginning of my talk, the year has been one of extreme confusion. We are trying to get ourselves out of the most severe depression that anybody alive today has ever seen in this country. The problems presented to the country, and, of course, therefore, to the Administration itself, are of a complexity and magnitude that we never dreamed of. Nobody thought a few years ago that this country would have to meet such an undertaking as the care of fifteen or eighteen million people resulting from unemployment, in a land of plenty where the opportunities seemed to be unlimited. Likewise, no one dreamed that we would ever reach the point of actually destroying crops that had been planted in order to try to equalize the situation that developed over a long period of years; or that we would have to go through this destructive procedure followed during the last twelve months.

I have mentioned the foreign situation to you when here before, and the importance to you, I felt, of having, at least once a year, at some of your meetings, a speaker who could tell you of what is going on in other lands besides our own. Due to the intimate communications we now have over the radio and in every other way; due to the close contacts, because of the fact that systems of transportation have been developed during the last fifteen or twenty years; the world has become a small place relatively and the intimacy that is now growing up between nations is adding very greatly to the complication of the internal problem of every country upon the face of the earth.

When you can sit in your office and listen to a voice from London tell of the immediate happenings in, and the procedure of that country, you can realize the closeness of the two nations, and understand that nothing of importance can transpire in any country of Europe, or for that matter in any country of Asia, or Africa, or South America without it having a very direct and immediate effect upon our own thinking in every community in the United States.

Therefore, aside from all of our varied problems over here, we have a world-wide problem. And with the social unrest that you find in Europe, partly as a result of the Great War, but more particularly as a result of the social experiments that are being tried in other countries, you can better appreciate the difficulty of coping with our present social unrest.

I have already mentioned to you the Russian situation, and how in extreme development, you get into a Communistic country where the situation becomes absolutely desperate, where no one has any of the comforts of life as we all know them here, where no one can tell from day to day what the results of their labor may be. While we think that it is no affair of ours, the question of Russia's development through the next twenty years is one that is probably as important as anything we have to deal with outside of our own boundaries. The Italian situation, the German situation, the situation in Spain, and even the situations in France and in England are filled with problems with which none of these countries have ever been faced before. So it is no wonder we have a serious time to deal with in these United States of America.

Having reviewed in a brief way the contact that I have had in Washington with the N.R.A., I am going to give you first a little review of the development that has been taking place in that regard in the past six or eight months during which I have been on the Advisory Board. Again I feel that this is not only a matter of national interest but of particular interest to the men in this club, because the future must certainly be affected by the development that is now taking place in this part of the industrial thinking of the nation.

The N.R.A., that is, the N.I.R.A.—the National Industrial Recovery Act—was, as I told you briefly last year, conceived originally to solve a labor problem. I think that was the sole reason for its first conception. In other words, the competition in certain lines of business in the country had become so great and the pressure in costs had become so extreme that manufacturers all over the United States had been forced through this competition to reduce labor wages to a minimum that was too low to permit people to live under it, and had increased working hours to the point where many people were being driven to the point of ill health. It was felt that if some formula could be developed that would permit of the payment of living wages, along with a reduction of hours without a reduction of the weekly wage, where business in turn could advance its prices sufficiently to take care of the increases that took place in the payment of wages, we would start ourselves on the road to recovery in this country, because we would create purchasing power among the employees of industry and business.

Now, theoretically, this formula seemed perfectly sound, and, practically, I am convinced that we have made real progress. There is no man in any phase of American life who doesn't want substantial living wages paid to all employees of every business. Likewise, no one that I know of, certainly no man or woman in this room, wants to have men worked more than a reasonable number of hours per day or per week. Certain hours should be given to leisure, and to proper home life, and to proper amusement. However, in the working out of a formula of this kind, the matter must be approached with extreme care, with real planning, and too much must not be tried too suddenly.

The only fault, gentlemen, that I have to find with the National Recovery Administration, after participating in the direction of it to some modest extent, is that too much was tried in an entirely too short a time. In other words, an attempt has been made in the past eighteen months to place under codes all of the industries of the United States, and almost all of the business of the United States, the result being that we have in Washington today almost seven hundred codes covering industries, with well over a hundred billion dollars concerned, and employing people to the number of at least twenty-two million. Now, you men know something about organization, and you know some of the problems of directing efficiently this department or that department in the paper industry; and if you can conceive of trying to organize twenty-two million people under seven hundred codes with rules and regulations affecting wages, and hours of work, and trade customs, and, in many cases, a minimum price below which goods shall not be sold, the rates at which services shall be charged, at which hotels of this sort shall be operated, and the number of hours, and in the charges for this and that service, you can begin to appreciate the job that has been attempted down in Washington. It was obviously impossible of accomplishment in the time that has so far passed, that is, of complete accomplishment, or, you might say, of really successful accomplishment. But, in spite of the magnitude of the job, and all the obstacles encountered, there has been, to my way of thinking, a real, and you might say, a vast improvement brought about in the situation. . . .

In our own paper industry the revision of the code has been proceeding along normal lines for many months. In other words, immediately after the signing of the code, mistakes were found to have been made, and these mistakes, in a future code are now being rectified. On the other hand, the government has found that there were very many things written into codes which could not possibly be enforced, any more than Prohibition could be enforced. So over the next few months, and in my judgment, over the next several years, there is going to be a revision of this code development along sounder lines.

You will hear people saying that the N.R.A. is a complete failure, that the administration will drop it at the first opportunity; or its opponents say the administration must drop it, that business will not continue with it, that labor is completely dissatisfied and will not continue with it, and that we must have new basic labor laws to take its place. But I think, gentlemen, that this is all beside the question. I think that the codification of industry along such lines as it has been conducted is going to be continued for many years. I think that the experiment is not really a new experiment, but is the culmination of thirty years of thinking, and I think that the development is here to stay; and because I have been so convinced of this, I have taken your time in reviewing the inside of the picture, because I think it may help you in focusing on what we have to do in the future, in the paper industry, as well as in every other industry.

I, of course, have been compelled to regard the paper industry as one of many, and when anything was brought before the board regarding it, I have been compelled to step out of my position as chairman of the board and ask the vice-chairman to take my place, because I did not feel it proper for me to pass upon the code details in which I was primarily a party to the making of, as I have been in all of the code work of the paper industry. But I have gained a great advantage, I feel, in my contact with these many industries, and have learned a great deal of the problems of industry in general, about which I think we should all do more thinking than we have.

We are inclined, when we go on a vacation, to stop and see a paper mill if we hear of one in the vicinity. We are always inclined to follow our own line of thinking, and I believe we would all do well to broaden our job by visiting steel plants, by visiting chemical or any other industrial plants when we have the opportunity of seeing them, to learn how other business is functioning. By so doing, perhaps, we can bring back to our own some new thought which will be much more beneficial than any idea we might obtain from competitive plants or units.

I am hopeful—I am not optimistic—that my contact in Washington and the work I have been thrown into will be of some direct benefit to the Mead Corporation because of the contacts I have formed with all other branches of industry, and because of the lessons I have learned from the experience of men in every branch of trade and business in the United States.

To return to our own affairs a little more directly and to review as I usually do, in a brief manner, the year in our company, I am compelled to immediately get back to the result of our own recent negotiations with the National Recovery Administration. I find myself very much disappointed that in our plant here at Chillicothe, as a result of the recent election, our own employees have indicated that they feel they can better serve their interests, (and I hope they take into consideration the company's interests) by the formation of a union as a part of the National Labor Movement, than by a continuation of the relationship which has existed for many, many years within our own company. Having followed the 'open door' policy, as we term it, where every officer of the company and every foreman, and every man who occupies a position of responsibility, has always had his office free to the entrance of any employee or group of employees for the discussion of any matter of either a personal or company nature, and either as an individual or collectively; and having had this policy and our men having availed themselves of it continuously, at least for the thirty years during which the present executives have been directing the company (and I have been told that the two previous generations have followed this policy), it seems rather unusual that our own employees should now elect to follow a different line of development. I must say that I am somewhat at a loss to understand the reasoning that has led to this conclusion, and, if any of the men of the Foremen's Club can enlighten me, I would greatly appreciate having them so advise me. I would like for them to write a letter to me, and if time does not permit of their writing their views, they can perhaps give them to some of the executives and thus let me know a little more directly than I have been able to learn up to the present moment what the psychology of our own employees has been that has led to this decision on their parts.

I told all of you men a year ago that I was in no way opposed to unionism. I think that in many situations in this country a fine development has been made by the union. In our Canadian contacts, when I was interested in the active management of the newsprint business, we always dealt with unions. When I went to Canada, we found unions existing and we had no inclination to make a change. It never occurred to me to say that I thought the situation was all wrong, and that we were opposed to unionism, and that we would have to eliminate them immediately or I would not have anything to do with the operation of the newsprint business. I was very glad to accept it, and my experiences were very satisfactory. I have found in the past that the union leaders were men that were reasonable in their viewpoints, and as I reported last year, I have the highest regard for the labor leaders I have met in Washington. They are an able, fine lot of men. The same applies to the leaders of the pulp and paper unions. But I repeat that while I think there are situations in which unions can be of direct benefit to the employees and to the companies that these employees work for, it seems to me that within our own corporation, the particular situation that they represent is not necessary, and certainly anything that is not necessary becomes superfluous and only complicates a situation.

Since we are dealing in labor questions, I would like to mention the matter of the thirty hour week, which has been brought forward by the American Federation of Labor. I have told the heads of the American Federation of Labor, whom I have the pleasure of knowing in Washington quite well, that I think they have made a great mistake in the position taken in this matter. It is perfectly obvious to anyone that you cannot have a thirty hour week in America and have it satisfactory to either the employees or employers.

No group of men that I know of want to limit their working to thirty hours a week. Certainly no man in this room has had such an idea. Certainly I have never had such an idea. There are weeks in which I might like to limit my hours to thirty, but I must say that over the past twelve months, along with practically every other executive in the United States, I have had a hard time limiting my hours to sixty a week. Particularly is this true during my service in Washington, where we usually work every evening as well as every day. Why the American Federation of Labor should recommend a thirty hour week to American industry, I am at a loss to understand.

There are economists and labor men, and business men who think that America is destined to continue in the unemployment situation; that we must always have a substantial number of unemployed from now forward in this country. I disagree with this very point. I am absolutely convinced that America has the power to consume everything that she can produce, that our present situation is only a temporary one, and that with proper thinking, and intelligence and cooperation put into planning and working out what is being attempted at the present time in Washington, it is only a question of a few years until we will be back in full employment in this country, when we shall have just as prosperous a time as the United States has ever enjoyed. Is there any reason in the mind of any of you men, after one hundred and fifty years of development in this country, to think that we are going to produce more than we can possibly consume, that we are going to go backward after having moved forward so long? It is perfectly outrageous to allow such a thought to cover the country according to my way of thinking.

But, gentlemen, we can never develop any prosperity, or any satisfactory operation of industry or business or our personal lives in this country on the basis of a thirty hour week. We will have the cost of production so high that people can't afford to buy the goods produced. Already, because of the reduction in hours that have been made, we have been forced to raise prices of all manufactured articles, and in our own immediate industry, we have curtailed production of paper because of the advances made in prices. There is no doubt in my mind that the plant in Chillicothe, and all the rest of our plants would be operating more days per week and more days per year if we had not been forced to increase our prices.

Every increase in price always meets with resistance, and this is so in every industry in the United States. Now, there is a stoppage in the progress that we have made in the last twelve months because of this resistance. I think it will be overcome. I feel that a fair and moderate increase in the price of all industrial production, to take care of a fair increase in labor rates and a fair reduction in hours of work, is perfectly proper, and as soon as we can get economically adjusted we will move forward and have advancement both in labor rates and in goods to be consumed; but I think to make a drastic cut such as is being discussed at the present time, in hours of work that are perfectly unreasonable to every thinking person, would create an advance in cost outdistancing anything we have ever conceived before, and would utterly destroy returning prosperity within the next several years. So why any group of men is prepared to advocate this as sound basic development, I fail to understand and I think that it shows that the thinking of these men has reached the point of unreasonableness. . . .

In spite of the fact that we have made several increases in the price of paper during the past year, we have been unable to advance to the point of taking care of increased costs that have been put upon us by reason of the proper labor increases that have been made. Now we haven't complained, nor have our stockholders, because we realize that we must have living wages. There must be a fair distribution of money between employees and capital represented in our own industry, and in our own company, as well as in all other industries, but there must be some profit to business or business will disintegrate, and we will have none in this country. The President of the United States and all others in authority in Washington have definitely stated that the Administration is squarely behind the profit motive in business.

I think the word capitalism is a thing of the past. The words "capitalism" and "labor" should be disallowed. That is, they should be forgotten as being opposed to one another, and the words should be eliminated from present economic thinking, for statistics prove that out of every dollar produced in America through industry, 87% is returned to labor. Out of every dollar's worth of business transacted in the United States, 13¢ represents the return to capital or investment in one form or another, and 87¢ goes to labor in one form or another. Therefore, the entire economic situation is built upon the basis of 87% labor, and you can therefore realize what great influence the cutting of the working hours in this country to 30 hours a week would mean.

The real reason for the present economic distress and depression in this country, I believe, is the inequality that has grown up over the past ten or fifteen years in the value of manufactured goods and raw materials. The farmers of the country in all productions have gradually been asked to accept lower and lower prices for their production, while the manufactured articles which the same farming group was forced to buy had been increased and increased in their prices up to the year 1929 when the whole structure collapsed.

Our problem is to get back the purchasing power of the farmer, and all of these experiments tried under the A.A.A. in Washington have been, for the purpose of trying to bring up the value of agricultural products—wheat, corn, cotton, tobacco, etc. The experiment is being tried of levying a processing tax whereby the manufacturer of flour has to pay into the Government a certain tax on every bushel of grain he absorbs. The cotton manufacturer has to pay a processing tax on every bale of cotton; that money to be distributed among the farmers to give greater return on their labor.

No one of us can tell whether the processing tax, or control of products, or allotments of land, or a number of these other experiments is the right one to bring about the leveling of prices so that this group, representing 45% of the population, can be brought back as purchasers of goods. But the thing that will destroy the entire procedure is the getting of manufactured articles on a higher basis so that we can never get this farm group into the proper alignment. Therefore, we must deal very cautiously and very carefully with the reduction of working hours and the increasing of wages in industry, beyond, as I said, a reasonable figure. Otherwise, we are going to destroy every hope of a return to prosperity, and we are going back into a worse situation than we are trying to get out of.

Now in spite of the blackness of all that I have been telling you and the great problems that we are trying to solve, I can say with a perfectly clear conscience and with absolute conviction that I believe we are making real progress. It is true that in the last four months business has been distinctly worse than the first six months of the year. It is true also that in 1933 we had a considerable increase in consumption and production, in all phases of business through the anticipation of higher prices as a result of the N.R.A. These temporary movements are natural to any return of more normal times from a depression. In previous depressions the history of recovery has been much as we now find it.

I have been disappointed along with all other businessmen, and all other people in the United States, with the slowing down that has seemed to take place during these last few months. If we had been able to proceed after July 1 with a normal Fall business as we proceeded through the first six months, we would all be enjoying our evening very much more than we are enjoying it, because we would have had a very much better five months of business since the first of July, but the complication of the problem temporarily overwhelmed us, in my thinking. Last summer we had all of the uncertainties of the A.A.A., and the N.R.A., and the unemployment situation which hadn't bettered itself along with the demands of labor and the strikes that were called unnecessarily. The whole picture was filled with an uncertainty which people didn't seem to be able to look through. However, as the summer passed and things began to clear up, I believe that a new light came into the situation.

Then we had an election in November which rather indicated that the present Administration was meeting with the approval of the whole United States. I heard the President say about a week after the election to a group of us who were talking over some matters, that he believed a certain part of the legislation under discussion could be put through. He said, "Of course, you all realize that I am only one branch of Government, but the indication points to my being able to perhaps persuade the other branches of Government to think somewhat along the lines I do." And one individual made the observation that in view of the recent election, Congress was likely to do what the President suggested. The President did not say this in a joking way, but in all sincerity, and I think that today, following this overwhelming evidence on the part of the country of confidence in him and in the Administration and the placing in his hands of more power than he had following the previous election, he feels even more seriously, if possible, the very great responsibility he has to this country in trying to direct it in a safe and sound American manner.

I can tell you with conviction that I am perfectly sure, after nine months of almost continuous residence in Washington and contact, while largely with the National Recovery Administration, but at the same time and to some extent with all other branches of the Government, there is no thought in the Administration of the United States to turn this country over to any Socialistic movement. The President and everybody that has anything to do with the Administration is thinking along truly American lines of trying to build up the country on the same foundation on which it started, and for the purpose of allowing men to have their individual liberties, and to make their own way in life, and to make their own profit as a result of their individual and collective work; and any belief or any rumor that is being spread around this country that the Administration has the idea of a bureaucracy or of Fascism or any one of a number of these ridiculous experiments, is absolutely untrue.

I took occasion last year to say that after the contact I had had in Washington as a member of the code authority I had developed a great admiration for the President and I spoke in the most glowing terms I could of the fine work he was doing there. I can add tremendously to that feeling now. The months that I have been in Washington have increased my admiration and my feeling that that particular man was doing the greatest job that any one could do for the benefit of the country. That feeling has become a sound conviction that nobody can shake regardless of politics, and I would like to tell you that in the entire N.R.A., I have never heard politics mentioned, nor have there been any political appointments made within the N.R.A. There may have been attempts made in a desultory way, but that group and many other groups in Washington are just as free from politics as any group we might select within our company here. I would like to say one word about this question. There was a thought some months ago that the Administration had attempted to assist in unionizing organizations of this country. I can find no such evidence in Washington.

I think that it is the right of every man to choose his own company, his own employer, and his associates. This right is considered inviolable. It is his constitutional right. While the vote of a majority, if overwhelming, may be the final control of the situation, as Mr. Van de Carr* has stated publicly and in every private conversation, the policy of this company remains as it always has been, that men can deal individually or collectively in one group or another, without fear of coercion on the part of the company in any direction, and by the same rule we propose to see that no men who work for us are coerced by anybody else.

Now that is just as final as I know how to make it, and I want to add my word, not only of real support but of great commendation, to Mr. Van de Carr for the position he has taken with the procedure in connection with our recent election.

The Directors and Executives of this company have desired to play this game absolutely fair and square, and above board. We do not want to interfere with the thinking of anyone in this room or in the company. Men are free agents, and if they feel that it is best for their interest to deal in one way or another, we will try to conform so far as we possibly can with their ideas, so long as they do not interfere with the welfare of the company, but we will not permit coercion by the Management, by labor, or by outside groups.

In a very desultory and disconnected way I have tried to review our development of this year. We had a better business for the first six months, but have had a less happy situation during the last six months. The company, I can tell you, because the financial statements will be available at the end of the year, has not been able to make a dollar profit during the last six months. One of the plants that has found it most difficult to operate is the Chillicothe plant because we have been unwilling to increase the price of magazine papers to anything like the price miscellaneous papers have been increased. The magazines have had a great problem of their own. The advertising of the country is placed on an annual contract basis, and the selling price of the individual magazine could not be increased on the newsstands. We have felt it part of wisdom to be very moderate to these large consumers of our goods, and in consequence, we feel that we have maintained a larger volume of business.

It is fair to say to you men that our whole year of 1934 is a better year than 1933 was. I think that applies to all other industries. I think that we are, as I said a year ago, gradually improving our position one month after another, and I asked you men at that time to use as the text of your talks thoroughness, feeling that it was absolutely imperative that we do things in a most thorough and conscientious way if we were going to make progress over all the obstacles we had to overcome. I think that this text still applies. I have nothing

---

*Charles R. Van de Carr, Jr. was then Vice President of the Mead Corporation. In 1948, he became President.

to suggest, except that our text for the coming year be thoroughness and economy in our operations. In other words, we should see that every phase of our operation is cut down to the minimum of waste with the maximum of production under the situations as they exist. We are not through with this problem. We will have, I think I am safe in saying, a continuing betterment, and I am hopeful that 1936 will be still better than 1935, but there is still going to be a great deal of mortality in industry.

Problems that have been developed under the New Deal, and under many factors brought into the picture during the last 18 months are so much more difficult of solution, that it will only be the very closest figuring in every phase of our appropriation, by the greatest energy put in the merchandizing of our product, by the turning out of a quality of paper that is better than anything we have ever conceived of before, and only by a combination of all these factors together, are we going to be able to force this company into a prosperous period which we will hope to enjoy for years to come, after we have gotten over this terrific period we are now passing through.

I think I should say that with the conclusion of the year 1934, I expect to conclude the active participation that I have had in the work at Washington. I have attempted to be freed from all participation, but it seems that that is impossible. It looks to me as if it has become a definite part of the work, of the obligation, of every executive in this country, that he give a certain portion of his time and thought in the future to the government of his community, of his state, and of his country, and this applies to the rest of you men in this room just as it applies to me.

In other words we have developed a great industrial nation in America. We no longer are able to do pioneering work. There is no longer any part of this country to which you can go and re-establish yourself and begin anew without competition. That day is gone by. We now have a completely unified country, a completely settled country. It has changed from an agricultural to an industrial nation within the past ten or twenty years. Twenty years ago the majority of the population was engaged in agriculture, while today the great majority of the country's population is industrial and the agricultural population is less than 45%.

One of the solutions is going to be unemployment insurance. I think most of the industrialists are in favor of it. I think the same applies to old age pensions. I doubt if anything can be done in that regard within the next twelve months. I think some steps will be taken about unemployment insurance. When we get back into more or less normal operation, we will have unemployment relief to take care of a temporary letdown, and that will help keep business on a uniform basis. It is not possible that legislation can solve the problem of unemployment as a result of a period of five years of depression, but it can be worked out gradually, and as I say, you men will all have to give more thought to the matter of how the money is expended in this community and state, and how we are going to assist in the direction of the affairs of the country. Without a stable and sound country our own industries and all others have no value.

Therefore, I am compelled to say that I will not give up any contacts that I have in Washington. I will not resign from the several boards that I have been associated with. I am, fortunately, relieved of the Chairmanship of the Industrial Advisory Board, and as you may well know the Chairman has a great deal more of the weight to carry than those who are merely members of an operating group. But it seems impossible for those of us who have contributed in even the most modest way to any of the development that has taken place, to entirely divorce ourselves and go back to our own individual occupations, and say that now our service is ended. This is true, because no man can give as much thinking to the discussions others and I have had, who have been there in these past months, and not be so convinced of the absolute necessity of our all giving time and attention to these matters, as to feel that he can eliminate himself just because of some personal or selfish reason. In spite of my desire to return and give all of my time to our company here, I say I am compelled to continue, but in a much less active way in some particular expansion in the work down in Washington.

FOREMEN'S CLUB, Chillicothe, January 13, 1936

I stated today, and I would like to repeat to you, because I told you at the last annual meeting that I thought President Roosevelt was doing a great job, a great many things that were most commendable. He frankly stated that he was experimenting, that we needed a change, and he was going to try this and that and something else, and if it didn't work he would try to find an alternative. We find this situation in the A.A.A. It has recently been declared unconstitutional by the Supreme Court. There are ways in which a similar result can be accomplished, and still be within the constitution. However, while we admit that we must have some similar plan for the moment to create a parity between the farm prices and other prices, in the long run we can't increase the wealth of this country in any other way than by producing it and we can only distribute it after it is produced. We can't take it from one hand and put it in another indefinitely. It has got to be produced by somebody, and it practically all comes from the soil and minerals of the country.

Regardless of party affiliation whether Republican, Democrat, Socialist or Laborite, there are certain economies to be followed if the country is to continue, and I think that we should see that the representatives who go to Washington in the future are men who understand that phase of the life of this nation. I stated that I had hopes that Mr. Roosevelt would see the necessity and would meet the situation. I have confidence that that may take place. However, whether it be Mr. Roosevelt or someone else, the necessity for economy in government and business has never been so great as it is today, and that brings us to our own problems.

There are in all legislative matters, and in political and religious matters, as well, two procedures. I heard the Rev. Dr. Fosdick stress this. He called one preventive religion and the other remedial religion, and I say the same applies to political and legal situations, and I say the same applies to the operation of industry. The distinction comes in whether we try to prevent an event or prevent something happening that is either good or bad, or, whether after it has happened we try to remedy it. We have, in the course of the past few years, spent all our time in remedial legislation. In trying to remedy a situation in which we are as a result of the economic condition following the war. I think the war has been responsible for 90 per cent of the disasters that have befallen us in the last five years. I feel that in national affairs, in political and economical and in industrial affairs, we should give our thinking chiefly to preventive legislation, to preventive thinking in our own operation.

I would like to have that the chief thought of the evening. We have tried over these many years in the discussions we have had together in the meetings of our Foremen's Club to leave with you some definite aim for the year, and I believe that we should all give our thinking to preventive work rather than remedial work. We have had some very serious naval disasters during the last year, I mean maritime disasters. When we read in the paper of a ship that has caught fire at sea, and how the other ships, being called by the great radio, came to the assistance. It is the heroism and the excitement that makes a great impression upon us all, and, at such a time, we often fail to appreciate that if somebody in a quiet way had inspected that great ship before it had left port, the disaster would never have occurred. All through our daily life, I feel that we are giving too much thought to remedial matters and not enough thought to preventive matters. In our own operation, if the foremen and directors of our different departments, if I, as executive of the company, along with Mr. Van de Carr, and other chief executives, can just have the foresight to prevent the things that are not beneficial to this company, success is assured. In the operation of all of our equipment, and the care of the lives of our employees, we have talked a great deal about prevention of accidents. This has been stressed and stressed well over these many years. We have the remedial treatment, but we have tried to prevent accidents. There is, at the present, a great wave of prevention of automobile accidents. Now, if we can apply that same psychology to our operation, and begin our day by thinking of methods of prevention in the manufacture of bad products and the breaking down of this piece of equipment, and that piece of equipment, instead of remedying it after it has happened, I think we will contribute more to the success of our operation than by any other thing that occurs to me at this time. I have been impressed with this thought, because, as I say, of the national situation, and the things I have observed over the last twelve months in connection with the political affairs that we have had to face.

I don't know that in my thirty years of business that there has ever been a time when the situation is so complex, either in political or business situations. We have had a better year in 1935 than in 1934. As you men know, in 1934 we were able to show a slight profit in our operation in the entire concern. I think that you all know that the profit came from the brown paper division instead of the white paper division. During 1935 we have improved. We have been able to operate our white paper division without material loss, and we have been able to increase somewhat the profits in our brown paper division, so that we will end the year with a modest profit, a very distinct improvement over 1934. While it is dangerous under conditions of so much uncertainty to forecast, I believe confidently that 1936 will be a material improvement over 1935. It seems to me that for the Mead future, we may look forward to a continuing increase in the business of this country; but as I stated to the clubs today at noon, the soundness of the business structure is somewhat alarming unless we may be perfectly sure of the financial position of this country. I am fearful that in the improvement generally of business conditions of the country, we may overlook the necessity for rigid economy, not only in government, but in our own operation. There is always a tendency, as you well know, when things begin to get better, to relax our vigilance, and our efforts, and at a time like the present, particularly, we must avoid falling into that weakness. It will only be, to my thinking, by the most serious attention to every detail of our business, that we will be able to do the things that should be done in the way of operation of these properties that we stand responsible for, and that is the reason I stressed a few moments ago the necessity for preventive thinking.

Competition is greater today than it has been at any time since the war. We need only hark back to those who were in business before 1914. There was great competition in those days. Mr. McVicker will support me in the statement that the competition between 1900 and 1914 was very severe in the paper industry, and in all lines of endeavor. When with the great influx of money into this country from the European nations as a result of the manufacture of materials and supplies, prosperity came to us and we all became careless and lax, we became that way in our personal habits of work and in the handling of our financial matters and in the handling of our businesses.

One of the greatest concerns that we have in America is a company that decided, following the war, to eliminate every chief executive, because they thought they had developed bad habits during the war period, and they pensioned all men of fairly advanced age. The executive who told me of this procedure told me that they had the largest pension roll of any company in America, and they felt that they had profited, and they felt that they could carry on the pension roll, men who had been executives throughout the war, and instill new life into the organization by the installing of new executive men who had not developed the careless habits that had come from that particular period.

This company of ours has always had the policy of keeping so long as possible, talent that has grown up with it, in having several generations of families continue with the corporation. We have prided ourselves on our advancement from within of the men who deserved advancement, and we have brought in very little talent from the outside, only when we felt that it was necessary. I would like at this particular point to say that the talent that we have brought in has been most beneficial to us. It has given us a new viewpoint. Mr. Van de Carr who has joined us in recent years has to my mind contributed more to the advancement of this concern than any group that we have been able to produce from within ourselves, including myself; not that I consider myself, and my talents of any particular value to the corporation, but I will say that along with the rest of you that I have given the best that I have in me and I have spent many years in the study of my art. The thing that is closest we often overlook. We have instilled new life in this organization in the last ten or fifteen years.

Mr. McVicker will remember my saying in a dining room in the old Masonic Hall to a group meeting such as this, only with a handful of men, that I looked forward to the day, and I believed that there were men in that room, who would live to see the time when this company had the largest book paper mill in America, in the City of Chillicothe. That was the statement of a young man who was optimistic beyond normal. However, some of us, including this fellow, have lived to see this. I think we have today as large a book paper mill as there is in the world, here, in Chillicothe. I think that many of us will live to see the largest mill that has come first from intensive hard labor, and second from trying to keep ahead of our competition by the type of thinking that I am asking you gentlemen and ladies to give to this organization during this next twelve months, in preventive work. . . .

I feel that, individually, I have been negligent in not impressing this organization from year to year with the necessity for more forward thinking. I do not mean by that, a lot of research work that seems intangible, but I mean in our everyday operation. The gentlemen in this room connected with our Brown Paper Division have, of necessity, to do more forward thinking because it is a newer art dealing with products never produced before. These chestnut chips were wasted in the past. We have been the first to put them into a saleable product. Since it was a new division it required more intensive work. I think gentlemen responsible for our white paper division should give more thought to improvement than we have in the past. I think you should try to impress on your men the necessity for improvement. If we can get that thought well into the whole organization. I believe that we will make such outstanding paper that the question of merchandising will be much simplified, and we will not only have larger production, but we will show better profit to the people who have entrusted money to us. . . .

We are always seeking new ideas as to how we can better improve the things that we are doing. I want particularly the men of this organization to give me suggestions. I want to obtain from the thinking of the whole organization the suggestions they all may have in mind. Now, this has been done in various ways, gentlemen, in organizations for many years, but in no way has anyone found a procedure that would compare with the sitting down in meeting, and discussing in the open and among ourselves, such procedure, and I would like the men of the different departments who are assembled here this evening to try out the procedure of discussing more frequently with the men whom they have under them, whom they think may have ideas and particular ability or may show by their work some outstanding accomplishment. Talk with those men. Be more communicative. We are inclined to let the days go by listening to this and that without enough intercourse, as it were. I have said to Mr. Van de Carr and Mr. Ferguson* with whom I am in contact frequently, that I have looked forward to the meetings that we three have with discussion of the policies of this company. I have found that my thinking has been greatly improved by my constant contact, and I have resolved to see more of other men, to enlarge the circle and, I find that it is of the very greatest help to me. I think that this same experience would prove of a great advantage to you, all the way down the line. It will accomplish another thing, gentlemen, it will allow the men who are working under you to feel that we have developed a new interest in what they are doing, in what they are trying to accomplish. Particularly, I find after a serious time such as we have gone through in these past few years, we are inclined to close ourselves up, to be less communicative. As I hark back to the years previous to the war, I realize that there was much more intercourse and discussion of every problem then than there has been in recent years. The discussions we are beginning to have in politics are not sound discussions. They are heated discussions; arguments rather than discussions. There is a certain bitterness creeping in. Throughout these twelve months that we are facing, we are going to find political discussions, on the stand, on the platform, will be filled with an attack of one sort or another, and bitter argument as to the merits of this or that, and during this period, we must be very careful to guard against allowing a similar feeling, although a much less evident example of that sort, to get into our organization.

---

*Mr. Sydney Ferguson was then Vice President of the Company. He became President in 1942 and Chairman of the Board in 1947.

We have to protect ourselves during these twelve months against the psychology that results from an improving situation which will seem to be bettering our whole outlook and yet which is only, to my thinking, temporary, and we have to prevent that new influence from allowing us to relax our efforts, and we have to, at the same time, steel ourselves against this outer influence of the political upheaval, and keep a particularly cheerful countenance, and a new interest in the men that are working for us.

FOREMEN'S CLUB, Chillicothe, April 26, 1937

Now it may seem to some of you men whose thoughts are devoted almost entirely to the white paper divisions, that it is unnecessary for The Mead Corporation to develop new mills at this time, or at any time. I have thought at great length about the future we all desire for The Mead Corporation, and, as I have told you many times before, this company is not being built with the idea of disposing of it, or selling it to some other corporation, or of its consolidation with some other corporation. I was alarmed a few years ago because I thought I could see from the tendencies then prevailing, that we might be forced into a consolidation. It looked to me for quite some time as if the successful industry of the future would be the consolidated industry, representative of a very much larger operation than anything we could visualize from our own developments, at least during my lifetime.

However, and fortunately I believe for this organization, the scene changed, and in recent years the tendency has been somewhat the other way. I am now convinced, and I believe that I can say to this group with a great deal of conviction, that the individual company with a number of plants is probably the soundest unit, economically, that can be developed in industry. The larger corporations have become too large. We now see, after thirty years of operation, some of the greater companies beginning to lose efficiency because of their very size. We see these units hindered by internal politics within the organization. I begin to find it impossible for any chief executive to cover the current work that is necessary for efficient operation in a big company. We also find that the ownership of these very large companies has become so diversified that there are no individuals heavily interested in the undertaking. Therefore, the big corporation begins to lose its personality.

Now, we have two safeguards against this possibility. One is that it will be a good many years before we reach the size which I just described. The second is that we have a personal name for our company, a circumstance which induces in any company a little more intense feeling about its success than if it were not so named.

I believe that The Mead Corporation is just beginning to show what it can really do. We have worked a good many years to make it an efficient, fine operating unit. We all know how many years it took to reach this point, and we are not going to stop here. We are going to make progress rapidly, Gentlemen, and we are going to make this company an outstanding and large company; perhaps not the largest—from the standpoint of size—but outstanding in such things as efficient operation and the production of high quality goods.

This company has been recognized as a quality company for many years, and come what may, regardless of other new developments, I want to point out that we have always kept in our minds this fact.

Those of us who are close to the Washington situation, and have worked the N.R.A., have contacted some of the labor leaders of this country, and by and large, they are a fine lot of men. However, there are a great many agitators throughout the United States who haven't the real interest of labor at heart. They are political agitators who are just dissatisfied, and are stirring up trouble for their own personal ends.

The Wagner Labor Act that has just been declared constitutional is a good piece of legislation, that many of us have always thought was sound. Other manufacturers felt that it was unsound and challenged it from a constitutional standpoint. One of the judges of the Supreme Court changed his position, and approved the act. I think he deserves tremendous credit, for any man who changes his mind when he finds out that he is wrong is deserving of credit. But he was not wrong before. He changed his position because times have changed, conditions have changed, and the state of the country has changed.

You men will all be asked sooner or later whether the Wagner Act demands that collective bargaining be used. There is nothing in that Act that demands collective bargaining. The Act states that, if the men want to bargain collectively, the employer is legally bound to hear them; but if the men wish to proceed individually, and, as in previous years, deal with the company individually, they have every right to do so. There is no compulsion of any sort to the contrary, and if that point is raised by anyone in your departments, Gentlemen, you can speak with conviction.

Of course, the union organizers will indicate, not say, that there is some wish that the men bargain collectively, but at a meeting I recently attended with labor leaders in Washington, it was freely stated by the labor men, and not contradicted, that there were many organizations in this country which did not want the so-called collective bargaining at this time. It may be that in the future they will, they may change their minds and their decision, but if they do not, there should be no coercion to make them try new ways.

There is nothing new in collective bargaining. This Corporation has always taken the position that if the time ever came when the men preferred as a group to employ collective bargaining, they should be free to do so, but I can't conceive of such a time arriving. . . .

FOREMEN'S CLUB, October 13, 1937

Last year I think I touched upon the question of whether or not in serving, or attempting to serve, the Government, I had somewhat neglected my obligations to this Corporation, which I am also attempting to serve, and I took the liberty of stating that I believed that in working upon this job in Washington I was rendering at least some service to the stockholders and the employees of this company, because I firmly believe it is the duty of every man in the United States to give some thought to his Government. As I stated last April, there is no use in building any industry or any other phase of national life unless we have a sound country, and a stable Government under which to operate it.

There could be no better time than this to take account of the situation and to make up our minds as to whether we want a stable and sound Government or not, because we see in every part of the world the disastrous results of unsound Government. One conclusion that I have very definitely reached about Government is that there is no such thing as a communistic government. Communism, if anyone had ever assumed that it might work, has completely failed during the last ten years. To my thinking, it is an impossible form of organization and it is equally impossible to believe that it ever could succeed. Communism completely lacks discipline and without discipline you can't develop anything. First, you must have self-discipline and then discipline in groups, and inasmuch as the very basis of communism is the complete lack of discipline, the results of this experiment, at least in Russia, is the development of the strongest dictatorship the world has ever seen. Therefore, it seems to me that it has been proven that the ultimate end of any communistic movement must be a dictatorship. . . .

If countries are not inclined to monarchies, which in the end are similar to dictatorships, then they must accept a democracy or one of the forms of dictatorship called Fascism or Naziism that we have seen set up in the central countries of Europe, and which we find also at the present time in Japan. The dictatorship in Japan of course is not so clearly defined as it is in Germany and Italy and we must admit that a dictatorship has certain distinct advantages. The President himself has mentioned in recent speeches that there are certain things which can be accomplished through dictatorship that we find most difficult to accomplish in democracy. However, in spite of the advantages that are evident from the type of government we have seen formed in Germany and Italy, and which is now being attempted in Spain, and worked out in a different way in Japan, I am more convinced than I have ever been that no country can obtain the maximum of happiness and the maximum of the good things in life without a democracy. We must have complete individual freedom if we are going to have true happiness in this world; that is, complete individual freedom of thought. Our freedom of action, of course, must always be dependent upon the obligations we have to the community in which we are living, to the country, and to our families and friends.

As an observer these past four years, I have constantly believed in my own mind that the Government is not necessarily as complicated nor the political situation as complicated as people generally assume. The Government of a country is not unlike our own business. If we properly conceive a business, if we properly plan it and build well, we have a foundation upon which to start. We then must operate that business. This requires the greatest care and consideration, a slow process of up-building, the greatest attention to detail and to our everyday work, in order to assure a fine product.

The greatest problem this country faces is the operation of the country itself. You all know that I have been very sympathetic to many of the policies of the President. I think his ideals and conceptions of the ultimate goal that we are attempting to reach in the United States of America are almost beyond criticism. But in the attainment of this goal we have a very great problem which, to my mind, is being neglected at the present time, and that is the operation of the country. Furthermore, I do not believe that it is possible to accomplish all of the things that any man conceives as the ultimate goal of this country in a short space of time. In dealing with a matter of such magnitude as the rearrangement of the United States of America we must take our time and we must exercise care. We must have patience and we must move slowly, for any attempt to hurry the situation and to jump too quickly from one position to another is likely to involve us in most serious consequences. We have worked for one hundred and fifty years to develop our Government in its present form. It is going to take us very many more years to build it to the ideals that the President of the United States has for it and that we all have for it. We all want the next generation to be better than our own and, for that end, are building a stronger Government than we now have. . . .

There is also no doubt in my mind as to the wisdom of the wage and hour bill. I am strongly for it. The working out of a practical bill is most difficult however. The President asked me, with two other men, to discuss the wage and hour bill with him and he asked us frankly just how we felt about it. One of the men was the president of the United States Chamber of Commerce and the other the president of a large banking corporation. I told him very definitely how I felt, which I think he already knew, due to my connections with the N.R.A., which I supported, and said that I thought it was a good piece of legislation and one which the country needed. I said that I believed it would be very much better for the states to legislate on this matter than for the United States to do so, but that I felt that a labor law which would serve as a standard for the states to follow would be a real contribution. I was subsequently asked to sit in on the formulation of the wage and hour bill which was finally presented on the floor of Congress. As in all legislation, there are certain groups in certain parts of the country who have objections to one clause of the bill, while other sections of the country have objections to another. Last night the President stated that he didn't think it proper for any section of the country to ask for exceptions to the wage and hour bill. I didn't quite agree with this, as in certain sections perhaps the men don't work as hard or as continuously as in other parts and there are differences in the cost of living in different regions. Therefore, all these inequalities must be given definite consideration and, if given proper consideration, the matter can be worked out. . . .

The question of economy in a community brings me to a matter which is not political but which I would like to touch upon tonight and that is the Community Chest Fund. I am a very strong advocate of the Community Chest. I have never been particularly active in Community Chest work because I have never been able to stay in one spot long enough. However, I have always been in sympathy with it and am a contributor to the Community Chest in Dayton which is my home and I have on occasion spoken in favor of Community Chest work and have been on a committee of industrial men to try to determine what the proper basis for giving is on the part of corporations in this country. I think corporations, as such, should contribute to Community Chests and I think that every man and woman who has a job should give something, no matter how small, to the Community Chest. It is an organized effort to take care of the requirements, in a community, of the people who are unable to take care of themselves; it builds character and is a part of the maintenance and successful operation of the community. I am delighted that Chillicothe has a Community Chest and only wish it were possible to fully express my views on this subject for, as I said, I am a strong advocate of this movement.

FOREMEN'S CLUB, Chillicothe, May 16, 1939

Now I am not being critical because no one who has been in contact with the problem of relief in Washington or anywhere else is unaware of the magnitude of the job and how hard it is to distribute the money and have it reach the right spot without some misappropriation or some bad management in the process. (I would like to say—and this is off the record—that several years ago in Washington I saw a great deal of Mr. Harry Hopkins who has had charge of relief until the last winter and no one I have ever met was more conscientious in his job or realized more keenly the weaknesses that were developing in the procedure he was forced to follow. He was most anxious to have a new relief procedure set up in this country because he knew the money, a lot of it, was not going into the right hands and that a lot was being used on the way down.) Some of these things are hard to control because, like N.R.A. and some of the other experiments tried in the last six to eight years, we have attempted to do more in a short time than could be done thoroughly in perhaps a lifetime. However, it is the temptation of any group of men, we would find temptation ourselves if we had the opportunity to follow the same lines, who have the handling of vast sums, to do it loosely. It is a great temptation to anyone handling great sums to misappropriate funds, for when you get to figuring in big figures you lose the value of money. . . . The President himself has become, in my humble judgment, careless, if you will, or rather indifferent to the question of money, because he has one great objective and that is a social objective; what he wants to try to do and what he wants to see is the lower third of the population of this country raised up to a level that will permit that group to enjoy the same experiences and same living conditions that we in this room are enjoying, or as near to it as possible. He is very sympathetic to people who have had difficult times and have been in distress. This is all that matters to him and, in his anxiety and zeal to try to accomplish it, he has gradually lost his sense of money value. You all know that I have been very complimentary to the President and that there are many things he has done that I have supported publicly and otherwise, and the reforms and objectives he has had are, in the main, I think, fine. However, there comes a time when you have to face a situation and do it honestly and clearly and the fact that he hasn't seen it yet disturbs me most of all. Therefore, the time has come, in my humble judgment, when this country has got to practice economy and every man in this room has to begin to spread the gospel, to each of the people who are representing us in the United States Senate and Congress and everywhere else, that we have to live within our means in government matters, just as in personal matters.

This same principle has to apply to our own company. Under the present management, we have passed through some thirty odd years of expansion and always trying to enlarge our properties so that we can get them into a balanced unit. So far as I know, and I have been the one responsible for this expansion more than anyone perhaps, The Mead Corporation has now reached the point where it now is a balanced unit. This doesn't mean that we will not add to our capacity in any way; but the big job is behind us. You in this room know that we have our steam plants, our plants to make soda pulp and raw materials fairly worked out. The only thing of any moment which we will have to depend upon from outside our immediate surroundings is sulphite pulp. During the last year we have completed and placed in fine operation, due to Mr. Van de Carr and his group, the sulphite pulp mill at Brunswick, Georgia. We have made Brunswick a real producer of very high-grade pulp so that we are not entirely dependent upon foreign sources. We have the opportunity, if the necessity should arise which we hope will not, in case foreign supplies are cut off we hope we can increase the production at Brunswick to take care of the demand. We think we are now protected from a sulphite pulp standpoint; we know we are protected on our soda pulp; we know we have balance in operation in our nine point mills. As you know, we went into the development at Port St. Joe, which I am happy to report is running very well due to the very hard work of the organization under Mr. Van de Carr's leadership and Herb Kidd's* immediate direction, and that operation is going very smoothly. Both of these operations are now in what we call the profitable period of their development. I told you last year the reason for going into the St. Joe development was because we had a large investment in our nine point mills and our customers began using liner so we felt it necessary to produce liner in order to meet competition. This was the reason and it was a sound one.

Now we have this balanced operation throughout the corporation and we are prepared for the first time to give our every hour and minute to the economic and intensive management of these plants. We are turning out better and better products at a cheaper and cheaper cost, and it is the first time in thirty-five years we have been in this position.

It is true, as you all know from the balance sheet you saw or if you didn't see it you at least heard about it, that the corporation operated in 1938 at a loss, or in red figures. This is the first time, except for the years of 1932 and 1933, that we have shown a loss under the present management. In other words, beginning back in November of 1905, we have been able to operate the company as it has grown without red figures until we met 1932 and 1933. We thought that at the end of 1933 we would never again find ourselves in red figures, that this period was past. . . . The reason, ladies and gentlemen, is largely psychological. We had a terrific beating in 1930 and 1931 with stocks dropping, banks failing in every community in the United States, all sorts of business disasters, and we were sharing in that situation. We then thought, at the end of 1933, that we had passed through the storm and we felt confident that in our lifetime we would never see another cyclone like that and we were out of the woods and beginning to improve in 1934 a little bit. 1935, 1936 and 1937 were pretty good years, nearly normal, and our corporation began to show a profit and money was spent in improving operations. Then, to the very great surprise of everybody in the United States and in the world, America suddenly went into a decline. Why in the world did this happen, after getting the country into the position it was in in 1937 with all the banks absolutely sound due very largely to government insurance on deposits (which was a good step of the present administration and which ought to have been done by the previous administration although no one seemed to be smart enough to see it; however, the present administration did see it and rectified it). The present administration, although they made a lot of mistakes, did a lot of good things that made it look as though we were about to come out of our difficulties. Then, for seemingly unknown reasons, the thing started to spiral the other way and we had to go through a losing year, and there seems to be no possible excuse for it in my judgment.

Furthermore, I will venture this statement to the group: If it had not been for the depression and the failure of the United States of America to maintain the progress that they had shown in 1937 through 1938 I don't believe we would have a world war scare at this moment.

I am just going to touch briefly upon the question of discipline. To get right down to our own affairs in The Mead Corporation, you men all have probably wondered in your own minds why the company management would permit the taking of certain orders of paper and manufacturing them here in the coating mill, or on #11 machine or on #5 machine, when it was perfectly obvious to you that it was a losing order. Then, we make the paper and have a terrible time and after turning it out and sending it to the customer, you get another order of the same sort and the question comes into your mind "What in the world is this management thinking of, what kind of Sales Department have we? But, after all, the Sales Depart-

*Herbert A. Kidd acted as manager of various enterprises undertaken by the Mead Corporation jointly with other companies. He became a Vice President of the Company in 1952.

ment is just one branch of our business, some fellow at the top must have slipped pretty bad." I decided that I had slipped and, therefore, we now have an operating committee composed of Mr. Van de Carr, Mr. Ferguson and Mr. Mead instead of just Mr. Mead, and it was two to one against me and I am hoping for improvement. But there are, in business, times when you have to do things that seem perfectly ridiculous in order to accomplish an end.

We can't choose to make nothing but magazine paper in this mill. Twenty years ago this decision was in order and we decided to specialize in this mill in nothing but magazine and gradually let all other business go, because we could make magazine paper best and possibly cheaper here. However, we couldn't do this for two reasons. A lot of other people who were envious of our position began competing with us and, if we had left ourselves in that position we might have reached the point where we had nothing left to do, for there would be no money left in magazine paper.

For the last fifteen or eighteen years, as I have told you before, this company has been trying to diversify its products, to get into various fields of paper, but we are interested in manufacturing only as many different grades of paper as we can possibly find to manufacture profitably. We ought to get the company to the point where every type of paper we manufacture is being manufactured at a profit. In order to do this job, we have to learn a new type of discipline in our own thinking. We have to learn a new type of discipline in our planning. And I want to tell this group that from the top on down (or perhaps top up—I think it is top up because I consider myself clear at the bottom after the showing of last year although I am optimistic enough to believe that we can lick this problem and I want the fun of being part of it), we have to practice a new type of discipline in all of our thinking. We have to think much more accurately and discipline ourselves and say, when we start a job, that we are going to do this job and do it more thoroughly than anything we have ever done before and I will pledge you the word of Mr. Van de Carr, Mr. Ferguson and myself, the so-called management committee of this business, that we are going to discipline ourselves and spend a great deal more time in planning the whole procedure. . . .

This merchandizing in a demoralized market is one of the most difficult things in the world. We will work for six months trying to save a dollar a ton on a certain grade of paper, or in the manufacture of pulp, and then we will go to the Sales Office in Chicago or Dayton and hear one of the salesmen talking to a customer and the customer tells him that so-and-so has offered him the same thing for two dollars a ton less than our price. Our salesman quickly tells him that we'll take five dollars off our price. Now this is just what they are doing down in Washington and it is perfectly ridiculous.

Unfortunately, but true, we are in one of these very demoralized markets now, but it has been my experience over these thirty years that such a situation can't last. We can't go on like this for very long. We have to rectify it some way and somehow it is going to be rectified. In the meantime, we have to exercise patience and keep our courage and all the vital energy we have not to lose confidence in the future of our own business, or ourselves, of this company and of the United States of America. . . .

FOREMEN'S CLUB, Chillicothe, May 27, 1940

Never in the lifetime of any one of us in this room has there been a more serious time than we are all seeing at present, in my humble judgment. The last war that happened in this world was so completely devastating that no one believed that they would ever live to see another. Certainly it was far beyond my own imagination to think that in less than another fifty to one hundred years could we repeat such an experience.

I, therefore, was unwilling to believe until very shortly before the present catastrophe overtook us that it was going to be a repetition. Now, that we have passed through six to eight or nine months of the recent experience, we see that nothing in the previous one could compare with what we are now being told, and I have reason to believe that the reports in the paper are in no sense exaggerated, and that much of the grief that is being suffered, both in the army and among the civilians of Europe, is yet to be explained to us. We entered into the last war under the slogan of trying to make the world safe for democracy. As we look back at the experience, I think we can all agree that we failed in our objective. The reason for our actually entering into the last war, while theoretically it was to save the world for democracy, was I think, in the final analysis, because we had the fear that if the Allies of that time were beaten we might possibly find ourselves involved in the fight without very much assistance left to us.

Now, if that were the case twenty-five years ago, this present situation is not twice as serious but at least ten times as serious as the one in which we found ourselves then. . . . I told my own family, my children in particular, that when this war started last September, that I believed it was a religious war, and I told my three boys that I thought they had better choose the branch of service they were going into because it was my feeling that all three would be called to some service and in a reasonably short time.

I think that is probably still a fact, and if it is, the quicker we declare ourselves in this country the better. It is perfectly obvious that from a material standpoint it would be impossible for us to assist the Allies with men or munitions, or with any other materials at the present moment, and it would take us so many months to enter the conflict in any sizable way that the war might be over before we got there, but the psychological effect upon Germany and upon the Allies, and upon Italy, in particular, who has not yet made up her mind as to what her next action will be, might be very, very beneficial. Now mind you, I am not advising that we do this, but I want to put it in the minds of everybody with whom I am associated, and I would like to have you give it honest thought, and I might come to you and ask your advice as to what all of our positions should be. At any rate there is no question but that this country is very close to such a decision, much closer than the people of America think. . . .

. . . I very much regretted the President saying . . . that he felt absolutely insistent that this country live up to the wage and hour laws and the other social laws that had been passed, no matter what our war situation and defense situation might be. I think this is absolutely wrong. Those of us in this room, and every industrial group in America believes in a short week as far as the hours of work are concerned. We have been in favor of minimum wages. When I was active in Washington as Chairman of the Business Advisory Council for the Department of Commerce, upon which I am still serving, the wage and hour bill was first brought before Congress, and the President asked me personally if I was willing to assist the movement, and if I thought the Council of which I was Chairman would also assist, and I answered him without question unqualifiedly. We discussed the minimum wage and maximum number of hours, and I agreed with him perfectly, and he agreed with the figures that we thought in the Council were perfectly fair and proper; but the Bill as it was ultimately passed was not the Bill we discussed. The original conception of this Bill was that there should be a statutory bill simply mentioning a minimum or maximum number of hours, exactly as our Ohio State law is developed for women's hours, and the same with the minimum wage—that there should be a minimum wage below which people should not be employed; and this floor and ceiling, as it is called, would be a statutory law and all we would have to do would be to provide proper inspection and see we lived up to it. However, in the drafting of this law everybody had a new idea as to what it should cover, and when they finished they had to have an administrator such as they had to have on a labor board, and we immediately found ourselves in a very complicated wage and hour situation which might have been entirely avoided.

Now in the greatest emergency this country has ever seen, when it is absolutely necessary that we do all in our power to protect ourselves, and to establish a defense that will keep this country from being attacked, I think these things should be set aside, and I think the President of the United States should say we will work as many hours as necessary to develop whatever in this country we need to protect ourselves. As soon as the emergency is over, we will go back to where we started.

. . . It makes us all stop and think when we see the possibility of France and England being swallowed up in the same way that the Netherlands and Belgium have been swallowed up, and the chance that there might be in this United States of ours being the next attacked, and I want to tell you within these four walls that there are not enough anti-aircraft guns in the United States to protect the City of Chillicothe from an air raid. That is a fact. I doubt very much if there are enough modern rifles in the United States to equip one army corps of 14,000 men.

I think it only proper for me to tell you people with whom I have been associated these many years, and with whom I feel very close . . . that I am unalterably opposed to a third term for any President, no matter what the emergency may be. I do not think that a tradition which has survived 150 years, and it is only a tradition—there is nothing in law to prevent a third term—a tradition that has stood up so well for 150 years limiting the service of any one man to the Presidency for eight years, should be altered. I think this for two very positive reasons: first, I do not think it possible for any man to give any more than eight years of service to that undertaking and give all that should be given to the job. It requires super-human strength to live through eight years of it and to contemplate even one more term is a mistake which I should not want to see any man make. The second reason is the statement made by the men who have refused this honor in the years gone by—they did not think it to the best interest of the country to be entrusted any more than eight years to any one man; and with our present example of what happens in European nations when one man does obtain control of the country and we drift into a new form of government, I cannot see how the people of the United States of America could ever submit their democracy to such a chance. Now, mind you, I am not speaking against Mr. Roosevelt, I am speaking against the principle, and I would feel exactly the same way no matter who the man was.

FOREMEN'S CLUB, Chillicothe, May 27, 1941

I took the liberty of telling this club last fall my own position with regard to the election, and I tried to impress on you all that in the remarks I then made I was attempting to give you a personal viewpoint without political bias. I regarded the election of last Fall as far above any political election that I had known or that we usually conceive of—I felt that it was the choice of a leadership at a time of great importance and national crisis, and while I expressed at that time my regard that you all know I have for Mr. Roosevelt and for many of the ac-complishments that he had made during the previous eight years, I felt that a change was advisable and almost necessary. I think I also told you shortly after the election in a few moments chat . . . that the election having been held and the majority of the people having chosen Mr. Roosevelt as the President of our country for the next four years, that I wanted the organization to know that I pledged myself and I felt that I was also pledging the organiza-tion unqualifiedly to support our chosen leader no matter what might develop, and I feel more strongly about that position today than I did even then, gentlemen. This is no time for quibbling and it is no time for a division of people within this country.

While I do feel intensely on this subject, I feel equally strongly that anyone who disagrees with me or disagrees with the President or disagrees with any of the policies that are being followed should have the full privilege of self-expression in the matter and should not be criticized for taking that position. . . . If we are going to come to an honest conclusion in our own minds as to the necessity of this situation, I think we too must listen to both sides and weigh the evidence as it is given to us, and then form our own convictions without bitterness and criticism. . . .

If we went into the last war to serve Democracy, we certainly did a very poor job. Democracy to my mind is a good deal like heaven; it is not a place, but state of mind, as some people have said of heaven, and to think that we could go to war and fight as we did in 1917 and 1918 and come out victorious and, with the reward of Democracy saved in our hands, begin forthwith to destroy, is, as I look back on it, almost one of the most serious crimes we have in civilization. . . .

Democracy as a way of life is being challenged in a manner that has never been challenged before. It has been said by a good many historians that there are only two things which men will finally fight for—one is their way of life, namely freedom, and the other is their home. Now there is no question, regardless of what Mr. Lindberg or anyone else may say but that we are fighting for our freedom and our way of life. . . .

There is only one way that people will live through the generations, and that is by helping one another as individuals; and every other philosophy of life has always failed, and any other philosophy, to my mind, will always fail. . . .

FOREMEN'S CLUB, Chillicothe, April 29, 1942

. . . During the last year I have had to spend a great deal of time in Washington. I hoped last Fall after serving on the Mediation Board for several months that I would not be called back for service of that kind. I made a special request that someone else be found to continue the job if a new board were set up, but for some reason or another my name was again suggested, and when I received a letter from the President asking me to serve on this board, on the 12th of January, I, of course, could do nothing but accept the command. It was simply a statement that I had been appointed a member of the War Labor Board and asked me to report at a certain time. . . .

I went back to work again in Washington in January, and the board is composed of twelve men—four representing industry, four representing labor, and four the public, meeting five days a week, permitting alternates for the labor and the employees groups of four men, which meant eight men serving on each of these groups. The public members are employed by the government, are permanent members, and must be there all the time;—Chairman, Vice-Chairman, and two other men. You probably have read about them. They are a very fine lot and are criticized very freely. Industry and labor are not always happy about the decisions, but I can tell you all with every assurance, that they are an unusually fine lot of men—I don't agree with them, but they are a fine lot of men. I haven't agreed with them yet—I may agree—we are coming closer, for your information we are coming closer and closer to seeing eye to eye and that goes for the labor fellows too.

I would like to make the statement that the labor representatives on this board at Washington are a fine group of men, trustworthy, straightforward, say what they think, and fight for their own cause, and they have my respect and admiration. I have told them so, and I am convinced from this experience I am having down there that labor in America is sound. It is like a good many of the other problems we have had to face in the last ten years; there has been a great deal of confusion developed, a great deal of uncertainty, but as we men know from our experience in this plant, and you men in our other plants, who are in contact with the workmen of this country—they think no differently than the group of us here in this room. Most of us have worked side by side and shoulder to shoulder with these same fellows so we know what they are thinking. Some are extreme, some have had unfortunate experiences and feel that they have been mistreated, and they have been told that men of importance in this country were accumulating wealth at their expense and were not entitled to what they were getting and did not play the game fairly. Some of them unfortunately have believed it.

. . . This labor work is very absorbing. When you start in on a Monday or Tuesday morning in the hearing of a case, as we do on the Board, the panel work is no longer carried on by Board members but by associate members. We have sixteen men to do that work, hear the cases before they come to the big Board—they do all the spade work and the hearing before the Labor Board itself is limited, both sides being allowed to present their case, and each side offer rebuttal just like the courts are carried on in Federal buildings in Cincinnati or in Washington. The work is very absorbing, the hearings last all day and in the evening the different groups have to get together to discuss the procedure to be followed the next day. Frequently I have found I work every day and every night to midnight for a week at a time, and when your mind is completely absorbed in that way it is just impossible for you to stop and take in the arguments that should properly be given to this particular business we are all interested in. I feel that if I am asked to make a decision under such circumstances it is just as likely to be wrong as right, and therefore in telling Mr. Ferguson and Mr. Van de Carr that I want to be relieved of any decision [concerning the Mead Corporation] for the few months I am completely absorbed in Washington, it is only proper that these gentlemen should be given full responsibility and that they should take over the active management of this company.

I think I might have a word with you about the country, because having had to spend so much time in Washington since the middle of January I have had an opportunity of learning certain things that the rest of you may not have realized. I attempted last year in this room to tell this same group about the seriousness of the war we were then in as I thought. I don't believe that from the remarks I heard subsequently, and from the general attitude that I knew existed in Chillicothe, that some of you realized the seriousness of the situation as it then existed. I was not able to impress it sufficiently on your minds, however, the Pearl Harbor episode created the necessary change in the thinking of nearly everybody in America, and we now find ourselves in a total war—acknowledged, declared, and we are all fighting in it. Some of us may be closer to it than others, those of us who have sons already started for the front at least; but come what may it is a job that has to be done and I am delighted that I happen to be fortunate enough to have two boys already in the service; one in the Marines and one flying; the third one coming along this summer. I know of nothing I would rather have my own flesh and blood do than try to defend America and maintain, preserve, or save for posterity the kind of a country that you and I have enjoyed and lived in.

We have all seriously neglected our obligations over the past twenty-five years. I have neglected mine, and you have neglected yours, and we are now paying a very severe penalty for our oversight. We have gone along in a complacent way feeling that democracy in America is a God-given situation that we were privileged to enjoy without doing the amount of work that is necessary to have the kind of happiness we lived in. We haven't given enough attention to our political structure, we haven't given enough attention to our local situation, we haven't given enough attention to our national situation; we have allowed a political group to control that phase of our national life which has done a pretty good job, but which can never do a proper job unless every man, woman, and child in America takes a part in it. It is because of a very deep conviction as to my neglect that I am giving so much of my time in Washington, and you younger people particularly will have to help to educate this community and every other community that we are a part of, to the idea that the larger corporations and the businesses of this nation in future will have to provide some way of having the executives of the business and the people who are responsible for your livelihoods and the stockholders' livelihoods—they will have to provide some way for these men to give part of their time to the national government. You can't run a democracy with absentee-ownership any more than you can run a business with absentee-ownership.

The only reason that the dictators, in my humble judgment, can temporarily whip the democracies is because the dictators demand at the point of a gun or bayonet that every man, woman, and child give the very best they have in them to the country. Now, of course, if you demand by force you will get results temporarily, but the country will never survive as a country, because when the dictator breaks and the group in control who have the guns and bayonets are changed, you have chaos. On the other hand, if you can get a group of individuals in this community, or in this State, or in the United States, who appreciate the responsibility they have, and give of themselves and their services because they know its their obligation and because they know it is the only way in which they can develop a nation of human beings who will live in the maximum of happiness, then you have something that cannot be broken, by any change that takes place at the top or the bottom.

FOREMEN'S CLUB, Chillicothe, April 26, 1943

. . . To you gentlemen who are here as guests tonight I think I should explain that my annual visit with the Foremen's Club and in more recent years with the Engineer's Club has been an informal one. I never prepare my remarks for the evening. I seldom give any thought to what I say because I want the whole evening to be just as simple and direct as if we were in a group of a few instead of a larger number. I dislike intensely making formal speeches anyway, and the worst part is writing it. Being the unfortunate president of the American Paper and Pulp Association last year and again this year, they told me . . . *I had to write a speech* because the paper trade journals and other important literary additions to our industry said that it had to be done and they had to publish it, since that was part of their racket, so with great difficulty I finally squeezed in the time to write a speech the minimum number of words it had to be and the proper length, and I had it all ready to deliver at the annual luncheon at New York, including all the people that they thought should talk (I didn't think anybody should talk but they thought so, and they run the Association); and by the time we had gotten through listening to all the other speakers, everybody was ready to go home. So when it came my turn to make the speech, I was just ashamed to ask those people to sit there and listen to it, but it had to be read because the paper trade journals had said so. I told the audience at the Waldorf Hotel that I was going to read it in the minimum length of time that a speech could be made. I went through it so fast I don't believe anybody heard it at all. Everybody was ready to take a nap anyway. So all of my hard work writing the damn thing went for nothing. And it certainly reminded me of the fellow who was walking up and down in front of the convention hall and they asked if a certain fellow was finished making his speech. He said, "Why yes, he finished the speech half an hour ago, but he doesn't know how to stop talking."

I have made a practice in appearing before you . . . to try to give you a brief review of the situation throughout the country, as it is part of my job to travel and contact people who buy paper and who publish magazines and other articles that use paper; and I have tried from time to time, as the record will show, to outline what I thought were the most important economic and at times political events of the year just past. And then I have dealt with activities of our own company and expressed a few hopes for the future. I decided today that it would be impossible in a short time to cover the economic situation as we see it in this country. The thing that most impresses me about this war effort, I have mentioned to you before—I spoke of it last year and the year before that—is the magnitude of the undertaking from the standpoint of the United States of America. I can't help but stress that again, and put it in first place tonight; particularly to all of you men who are in the development and research and engineering end of our business this year in Chillicothe and also the men who are responsible for production.

The figures and accomplishments of the past twelve months are just beyond my comprehension. The organization built for accomplishing the work that is being done in America is beyond anybody's imagination. We all know of problems that we have had in our various businesses and departments in times past, and that we think we face in the future. They just pale into insignificance when you think about the problems that other men are having in connection with the war venture. . . .

There is no question in the mind of any man or woman that I know in America but that we will win it, the only question is one of time. It would be foolish to say as to how long a time it may take. I think we must all plan for a long war. It is the only safe thing to do in our personal activities and in our business activities. By a long war, I mean another couple of years. It seems to me there is always a chance that it may take less. The time it takes to my thinking, is directly dependent on the effort and the mental attitude of our people.

It has always been a great relaxation to me to come back to Chillicothe from the busier sections of this country because I felt we have a very stable, happy community here, and it has been particularly pleasant to me in the last year or two to come back from the work I have been doing in Washington as a member of the War Labor Board to a community that I have always felt was free from labor controversies and where we have been free from them for a great many years, almost a hundred of them in the history of the paper mill, and yet but recently I received the distressing news that our paper mill was shut down because of a labor difficulty which seemed petty to us and which was entirely uncalled for to my thinking.

. . . We have stressed democracy in the United States of America very vigorously for 150 years and yet I doubt if any of us have realized just what true democracy was. We have urged the education of all people, and have encouraged the thinking of the individual. I am convinced that this procedure is correct, but we failed to realize that in the stressing of individual thinking we have created among all people in the minds of the youth of this country and those same minds as they have grown into womanhood and manhood a desire to know more about what was being done for them and to them and now we find ourselves almost overwhelmed by this great desire of each and every one of these people to know what is being thought of for them and what is being planned in their lives, and the job of those of us who have the responsibility of directing others has become one of trying to analyze what is in the mind of each and every one of these individuals, what questions they may have to ask, and letting them ask them and trying to satisfy the yearning they have for information.

One of the greatest weaknesses of industry over the years has been that it has carried on its business within itself and felt it concerned nobody else, as to what that particular business might do or think. In certain areas, such as we have here in Chillicothe, our company and the Chillicothe Paper Company have always felt a direct responsibility to the community, we were the chief employers in the town, and the activities of our companies supplied the dollars and cents with which the traffic and merchandizing of the town was carried on. I know I have always felt, and I know Mr. Story* has always felt, and Mr. McVicker* before him, that it was imperative for us to, so far as possible, get the business that was necessary to run the plants the maximum amount of time they could be operated. Now we felt that because we wanted to have profitable undertakings, but we also felt it because we felt it important that the men who were working in our establishments, and the women likewise, should be able to work just as many days in the week, weeks in the month, and months in the year as was possible. But we haven't talked much about it, and that has been true throughout all industry in this country.

When, in the early thirties, the human cry was raised against industry, that it had been responsible for the great boom and great collapse, there was no one who talked about the converse of that argument. Of course, industry was no more responsible for the boom of the twenties and the collapse of the thirties than any other segment of our whole society. Real estate speculations, stock speculations, all kinds of financial undertakings that were of the wildest sort, a lot of the political activity of those days, all of these various factors contributed to the boom we had, and the ultimate collapse; but because industry was the employer of a very great amount of labor, industry was blamed when the jobs were not forthcoming.

On that basis, the political party that was in power at the time of the collapse received its proper share of the blame, and was put out of office, and the so-called "New Deal" developed. I need not tell a lot of you men in this room who belong to our own organization that I have said annually to you that there was a great deal of the thinking of the present administration that I have had great confidence in, and that I supported. There are other phases of the administration that I have not had equal confidence in, and have spoken against; but I think that President Roosevelt is a very great man; I think he has done a very great good for this country. I think at the present time that he is a magnificent leader. . . . I think that the Lend-Lease conception, and the putting of it into effect as quickly as was done by the President (and it would not have been done except for him, in my judgment) probably saved England, and saved us, from a whipping at the hands of Germany at that particular time. I think that the President's visions in handling the affairs of this country during the war period have been magnificent. I think, however, that our own domestic economy and the management of our own internal affairs . . . have not been well handled. Whether we should expect the same man who has this great vision and who has exhibited such fine illustrations of the ability to take care of all the international affairs to take the same responsibility in handling domestic affairs, I don't know. I leave that to you to judge. . . .

---

*Mr. Story and Mr. McVicker were executives of the Chillicothe Paper Company, whose organization was assisted by Mr. Mead, and which was later merged with The Mead Corporation.

. . . I feel it an obligation, as I usually have, to tell you who are associated with me in this paper venture the problems as I see them that we face in the immediate future. One of the greatest of them is this labor problem to which I referred a minute ago. As you know, we have at the present moment in this country the most serious labor controversy that has ever developed. I unfortunately am sitting on the Board in Washington that has to finally deal with Mr. John Lewis in this matter. I think it is important that we clearly understand the issue. The issue is not one of wages and working conditions, but whether this country shall be directed by the Commander-in-Chief of America and the administration, or by other groups who are not willing to accept their full share of the responsibilities.

I think, and I believe you are willing to agree with me, that the American people at the present time are going to see this war through and are not going to let anything interfere with it, and that the expressed wishes of the President of the United States are going to be followed whether or no. I would like to know if I am wrong, but I believe that is the attitude of the people of this community and of every other community in the United States. . . . I think that not only over the next few weeks will we have a crisis in North Africa through which we are going to pass successfully, and which may be the turning point of the war; but I think that we are going through a domestic crisis which is going to be just about as serious, and through which we are going to pass equally successfully, and that we will find ourselves better off for having made the fight. . . .

Now, I really feel as I have grown older and have spent more time in Washington over these past ten years, that the people of America know a great many things down deep in their hearts that they never give expression to, and that each one of us in this room will always rather take the easier road and say that we know some things go on, but why talk about it? I think the time has come when each one of us must take a position in this matter [allied unity], and there isn't any one of us that isn't equally important to the whole. Unless we do it the country as a whole is going to suffer desperately. If, after all the blood and agony we have gone through to win this war, we are stupid enough in America to allow ourselves to be divided in our allegiance after the war is over to the people who have fought with us, and to begin to feel that because of their selfishness we are not going on to protect this world, we have just wasted a lifetime. . . . In some way somebody must start it, to try to develop a relationship particularly with the British Empire, and nearly equally with Russia and China, to see that no set of people in the world can pull us apart after this victory is once won. . . .

Now, I haven't anything to say to you, ladies and gentlemen, about The Mead Corporation, except that it has managed to pull through a very difficult year and keep its head above water, and is in good sound financial condition. . . . I am disappointed, on your account more than on mine, about this labor situation that we seem to have run into. It is due to misunderstanding; it is exactly like the situation that I am pleading to avoid in connection with our own allies. If you let a misunderstanding start and grow and expand itself, you will finally get to the breaking point where something happens. . . .

. . . I have made the statement to you men that I have no objection to labor organizations; if it ever seemed to our men best, we wanted them to have a free choice in the matter. We want it to come by their own inclination, and not by pressure, and we certainly don't want it to come by a misrepresentation and abuse of those of us who have tried to lead a decent, straightforward industrial life.

. . . This is all a phase of our labor problem, just as different as the type of war that we are carrying on is different from the previous war, and you men and all of us have got to learn to adjust ourselves to an entirely new type of thinking.

FOREMEN'S CLUB, Chillicothe, May 29, 1944

I suppose that Washington today is the most important individual location in the world; the other capitals of the Allied countries are, of course, of great importance to us all, but when it comes to the interest and very great value to all of the face of the earth, I think Washington stands almost alone at the moment. And while the experience I have been having down there is awfully tiresome and at times a little depressing, it takes a great deal of effort and has its discouragement, I think the privilege of being in this particular spot at this particular time—these last three years—is a very great one; and it seems to me I have a real obligation to all of you who are making it possible for me to be there, and to give you the things that I am seeing and that I feel may be of real interest as coming from a first-hand source rather than through the press or radio or the many other channels that you have open.

In thinking over what might be of most interest to the group, I thought that you might enjoy hearing something of the personalities involved down there. I don't know that I have ever talked particularly in the past about the individual men that I have come into contact with during this period, but as time goes on and you watch these men in action, and realize the tremendous pressure they are under and the hours of work that they all put in, the hours that they must have at home with their minds intimately filled with the great problems that they are feeling through the day, you can't help but have an increasing respect and admiration for the individuals and also a great pride that we have such people in America. The people from abroad that come to Washington that we meet are the same type, of course, but those of us here in this country can't help but feel that our group, after all, is the top.

To my thinking, the war effort has produced two or three very great men in addition to the President. I put him first because the more I watch his operations and I think the more that we all see of his accomplishments, the greater must be our admiration and affection for him, and political thinking makes no difference in my mind at the present time. I have been asked by several people since I came west . . . what I thought of the coming campaign and I said I was not much concerned with the election next fall. I for some reason can't regard it as of very great importance. Now, that doesn't sound very conventional, because so many people in this country have stirred themselves to an unreasonable limit, to my thinking, because of the coming election. The problems of the world and of this country are so much greater than the individual problems that I feel that the composite thinking of America is the factor that will save, make or break, the situation, and not any one individual.

. . . As I say, the admiration for the President of the United States is very great; I think he is a very wonderful man. He has many weaknesses, as we all have and every human being has, but in all of the major issues that the world and the country have faced during this war period, I think he has been as nearly right as a man could be, and his willingness to give of himself and every ounce of his life and energy to the country at this time is most generous; and with it all he keeps, as you probably know better than I can tell you, a smile and a patience and a forbearance that is always beyond belief. . . .

I think perhaps the greatest man in America, and I am not sure that he is not as great as any man in the world today next to the President, is General Marshall. I don't know that I have ever seen a finer man than that man; he is simple, straightforward, direct in everything he does. He moves, both mentally and physically, with the greatest ease, right to the point, every word he speaks. He always seems to have time to stop and say a kind word to anybody that he knows, and he has built up the greatest army I believe this world has ever seen in an incredulously short time. When you think that a number of times we have had to multiply the original standing army of America of a few years ago, and how we have had to equip, to train it, get a lot of it abroad, do a lot of things the Army has done—and that not only the man that is responsible at the head, but the man who is responsible for the complete organization in my judgment, is this one fellow Marshall—you can begin to somewhat imagine the quality of the fellow. And you just can't overestimate him, you just can't; he seems to be almost superhuman.

The General was with a group that I happen to be a member of down in Hot Springs last fall; he had Mrs. Marshall with him. He spent two days with us and chatting informally part of the time; he was the guest speaker of the evening on Saturday night at a dinner at which many of our wives were present, a dinner of about seventy, I should think. He talked of the future, the problems he was facing, just as frankly as I am talking to you this evening, and just as simply. The next morning, Sunday morning, he got up and went out, took a horseback ride, started out all by himself; and the man who was responsible for his being there, the chairman of this group, was so astonished that he asked the General if he would wait a few minutes until he slipped on his riding clothes and he would ride with him. He rode with him, and when they returned this man said to me, "Is there any other place in the world, or any other country in the world where the General of the Army, the top man who is responsible for the welfare of the country, would get on a horse and go off by himself on a horseback ride in the woods!"

. . . A very great man in America today that you have been reading about lately—he is a product of the last war as well as this war—is Mr. Baruch. I don't know of anyone outside of the government in America that has anything like the confidence of the country that he has, and it is well deserved. He too is a very great man, simple as all great men are in my judgment— that is, all that I happen to have any knowledge of—a man of great mind, unlimited capacity, who at pretty advanced age as you know is giving everything that he has to the country in the way of his own activity, instead of staying in retirement and resting as he is perhaps entitled to. He is at work every day, without any reward of any sort, of course, except that he feels that he owes a great deal to America and any debt that he can pay at a time like this he should pay. I think we are tremendously fortunate in having him as near the top of our advisory group as he is.

Associated with Baruch's name is of course Mr. Justice Byrnes; at the present time Baruch is Justice Byrnes' advisor on all business and economic questions. Justice Byrnes is well up in the class with the three men that I have just named, in my thinking, one of the same type who is almost above reproach. He, too, has made so few mistakes since he left the Supreme Court Bench and came into the administration that it is almost unbelievable.

We could go on naming a dozen men who, while not quite so much in the press or so near the top, are doing equally fine work—in fact, you can find hundreds of them in Washington, nearly every one of them placed in the position that he is best qualified to fill and almost without a peer in that position. Now, the President has been criticized in this country a good many times because he was not an organizer, he was not an administrator or executive. . . . But when the President has to, when the conditions demand it as they do in world war, when the country is at war, and he knows that the right men must be found for the job, I can't help but feel that he has done a most outstanding, an extraordinary piece of work in the selection of the men he has placed in these very critical positions. Almost without exception, as I say, the men who are in the places of importance in this government and in our war effort are, to my mind, the best selection that could possibly be made, and I don't think that the people of America give this fact anything like the proper weight.

We have heard a great deal of criticism of Mr. Nelson, and yet if you ask any industrialist, any man of importance around the country, whom he would put in Nelson's place doing the job he has to do, and you fail to get a response. Mr. Nelson has as his chief deputy Mr. Charles Wilson, president of General Electric Company, and he is doing a magnificent job; but I don't think, as fine as Mr. Wilson is, and as capable, and as great an executive as he is, I don't believe he could do Mr. Nelson's job. In fact, I don't think he would do it, more than a week, so that you have to take the temperament of all these men and their different characteristics, and weigh them most carefully before you put them in the spot if you want them to stay. In other words, a man who is misplaced doesn't stay very long; and you can go right down the scale in Washington situation and, as I say, you will find almost without exception the men who are doing the great jobs are men who were carefully chosen by the President and put in these positions, and, with very few exceptions, without a mistake on his part in selecting them.

I would like to speak just a word about one of them who has recently passed away, Secretary Knox, Secretary of the Navy. He was a great character, a magnificent man. I have heard a great many Republicans speak ill of him since he accepted a position in the cabinet. President Roosevelt announced he was going to pick two men from the Republican party for his Secretary of War and Secretary of the Navy, and a lot of people criticized Mr. Knox and Mr. Stimson for taking these positions. We heard from a number of partisan Republicans that after all they weren't particularly good Republicans anyway. But a few years back when Mr. Knox was running for Vice President, the same men said that Knox was one of the greatest Americans that ever lived. Secretary Knox had a wonderful physique, he was a powerful man in every way. He did a great job as Secretary of the Navy, and he just worked himself to death; there was no other out to it. He was a perfectly well man a year ago, and as his health began to decline and people, his intimate friends and family, begged him to stop working at the great pressure, he paid no attention to them. "I am going to do this job to the limit of my ability." No human being could stand the pace that he was driving himself, and I think the country owes him a great deal of gratitude. He was a very good friend of mine, and, as several of his friends who knew him at all will say, we felt the deepest sense of loss; and I want to express right here and now to these intimate friends that I have in this room the intimate feeling I have of regret that he had to step out of the picture before the war was won, because he played a greater part than the people generally realize.

To get a little bit closer to the work that I have been attached to, I want to mention Walter Davis, chairman of the War Labor Board. Like all others, he has some weaknesses, and as it is he is subject to particular criticism because all of us on the War Labor Board seem to be subject to that. We have had our ups and downs and we have had many fights of all sorts, as you naturally would on a partisan board, but through it all Davis has remained fixed in his purpose and straightforward in all of his dealings both with labor and industry. With un-limited patience and tremendous ability he has been able to keep the War Labor Board alive, and that is some job. I don't believe that there is any more intensive work going on in Wash-ington, because of the peculiar labor situations we have in America.

... It incidentally happens that Mr. Sewell Avery is a friend of mine. He and I were co-directors on the board of the Container Corporation of America for two years during the depression, and I saw a good deal of him; I haven't seen much of him in recent years. I was a little embarrassed when I had to vote to impose a maintenance of membership on him.

When a vote is split, no matter who the winner may be, the rest of the Board supports that decision one hundred percent. Now the original industry members of the War Labor Board, of which I happen to be one, decided that that would be our position at the beginning of the undertaking. On the very first decision that the Board made, the industry members were voted down, the four labor members and four public members voting for a maintenance of membership and the industrial members voting against it. Then the question came, when the employer said he would not abide by the Board's decision, as to whether the Board should apply pressure or not; and we decided to make up our minds as to whether we would support the Board's decision or continue to vote against the other two factions. We decided, and I think properly, that no matter how the vote went, once made, we would unanimously support it and insist that, regardless of whom the vote was against, either the employer or the em-ployee, he would have to accept the decision of the Board. I know, gentlemen and ladies, of no other way to run a board in this country or to run a government. If a majority votes for a situation, no matter how some of us felt, we must support the law.

I will admit that we haven't always lived up to that principle in this country, nor have I. ... The only way we can save this democracy of ours is to support the government, and from now on I am going to support it no matter how I feel about the decisions. That is what we decided to do on the War Labor Board, and we have never varied from that position, and I am happy to say that the labor men have never varied from that decision; they have supported every decision that has been made, whether they objected to it or not. We are now accused on the industry side of being inconsistent, because we are opposed to maintenance of mem-bership and yet we say that when a maintenance of membership is imposed against an em-ployer that he has to live up to it, and we are being criticized by industry. I am happy to say that the vast majority of industry, in my judgment, are of the same mind when they under-stand the question. They believe as we do who have stood by this principle.

The Montgomery Ward situation, ladies and gentlemen, is a pretty simple one when you know the facts, but it is awfully hard to explain them in writing and then read the description and know what it says in the end. But I think I can tell you in just a few words what the situation is. This War Labor Board was set up by an Act of Congress, a Directive of the President, three years ago, and in that Act we were instructed by the President to settle any wage dispute that had any influence on the production for the war effort. Those are not the exact words. It was left to the War Labor Board whether a labor dispute in question had any influence on the production for the war effort, and that is a very hard matter to decide.

One of the early situations was the San Francisco Hotel strike, which was completely broken by the local authorities, so that the hotels were operating but were being picketed. The pickets could not be taken off the streets; under the present laws pickets are allowed properly. The United States Army came to our Board and said, "We think you ought to settle this labor question in these San Francisco hotels because it is interfering with the shipbuilders; it is demoralizing. Furthermore, we fellows in the Army don't like to drive up to a hotel and get out of a cab and go into it with pickets out there. We think you ought to clean it up." We had voted before that it did not involve enough war production to warrant our taking the case up, thinking we were following the law, do you see; but the Army wanted us to do it, the local authorities in San Francisco wanted us to do it, and finally we had to reconsider the matter and agree that we would take up this hotel situation and try to make a contract between the union and the employer. The moment we made that decision, we opened the door to almost every labor controversy in America, and therefore under the law we were compelled to take any labor dispute on our Board for final determination that had any indirect influence on the war, do you see; so that there was no way that the War Labor Board could avoid taking on the Montgomery Ward dispute, regardless of the merits of the case. We had to take it; we had to make a determination.

After the original Act setting up the War Labor Board, last summer Congress passed another act called the Smith-Connally Act, or properly called the War Labor Disputes Act. It was very hastily put together under great pressure when prejudice was at its highest during the coal situation, and it was probably the poorest act Congress has put on the statute books in the last five years, because nobody that really knew the labor situation had anything to do with it; and the act, in our judgment on the War Labor Board, has not been a helpful act in the main. There were some features of it that were, but generally speaking, no, we would be better off if we didn't have the act. In that act, it was specified that if the War Labor Board decisions were not maintained or lived up to by an employer or a labor union, that the President could take over that property and the War Labor Board's determination would be, therefore, in the hands of the government rather than in the hands of the individual operator. Now, it said in that Act that the War Labor Board had the right of determination only in certain producing companies, that is, companies producing for the war effort, the word was used. So here we had two acts, one passed at the beginning of the war setting up the War Labor Board, and the second act which was supposed to cover the activities of the Board, but covered only a small part of the activities. The question is which act the Board would follow. The War Labor Board decided that we would follow the original act that set up the Board—what else can we do?

Sewell Avery says that the President had no right nor authority to take over the company, because it wasn't specifically stated in the second act. But if it isn't specifically stated, what is a War Labor Board going to do with the thousands of employers in this country who are not producing war goods? It is a legal technical point the Montgomery Ward Company is standing on. I personally do not think the Montgomery Ward Company has any right in the height of a war effort to stand on a technical point in the handling of any dispute. I think Mr. Sewell Avery is wrong in his position. He has brought out the fact that the President, if given this broad act, can take over the dry goods store downstairs. I think the President, as Commander-in-Chief, can do anything that he thinks is necessary to the fulfillment of his task in winning this war, and it becomes a matter of judgment whether a decision of Montgomery Ward is necessary or not; but certainly the War Labor Board is of no value in this country unless somebody can enforce its authority. The War Labor Board can't. We have no enforcement power given to us, so that we must depend on somebody else to do the enforcing, and the only way it can be done, whether the union is at fault or the employer is at fault, is for the President to take over the plant.

. . . Operating under the laws that we have at the present time, the procedure being used is the only one that can be used; and until Congress passes some new laws, we have to go right down the road we have been going or give up the War Labor Board. There are a great many people that think that would be a great idea, and I am one of them. That would tickle me to death. But a great many of you who study figures, and remember the last war, know that commodity prices have advanced in this country less than one-half as much during this war as during the last war. There have been two factors in stabilizing the prices and wages in this country; one is the Office of Price Administration and the other is the War Labor Board. Under the second act passed a year after the first War Labor Board Stabilization Act the War Labor Board was given full authority for fixing all wages in this country. These are the only two authorities in the industrial field—we have the agricultural group that fixes food prices.

During the early part of the stabilization program the Office of Price Administration was much the stronger influence in keeping prices from advancing. That was during Leon Henderson's time, and I have made the remark on a good many occasions that he did more as an individual to prevent inflation than any man in America, and I think that will be written in history. He has made himself unpopular, like a good many others, worked himself completely out. His retirement was forced by Congress and public sentiment—it was also forced by his health as well. But so long as his health lasted and so long as he stayed on his job he did a wonderful heroic piece of work.

. . . During that same period, the War Labor Board has had to try to stabilize wages, and since the act was passed the Board has done an outstanding job in the eyes of the Administration, I think, and in the eyes of a good many people who are students in keeping these inflationary prices from going into the sky; and if they had gone as in the last war I am convinced that America would have been a bankrupt nation by the end of this war. Prices are reasonably stabilized and being held to the end of the war. I think that any wage increases will be extremely moderate, and I think that the national debt will not be too big for this country to survive, so that our economy will be saved. I think the credit for that accomplishment goes to the Administration in Washington, not to say one group, but to the whole administration, and I think it is a very great feather in the cap of the President of the United States; and as I say, in my thinking I have gotten over any partisanship and I think we must give credit where credit is due—that no matter whether it be Republican or Democrat or some other political group I believe you can't deny that great things have been accomplished in this war period.

I am asked by a good many people, and perhaps it is in your mind, as to how I feel about Lend-Lease. There is a great deal of comment going around this country on the fact that we have been a lot of suckers in giving liberal assistance, financial and otherwise, to Great Britain, Russia as well, and to the rest of our allies, and that the lease-lend program has not been a really successful venture. I don't know how you all may feel, or how much thought you have given to it. I would like to say, for my part after watching it carefully, seeing it under operation, and knowing what I do about it from study right on the ground, I think it is probably one of the greatest outstanding developments of the generation. I think that without lease-lend, this war would have cost America so much more than it has in lives and in disaster, that there is no possible way of estimating, and I deplore the idea of now, when we are on the verge of victory as we are sure we are, having people of this country feel that England has in any way taken advantage of us, or that we have been lax, unbusinesslike, or overgenerous in the lease-lend project.

And again, you have to give credit where it is due, and I am quite certain that, along with a few others who now contribute to his thinking, the President was responsible for lend-lease, and it has been carried out by one of the great men of America whom you will hear much of, in my judgment, in the future, Edward Stettinius, new Undersecretary of State. He broke his health in the middle of it, and an intimate friend of Charlie Van de Carr's and mine, a man in the paper industry—Tom McCabe, President of the Scott Paper Company, who is an associate of our company in Brunswick Pulp and Paper Company—Mr. McCabe was Mr. Stettinius' right-hand deputy from the beginning of lease-lend, and all the time Mr. Stettinius was out of his office for months with broken health a year or so ago after working eighteen hours a day for many months to get the thing straightened out and going as it should—all during that time Mr. McCabe was running that department. Yet his name has never been seen in the press, nobody knows anything about him. Stettinius, you may remember, at the beginning of the war was one of the men chosen with General Knudsen to head the O.P.B., or O.P.M., as it then was, and was then set aside for Mr. Nelson to take that job, and the common expression in Washington that was used about Stettinius was that he was "kicked upstairs" by the President and put in lease-lend because the President did not know what to do with him—all of which is ridiculous if you know the facts. The lease-lend was the most sensitive area that we had in America, one of the most difficult to handle, and the President picked the man who he thought could do the job best, realizing that it was more important than the production in the war effort. Unless we were able to support England and give her all the help she needed, the war would have been lost in six months. In picking Stettinius, the President unquestionably picked the best man in America to do the job. That is proven—Russia thinks he is a great man, England has confidence in him, and Congress will give him any amount of money he asks for.

I had luncheon the other day with the head of the British Industries—he occupies a position not unlike our president of the Chamber of Commerce on the British side. He is a nice fellow, Sir John Forbes Weston, and he told a story about one of the British Cabinet he knew well, traveling a short time ago, and he got on the train and the conductor came through and Sir William started to fumble in his pocket, but couldn't find his ticket, and the conductor told him he would go on and come back in a little while. When he returned Sir William was still unable to find the ticket and he said, "Sir William don't you worry about that, I know you well and I've seen you lots of times, I know you're an honest man, and if you find the ticket you can mail it to the railroad, I know you will take care of it." And Sir William replied, "That may be all right with you, but I've got to find the damn ticket because I don't know where I'm going."

That is the way I feel about this subject tonight. Well, I had no set speech. If I had had, I would have left it in my coat pocket. That is one reason for leaving your coat downstairs. I could claim that my speech was put away in my pocket, but I have never delivered a regular speech, and I can't get over with that one.

However, as I say, I just wanted to tell you about a few of these things that I hope are of some interest to you in Washington, and felt, never having talked about the personal side of those, that might come closer than anything else. It ought to give us all the greatest confidence in this country, and in our democracy, and our present form of government, in spite of all its weaknesses, and the fact that we say things are in a terrible muddle and we don't know where the end is and we sometimes doubt that our democracy can survive this terrific period in our history. When you see it at work, when you are an intimate part of it, it gives you great confidence and strength and implicit belief that America not only will survive, and our form of government survive after this war is over, but that we are going to find equal talent in developing the future.

Now I am just going to close with a few words about that phase of our present situation. Unquestionably, this year of 1944 will go down in history as one of the greatest years of all time. Here we have the greatest of all wars, we are about to enter the greatest offensive that has been known in the history of the world. If George and General Eisenhower will only make up their minds, we will have an extraordinary situation this summer and fall. There is a deep conviction on the part of everybody that has any part in it that it is going to be successful. There is no question in anyone's mind about that. How disastrous it will be, what toll of lives, how terrible no one of us can tell, but my only fear about America and about those of us in this room, and about our company, and about this community, and about other communities, particularly, about the middle country, where we are farther removed from the activities than they are on the East and West Coasts, is that there is still too much complacency. There isn't enough realization of the sacrifices that are necessary in a war. There isn't enough intense feeling about the situation. My feeling is that we may have the victory and not along with it the depth of feeling that is necessary to save us in the future.

FOREMEN'S CLUB, Chillicothe, April 23, 1945

I think I should first tell you what I am supposed to be doing in Washington, because there is some confusion about it . . . I don't want anything publicly said about what I am supposed to be doing. At the end of last year I terminated my work with the National War Labor Board. I asked to be relieved the middle of the year, feeling that I had served long enough, having been there already three and one-half years at that time, one year on the first board that was appointed, that is the National Mediation Board, and two and one-half years on the subsequent National War Labor Board. The last year and a half I had been the Chairman of what we know as the Industry Group of the Board, representing Management against Labor. As you know, the Board was composed of twelve persons, four representing the public, four labor and four management. I was promised relief from that activity each month during the Fall, but it didn't materialize.

Now, on account of my closeness to Mr. Byrnes, last fall he called me up one day confidentially when I was in the West on a trip, and said that he would allow me to retire from the War Labor Board at the end of the year if I would accept another appointment. I told him that I would do so after a good deal of argument over the telephone. I tried to talk him out of it, I thought there were other men in America that should be chosen in my place and I told him that I would try to get one of them, but he said "No," the decision had been made, and that I was to become a member of the Board that was set up in the Act of Congress passed last fall determining the Director of Reconversion. That act made one man not only War Mobilization Director, but the Director of Reconversion, so that office was combined. That seemed to be necessary because of the transition from war to peace through the Japanese phase being contemplated. It is quite a long one and obviously you can't have one man prosecuting the war while another is setting up the peacetime economy, so that Mr. Baruch, who formulated the act, along with his assistant, Mr. Hassett, and the Congress in passing the act, agreed . . . that the job should be given to one man. But it was seemingly such a colossal undertaking and such a great responsibility to be in the hands of one individual, since it covers all the other war agencies in Washington and peacetime agencies that are still to be set up that it was determined by the Congress that a board of twelve men, twelve persons, should be appointed by the President and confirmed by the Senate, and that is called the Advisory Board to the Office of War Mobilization and Reconversion, and is the Board that Mr. Byrnes and the President asked that I serve on. The public is represented on that Board by three persons, one of whom is the Chairman of the Board; the law reads that three persons shall be familiar with labor, shall be experienced in labor matters, three experienced in management matters, and three experienced in farm or agricultural matters. We have represented on the Board the public by Governor Gardner, Governor Max Gardner, a former Governor of North Carolina and now a practicing lawyer in Washington, as well, and Mr. Davis who was Chairman of the War Labor Board, and who has now been made Economic Stabilization Director, and Mrs. Anna Rosenberg of New York City. The Industries, or Management representatives are Eric Johnston, Nathaniel Dyke of Little Rock, Arkansas of the Smaller War Plants Corporation in Washington for several years, . . . and I am the third member of that group. The three farm organizations are represented by Edward O'Neal, Albert Goss and Jim Patton, and for labor we have Murray, Green and Cashen who is the president of the executive group of the railroad unions. That Board sits every other week starting Monday morning for two days and sometimes three, and so far practically every member has attended every meeting. There is no chance of substitution because we were confirmed by the Senate, which means that the individual name has to appear or else the place is empty, there is no chance of substitute votes. You can perhaps visualize the activities of the Board since I have told you some of what the Director has to cover and the Director sits with us during the two day discussions and we try to give the best we can of our judgment and experience to him in helping him make the decisions which he has to make to carry on his work for the next week or ten days. We are also subject to call at any time.

After accepting that responsibility, Mr. Davis who has been Chairman of the War Labor Board ever since the war started, and with whom I have had a very close association—Mr. Davis when he was made Director of Economic Stabilization had a vacancy caused by the resignation of Mr. Ralph Flanders of New England in his Board, and asked me to take that job because it comes the day after these other meetings and didn't seem to require very much more time, and I was persuaded to accept that responsibility also.

However, I can assure you that this is the limit. I have gone to the end of the road and it means that I am in Washington four days every other week and the rest of the time I am happy to tell you I am coming back to Ohio to live and I am going to get to the paper business. My wife and I have given up our house in Washington the first of the year with the idea of getting back where we belong. . . .

. . . We read a great deal about strikes, about loss of time, and the way men are misbehaving, but it is a well-known fact that this country has lost less hours of work through stoppage than any of the other countries that are supplying war goods except Russia and for both England and Canada the record for lost time is greater than ours. And I think by and large the American workman has done a fine job. It is a fact that they have become more critical—labor —they are harder to handle and that makes the work that you men have as directors and advisors of these men twice as difficult but it also makes it twice as interesting. The day has gone by in America when we can drive men and tell them what to do and expect them to do it, without having them question not only our authority but our judgment, and that is the result of education.

You cannot, in my humble judgment, ever develop a dictatorship that will equal the democracy that we know in America, because the composite thinking of a lot of individuals such as we have, people who respect one another, is always bound to be greater than any group of men that can be put into one room in some other country, or in this country, and direct from that room the activities of millions of people. It is just as clear to me now as the nose on your face why democracy is winning this war, and why democracy must survive over the next generation, and why it will continue to lead the world. . . .

We have got to learn many things. The first one is to give more of our time to the political situation and the social situation. By that, I mean looking after the people who need looking after, all through this land. You all have got to give more thought and time to the direction of the affairs of Chillicothe and the State of Ohio, and more thinking and discussion, have more discussion, about all of our political affairs. America has got to learn to talk politics without emotion. In discussing politics a few people sit around and begin to talk about the election or about something that has to do with the policies of the country, and everybody gets mad, and the evening's over, that's all there is to it. The discussion lasts about ten minutes. That's something that we can't permit any longer; we have got to learn to discuss politics; they have done it in England for a great many years, and they have done in many ways an outstanding job in the development of government; but we will learn it; we will get there.

. . . Of course the winning of the war in Europe is the greatest event of the past twelve months, and it is won, I am sure about that. I think that there is not going to be any victory in Europe in this war, because the situation is so terrible, and certainly there is no merit in being victorious over a country that is as devastated and demoralized as the German people are to-day. It is a matter of sympathy rather than anything else. I don't mean by that that I am one who wants to be soft in the treatment of Germany; they are our enemies, and they are very bitter against Americans, and they are going to continue to be bitter as long as the Nazi Party, which will continue underground for many months and probably all of our lifetime, will keep that bitterness alive.

I am asked, of course, by people I meet outside of Washington, what the general feeling is about the Japanese war. Nobody knows. There are two arguments, two sides, one that Japan after Germany's conclusion may decide that she can't possibly stand up against the world, and therefore the quicker she capitulates and turns herself over to the Allies and asks for whatever terms we impose upon her, the better off she will be; and there is no question of that, if Japan tomorrow would say she was through, and "Here I am, what are you going to do with me?" I don't know what we would do. That would be a terrible thing to put to America, and if they were smart, they would do it; but I don't think they are, and the war will have to go on for some time. But Japan, we know now, is whipped just as Germany is, and it is merely a question of time.

The problem of supplying an army in Japan is colossal, as you can well appreciate. I think that some of the figures are interesting to know. I had dinner the other night in Washington with a man who had just come back from Europe, who is one of the top men in the Supply Division of the United States Army, and he was telling a few of us the problems they have had to overcome over there in the last twelve months ever since D-day, and I don't know whether you men realize the magnitude of the undertaking that the United States, the Allies, had in D-day. He said that the supplies that were landed in France on D-day and the following few days in that first week of the attack corresponded in tonnage and in extent and size to the moving of St. Louis, the whole City of St. Louis, at least one hundred miles. Now if you can conceive of going and taking the whole City of St. Louis and moving it one hundred miles, you would have a picture of what they transported from America and from the British Isles across to France in that first drive they made in the landing. Furthermore, the Allies moved in the first ten days, they covered as much territory as the Army had planned for them to cover in the first forty days, so that they took that City of St. Louis and moved it that much further inland than they had expected to in that short a time. By the time they had got across France, in the next one hundred days, the city had trebled in size. In other words, by that time they had a city the size of Detroit, which is about three times the equal of the city of St. Louis, and they were moving that much stuff across the country. It just seems unbelievable, beyond anything; we can't use those figures, because they are not public yet. But in this recent attack on Iwo Jima, that small island, they required 640,000 tons of shipping in the first thirty days. Just think of it, the first month they had to transport 640,000 tons of material and put it on that small island, in order to win that one position; and the next month they sent something over 200,000 tons more; so that you can imagine the undertaking that this country now has in trying to supply an army in China and Japan and over all that part of the world. It will require four times as much shipping to take care of an army in the Pacific area as it did in the Atlantic area, so that if the Japanese war continues to last, this country will have one of the most colossal jobs of supply that human mind can conceive. But it is all well in hand and being wonderfully done. I think that the accomplishment of the United States Army and Navy in this war has been perfectly magnificent; I am sure we will all agree on that.

In this last twelve months since I last talked to you was the death of the President. I would like to explain to you that I am still a Republican, but as a member of the opposed party, I have as you all know, from the beginning of the administration of Mr. Roosevelt been appreciative of his fine qualities, and have felt that he should be supported in this great experiment that he put before the American people. . . . He had no illusions, in my judgment, about his own peculiarities, but he had a great vision, there is no question about that. He had a great vision back in 1933 when he started to turn this country from its serious depression to a better direction, and he has done a great job for America. . . . The people who were for him, and particularly anybody who had ever had any contact with him, felt the greatest sense of loss and grief, and I must say that I shared to a considerable extent in that feeling.

Now, Mr. Truman is a very fine man. He is a man of ability and great integrity, is a great believer in the democratic plan, and is just the type of fellow that I believe can from now on carry forward this work, and close in the open spots that we had, and make this country sound again after this terrible war experience; so that I can tell you men that I face, look forward, to the next few years with a great deal of confidence, and I think we have every reason to feel very fortunate that the situation is as it is. Mr. Truman is the kind of man who uses every possible opportunity to learn about every situation; he is careful and cautious, and he wants the benefit, so I am told, of all the advice he can get. He too has no illusions about his limitations. He is perfectly willing to surround himself with the ablest men, I believe, that he can find in this country, and everybody that I have talked to is most anxious to do his share, so that the country, in my judgment, finds itself in a very happy position from that one standpoint.

As to the immediate future, I don't know how much you all are thinking about the international situation, but that is extremely important. One of the things that we can't do now is to slip backwards. It is one of the things that the President would not have permitted the country to do, because he had the quality of leadership which kept the pressure on at all times. Mr. Truman, I don't believe, will do that. He wants to leave the decisions more to the people; he is going more particularly in the Congress and the Senate, and asking for the advice of the people in the country, and that means the people in this room, and we have got to realize that the world must become economically prosperous if we are going to have peace. Now, I feel that any accomplishment I may have made in my modest business career is insignificant, compared to the shame I feel in having permitted this country to have a war after twenty-five years following the last war. I think we are all just about as dumb as we can be to have permitted that sort of thing, and if we do it all over again, the country, I don't believe, even this great nation, can stand another world catastrophe like the one we are passing through now. Everyone in this room has to do all that he and she can to see that something is done that will prevent our having another war, and that means having a sound peace now. There may be a lot of things about it that we don't like as it is being set up. Here and there there may be criticism of the way the Dumbarton Oaks plan was formulated, and we will have trouble with Russia and England and the rest of the world in formulating a procedure; but we have to start with something, and if it isn't just right, we will go on and make it right as the years go by. The trouble with America is that we want everything done at one time, and that just can't be handled in as big an undertaking as we have ahead of us in that way . . .

I do always close by talking about The Mead Paper Company . . . We have a lot of plans, postwar development plans. We have had our postwar committee working for the last two years and they have done an outstanding job in thinking and looking forward to the future. Our research and technical group have done an outstanding job in spite of very limited facilities and personnel, and I believe that the next five years in all industry will be tremendous, one of tremendous changes and tremendous progress and I am very certain that The Mead Corporation is in a position to move forward just as rapidly as any of its competition and I am sure that applies to the Chillicothe Paper Company too. I will predict that along with the success of the country, our own company is going to have in another few years an establishment and a reputation that will just be surpassed by none . . . .

COMMENCEMENT ADDRESS, Miami University, June 7, 1954*

In addition to the responsibilities I have noted [financial responsibilities and human relations], there now comes to the business executive a new problem which, in my judgment, transcends all others. I refer to the responsibility for the maintenance of a sound national government and the development of new and wise policies in our international relations extending far beyond the horizons we have known in the past. Indeed, the political implications involved have become so vital to the survival of our country that they might well be put in first place.

---

*Mr. Mead spoke frequently between the years 1945 and 1954, but, because of the loss of files by flood, no verbatim accounts exist. The commencement address at Miami University was the only speech Mr. Mead ever composed ahead of time. He did so only under pressure from the University. His subject was "Observations on the Social Role and Responsibilities of Business Executives."

The great institutions we have built and all of our technological, industrial, cultural, educational and spiritual growth of the past 175 years stand in immediate danger of destruction from without. Yet we seem nationally unprepared in thought and action to meet this great issue.

It seems incredible that those of us who have carried on an active business life in executive work should have experienced two great wars and still have done so little thinking on how to meet the great challenge of preventing a third world war.

I am convinced that world war two might have been avoided, and I am perfectly certain that a third one can be avoided. It must be avoided if you, the members of the class of 1954, are to live in a free country and enjoy even the bare comforts and privileges of the generations that precede you.

Avoidance of a third world war will require more understanding, more diligence and more sacrifice than my generation has been willing to accept. There can be no such word as "Isolationism," nor can there be partisan politics in the solution of our great international problems. Whether we like it or not, the United States has inherited the leadership of the free world. That means great responsibility for the graduating class of Miami University and for the graduating classes of all colleges and universities in this country.

It has been my belief for many years that when the majority of the people in the United States elect a President to direct their destiny, all of us should do all we possibly can with good conscience to help and support him. Although a Republican, as some of you may know, I have given a modest portion of my time to serving on more than a dozen committees and commissions in Washington over the past 20 years, from 1933 through 1952, because I felt the impact of Government on all business and other segments of the economy was becoming increasingly important and must be accepted as a subject of major consideration by every business executive. Few people in our country yet realize the magnitude of the operations of our Federal Government or the importance of its successful functioning not only to our economy and welfare but also to our very lives.

The economic stability of the free world and a continuing enjoyment of international trade now depend upon the economy and prosperity of the United States. This Miami University class of 1954 and graduates of all other colleges are entering the business, industrial and professional world at one of the most critical moments in history. Your leadership must play a great part in the solution of the many complex problems facing our nation.

I would advise tolerance of and confidence in your fellow men and women. The vast majority of our people are honest, forthright, patriotic and of sound judgment.

I should like to summon greater cooperation in national efforts. Politics have a very definite and proper place in our domestic affairs, but in developing international policies, much greater unanimity is imperative. Partisan politics should be definitely set aside.

Remember that this means each of you, as intelligent individuals, can, if you only will, be a constructive force in building a better, finer world.

God's power for good has, throughout all history, won over the power of evil, but it has taken and will take from each one of you men and women hard work, sacrifice and deep faith.

RESEARCH AND DEVELOPMENT MEETING, Chillicothe, January 17, 1955*

Nineteen-fifty-five is more than a new year. It marks the end of the first post-war decade, and the beginning of America's long trial of endurance in the cold war.

The physical if not the moral reconstruction of Western Europe has been achieved. A divided Germany and a truncated Japan have revived, and the enemies of yesterday are the allies of today.

The changes are almost beyond belief. The location of decisive power in the world and even the very nature of power itself have altered. Asia is in revolt. China, the drowsy giant, has awakened and tipped the balance in the Far East toward the Communists, and the United

---

*As recorded by *The New York Times.*

States and the U.S.S.R. have abandoned isolation and confront one another across the whole face of the earth.

This is the somber image that confronts the President and the new Congress as they return to the Capital in 1955, and yet there are sound reasons for saying that if America does as well in the next ten years as it did in the last ten, free men need not fear the future.

The most important political fact of this past decade is that America has demonstrated that it will oppose aggression regardless of which party is in the White House. . . .

All the bickering on Capitol Hill in these past ten years, all the squabbling among the allies, all the doubts and hesitations, all the disappointments in Asia are subordinate to this fact: America is unified on opposing the new barbarism; the old world has found in the new world a power equal to the power that threatens our common civilization.

This is not meant to minimize the contributions of other nations. It is said because it is true and because one of the tragedies of our time is that America is not sufficiently conscious of what she has already achieved in the post-war era.

At the end of this century, historians will never understand why, in the midst of one of her most glorious chapters, the United States was so self-critical, why, in the moment of success, there was so much talk of failure, why the architects of her salvation were treated so shabbily.

The explanation of this lies very largely in the peculiar habits of Washington. It lives from day to day, one problem, one issue at a time. It dwells in the pit of controversy, with very little philosophy or sense of history, and loses sight of its progress in the battle.

Washington does not recognize success, and therefore, loses its hard-earned sense of participation in great achievement, because it lives with the illusion of perfection. No victory is true victory but total victory: so Korea, which was one of the great achievements of our history, is said to be a failure, and the diplomacy which kept 175 Red Army Divisions from running over twenty allied divisions in Western Europe is condemned. . . .

The past generation has been a period of unbelievable confusion and change: a convulsion of economic maladjustment, of mass slavery and death, of war and deceit in which the qualities of pity and love have been largely overwhelmed.

Nevertheless, the United States has adjusted enough and sacrificed enough to avoid the holocaust. It may seek a perfection which can be found only in heaven and a finality of solution which comes only in death, but it is moving and learning. It has the capacity to mature and yet stay young if it is well led, and that is a pretty good state for any nation to be in.

INDEX

Index

54257

Designed, printed and bound at
The Lakeside Press, R. R. Donnelley & Sons Company
Chicago, Illinois and Crawfordsville, Indiana
The text is set in Linotype Caledonia
and is printed on Mead Publishers' Offset

INVENTORY '80